SOCIAL JUSTICE IN SPANISH GOLDEN AGE THEATRE

Edited by Erin Alice Cowling, Tania de Miguel Magro, Mina García Jordán, and Glenda Y. Nieto-Cuebas

This collection of original new essays focuses on the many ways in which early modern Spanish plays engaged their audiences in a dialogue about abuse, injustice, and inequality. Far from the traditional monolithic view of theatrical works as tools for expanding ideology, these essays each recognize the power of theatre in reflecting on issues related to social justice. The first section of the book focuses on textual analysis, taking into account legal, feminist, and collective bargaining theory. The second section explores issues surrounding theatricality, performativity, and intellectual property laws through an analysis of contemporary adaptations. The final section reflects on social justice from the practitioners' point of view, including actors and directors.

Social Justice in Spanish Golden Age Theatre reveals how adaptations of classical theatre portray social justice and how throughout history the writing and staging of *comedias* has been at the service of a wide range of political agendas.

ERIN ALICE COWLING is an assistant professor of Spanish at MacEwan University.

TANIA DE MIGUEL MAGRO is an associate professor of Spanish at West Virginia University.

MINA GARCÍA JORDÁN is an associate professor of Spanish at Elon University.

GLENDA Y. NIETO-CUEBAS is an associate professor of Modern Foreign Languages at Ohio Wesleyan University.

Social Justice in Spanish Golden Age Theatre

EDITED BY ERIN ALICE COWLING,
TANIA DE MIGUEL MAGRO, MINA GARCÍA
JORDÁN, AND GLENDA Y. NIETO-CUEBAS

UNIVERSITY OF TORONTO PRESS
Toronto Buffalo London

© University of Toronto Press 2021
Toronto Buffalo London
utorontopress.com

ISBN 978-1-4875-0765-7 (cloth)   ISBN 978-1-4875-3668-8 (ePUB)
ISBN 978-1-4875-2528-6 (paper)   ISBN 978-1-4875-3667-1 (PDF)

___

Library and Archives Canada Cataloguing in Publication

Title: Social justice in Spanish Golden Age theatre / edited by Erin Alice Cowling, Tania de Miguel Magro, Mina García Jordán, and Glenda Y. Nieto-Cuebas.
Names: Cowling, Erin Alice, editor. | Miguel Magro, Tania de, editor. | García Jordán, Mina, 1972– editor. | Nieto Cuebas, Glenda Yael, 1975– editor.
Series: Toronto Iberic ; 54.
Description: Series statement: Toronto Iberic series ; 54 | Includes bibliographical references and index.
Identifiers: Canadiana (print) 20200279963 | Canadiana (ebook) 20200280155 | ISBN 9781487507657 (hardcover) | ISBN 9781487525286 (softcover) | ISBN 9781487536688 (EPUB) | ISBN 9781487536671 (PDF)
Subjects: LCSH: Social justice in literature. | LCSH: Social history in literature. | LCSH: Spanish drama – Classical period, 1500–1700 – History and criticism.
Classification: LCC PQ6105 .S63 2020 | DDC 862/.3093552–dc23

___

University of Toronto Press acknowledges the financial assistance to its publishing program of the Canada Council for the Arts and the Ontario Arts Council, an agency of the Government of Ontario.

Contents

List of Photos ix

Foreword: Theatre for Justice xi
    FERNANDO VILLA PROAL

Acknowledgments xv

Introduction 3
    ERIN ALICE COWLING, TANIA DE MIGUEL MAGRO,
    MINA GARCÍA JORDÁN, AND GLENDA Y. NIETO-CUEBAS

Part One: Readings of *Comedias*

1 The Poetics of Tragedy and Justice in Vélez de Guevara's *La serrana de la Vera* 15
    HARRISON MEADOWS

2 Utopian Divorce: *El descasamentero* by Salas Barbadillo 34
    TANIA DE MIGUEL MAGRO

3 The Voice of the Voiceless: Towards Equality and Social Justice in Sor Juana's *El divino Narciso* 53
    FRANCISCO LÓPEZ-MARTÍN

4 Staging Strikes, Depicting Merchants, and the Morisco Problem in Valencia 68
    MELISSA FIGUEROA

5 Notes on an Ethics of Theatricality in Cervantes: *El gallardo español* and *La Numancia* 82
    MOISÉS R. CASTILLO

6 Using Shame and Guilt to Impose Social Injustice in
Ana Caro's *El Conde Partinuplés*   98
JACLYN COHEN-STEINBERG

Part Two: Adaptations

7 A Social Justice Framing of the *Comedia*: EFE TRES
Teatro's *El príncipe ynocente* Adaptation   119
ERIN ALICE COWLING

8 Systemic Oppression in Morfeo Teatro's Adaptation and
Production of *El coloquio de los perros*   137
GLENDA Y. NIETO-CUEBAS

9 *El Trato de Argel* and the Immigrant Crisis   157
MINA GARCÍA JORDÁN

10 Chirinos and Chanfalla Go to America: Social Justice in
Adaptations of *El retablo de las maravillas*   175
CHARLES PATTERSON

11 Social Networks, Social Justice, and the People's Right to the
Golden Age Canon: The SGAE or the *Comedia* Villain of
the Digital Age?   191
ELENA GARCÍA MARTÍN

Part Three: Interviews

12 Ben Gunter (dramaturg and director), Theater with a
Mission, Tallahassee, Florida   211

13 Harley Erdman (university professor, director, adapter,
and translator of early modern theatre) and Gina
Kaufmann (university professor, director),
University of Massachussetts, Amherst   217

14 Sandra Arpa and Paula Rodríguez (founders, actors, and
directors), Teatro Inverso, Spain   223

15 Fernando Villa Proal and Allan Flores (founders and directors),
EFE TRES Teatro, Mexico City   227

16 Ian Borden (associate professor of theatre studies), Johnny Carson School of Theatre and Film, University of Nebraska   232

17 Natalia Menéndez (director, actor, dramaturg), former director of Almagro Festival, Spain   237

Bibliography   243

Contributors   261

Index   265

Photos

Photo 7.1   Fernando Villa Proal and Fernando Memije of EFE TRES Teatro on stage during a presentation of *El príncipe ynocente* 125
Photo 8.1   Francisco Negro and Mayte Bona of Morfeo Teatro on stage during a production of *El coloquio de los perros* 146
Photo 8.2   Francisco Negro, Mayte Bona, and Felipe Santiago (centre) of Morfeo Teatro during a scene of *El coloquio de los perros* 148

Foreword: Theatre for Justice

FERNANDO VILLA PROAL

"Ella [la utopía] está en el horizonte," dice Fernando Birri. Me acerco dos pasos, ella se aleja dos pasos. Camino diez pasos y el horizonte se corre diez pasos más allá. Por mucho que yo camine, nunca la alcanzaré. ¿Para qué sirve la utopía? Para eso sirve: para caminar. (Galeano 310)

"Utopia is in the horizon," Fernando Birri says. I move two steps towards it, she walks away two steps. I walk ten steps and the horizon moves ten steps further away. For as much as I walk, I'll never reach it. What is utopia good for? Precisely for that, to keep us walking. (my trans.)

Justice.
   Theatre.
   What is justice?
   Is there a way to achieve it?
   Just as utopia is always out of reach, so too is justice. Still, I like to think that justice and utopia are reachable. I don't think I will actually see it happen, on a global scale, but I do what I can as an individual, as an actor, and as a director.
   Is theatre a tool in the path towards justice?
   It awakes consciousness: through emotions (empathy, laughter, terror); through intellect, an invitation to insight, thoughts about specific ideas and situations; and through action.
   Theatre reflects reality. This we all know; it has been told to me ever since I first stepped into drama school ... I have, now, had the opportunity to corroborate that. It shows our particular perspective, no one else has it. Some may share a few ideas, some may seem very much alike, but no one will have the same eye, the same aesthetic approach. Since through art we are able to find a voice for ourselves, we want to make sure of what it is that we want to say, and how. It is in art where we

have a bubble of freedom, absolute freedom. In life we are attached to so many things and ways that it is hard to follow our desires, to stay true to ourselves. We are bound to so many duties and "needs" (I use quotation marks because, for the most part, these are created, or are constructions and manipulations of this world we live in). I have to pay rent; I need to have a big apartment, in an expensive area; I need to have a dog, I need to have a family; I have to stay married, for the children, even if it hurts; I have to stay connected; I need the latest phone; I need the biggest and brightest TV; I need the most comfortable, fast, state of the art, flashiest car. I have to take care of my elderly, ill father, I have to … I need to … whatever. Each one of us knows our personal boundaries and "obligations." In art, there is no other obligation than to stay true to oneself.

When we are searching for rewards other than the pursuit of our own truth, the art we create feels like it is lacking something. If we begin our artistic creation looking for recognition, or for money, or to replicate another piece (our own or someone else's), or searching for specific reactions/emotions for a specific end, then our creation is compromised. It's like beginning a conversation that is meant to be honest with someone else's speech, saying it's ours, or trying to be earnest through manipulation. I'm not saying such a creation can't be beautiful or functional but it will not be truthful. My question is then: if art (theatre in my case) is a place for exploring my deepest desires, fears, thoughts … my deepest me, why wouldn't I explore that, instead of creating without looking inwards? Why wouldn't I choose a path without ties or boundaries for my creation? Even if sometimes this requires effort, it is worth it. Even if sometimes I get off track (because I need the job, I have to show I'm great, I want people to like it …), coming back to truth is essential to art, as Paula Bonet explains:

> El arte es el lugar en el que se hacen preguntas y se intentan encontrar respuestas. Es donde debería haber más libertad para poder denunciar y alzar la voz. Es una herramienta de comunicación que funciona, creo que tenemos que hacer uso de ella. (Bonet qtd. in Sánchez Seoane)
>
> Art is the place where questions are asked, and where we try to find answers. It is where there should be more freedom to accuse and raise one's voice. It is a tool for communication that works and I believe we have to use it. (my trans.)

It is inevitable to be more myself once I know myself. When I have explored what is in my head, what I believe, what I'm comfortable with, and what I don't like, then I tend to be more congruent. Therefore, it is nearly impossible to not be a model of the theatre I stage. I create theatre and theatre creates me in return. The person I am will be an agent of change; how I treat people, what kind of example I set, how I react to the people around me ... If one person can make a change with his or her behaviour day by day, what kind of change or influence can be achieved by something that is meant to have an audience?

I believe in the idea that art is subversive, for it is an expression of freedom. To be free in a world like ours is in itself a rebellious act. And creating, performing, and teaching are responsibilities we should embrace, for they will show others the path to freedom. Theatre inspires and shows others the possibility of creation in themselves. As Joseph Beuys said, "every man is an artist," and he believed that we all have the creative capacity for autodetermination, while also supporting the idea that true capital was not money, but creativity (qtd. in Gutiérrez Galindo 100). Theatre (art) invites spectators to create, to be agents of action (to determine themselves and their surrounding); theatre invites people to be free.

Whatever I do has an impact in society, micro or macro. Paula Bonet has said, "Creo que todo – absolutamente todo – es político: lo personal es político, cada decisión y acto lo son. Incluso decidir no actuar es un acto político [Everything – absolutely everything – is political: The private is political, each choice and each action are political. Even the decision of not acting is a political act]" (qtd. in Sánchez Seoane; my trans.). Following this line, there is no way a play wouldn't be political. Even choosing to make a non-political play is itself a political decision.

If the audience doesn't find direct meaning in what they see, they tend to search for it ... and eventually they will find it. People will try to make sense out of art. It is not a matter of what is right and what is wrong. In art there are no wrongs. It is a matter of what you are saying. What speech do you want to deliver? How specific or how open to interpretations do you want it to be? Just be aware. Anything you do is open to interpretations.

And again ... everything you do is political. What kind of world am I helping to create? As Galeano said about utopia, you have to keep walking the walk. Maybe raising my voice will not change everything, but I'm certain that someone will listen, and maybe, then he or she will raise another voice ... and so on and so forth. Theatre is my megaphone, my place, from where I try to make my voice reach further.

When engaging in an artistic endeavour always think: What kind of society am I procuring? What am I criticizing? What kind of ideas do I want my audience to wonder about? What do I want – or not – from my play? These questions are also applicable to me, as a family member ... as a professional ... as an individual ... as someone who has an active part in a society. As someone who wants justice to be achieved, even if not in my lifetime.

Acknowledgments

The co-editors would like to thank all of the authors and theatre practitioners who have contributed to this volume. It has been a pleasure to work with the University of Toronto Press and we are particularly indebted to Suzanne Rancourt, Manager, Humanities Acquisitions, for enthusiastically supporting this project from the beginning; the co-editors of the Toronto Iberic series, Robert Davidson and Frederick A. de Armas; Barb Porter, Associate Managing Editor; and Anne Laughlin, copyeditor.

This volume would have not been possible without the financial support of the following: the Eberly College Publication Subvention program at West Virginia University; the SARIF program at the University of Tennessee, Knoxville; and publication grants from MacEwan University's Office of Research Services, Ohio Wesleyan University, and Western Washington University.

SOCIAL JUSTICE IN SPANISH
GOLDEN AGE THEATRE

Introduction

ERIN ALICE COWLING, TANIA DE MIGUEL MAGRO, MINA GARCÍA JORDÁN, AND GLENDA Y. NIETO-CUEBAS

Over the past few years many articles have been published on the "crisis of the humanities," attributing its development to lack of economic support, lower salaries, and cuts to academic programs and government-funded and endowed organizations. This crisis has awakened extensive and profound discussions about the humanities' future and why it matters. The humanities are often used as an umbrella designation to refer to the study of several subject areas including the visual arts, history, music, theatre, literature, philosophy, and languages. In defence of the humanities, training in these various fields has been associated with increased critical and creative thinking; it has also been credited with teaching and inspiring individuals to ask questions, to learn about other cultures, and to reach a deeper understanding of how different societies live.

The humanities take their maximum expression through the arts as a pathway to expressing human thoughts and emotions. Within the arts, theatre especially can be considered a genre that highlights how fields within the humanities can work together simultaneously to achieve specific goals. As they evolve into productions, theatrical works encompass elements from the visual arts, music, and architecture in order to bring texts to life and explore human complexities. Eugenio Barba claims that the twentieth century repeatedly asked why theatre might still matter, while promoting the idea that meaning can only come from the individual, be it performer, spectator, or even researcher (206). As we ask why the humanities matter, we believe the theatre can provide a space to show its constructive educational and social effects through the re-enactment of the human experience. Theatre can inspire audiences to doubt, question, feel uncertain, and react to subversion. It can also encourage them to think about social problems, to challenge authority, and to reflect on human nature in all its diversity.

Humanistic training gives us a foundation to understand different political systems, the significance of democracy, and matters of social justice, as well as to learn how to solve problems and make new discoveries. In a recent article published in the *Chronicle of Higher Education*, Rens Bod explains:

> A closer look at the general history of the humanities shows that besides demonstrating value and interpretation, humanists have also tried to solve many concrete problems: the problem of reconstructing a text from extant copies, of comparing different art works or literary works to figure out the origin and author, of determining whether a tale about the past is trustworthy, of finding general principles underlying different languages. In all these activities, humanists sometimes make discoveries, some of which have applications for entirely different fields. These discoveries are too often erroneously credited to the sciences.

The knowledge and discoveries produced within the humanities matter because they involve the development of human expression and help expand our understanding of our societies and ourselves.

Likewise, our own field of studies, the so-called Golden Age of Spanish literature – and even more specifically, the *comedia* and theatre – has been under siege in recent years. This project was first conceived at the 2016 Association for Hispanic Classical Theater's annual conference in El Paso, Texas. Matthew Stroud (Trinity University) gave a plenary speech titled "Why the *Comedia*?," which discussed the challenges facing the humanities in general and our own subdiscipline of Spanish *comedia* studies specifically. Many of the statistics he outlined portrayed a discipline in decline, forcing us to wonder what, if anything, could be done to remediate the situation.

Not all is doom and gloom, however. Stroud makes three recommendations that we – the co-editors of this edition – have taken to heart. The implementation of the first recommendation, to establish links between the social, economic, political, and cultural aspects of the Golden Age *comedia* to those of today, is the backbone of this volume. Although the language can sometimes be difficult for students of more modern Spanish, the issues of gender, race, politics, and war that are at the heart of many early modern plays are still very relevant and allow modern audiences a locus of identification. By including modernized adaptations of these plays in our classrooms and on our stages, we are adhering to the Brechtian understanding of epic theatre, and to techniques already employed by marginalized groups as early as the 1970s, as they strove not only for acceptance but also for representation in their performances both in Europe and North America (Borowski and Sugiera 76–7).

Stroud's second recommendation was to encourage collaboration. This volume includes chapters written by academics, at different stages of their careers, that address social justice issues from a variety of perspectives; it also takes into account the point of view of theatre practitioners: both actors and directors. The humanities have long been thought of as a solitary endeavour – the lonely scholar in an ivory tower, writing for an audience of three or four like-minded academics. By collaborating we are not only getting out of our individualistic mindset, we are also opening ourselves up to new ideas, widening our audiences, and bringing humanities to the forefront of public knowledge. Although these plays may seem out of reach for the average theatregoer – what Barba calls "the archaeological remains of another time" (218) – we aim to show how they can be adapted to a variety of settings and teach all of us about society both then and now.

Stroud's final recommendation, to underscore the relevance of these plays, leads us to ask the following question: What is it about the *comedia* that makes us study it, even now, four hundred plus years after Lope de Vega wrote his *Arte nuevo de hacer comedias en este tiempo* (New Art of Writing Comedias in This Time)? We need to explore why it is still important for it to be a fundamental part of an undergraduate major in Spanish literature or theatre, and why we need to expand the list of so-called canonical works so that theatre groups can put on performances that reach a modern audience.

Taking into account all three of Stroud's recommendations, we decided to start working collaboratively, and look for ways that we can connect our love of the *comedia* with our students' needs, as well as the desires of modern audiences to identify with the stories and people onstage. As college campuses become more politically and socially active, we believe that the issues of social justice present in the *comedias* provide a sound starting point to connect with students and audiences around the world. We have seen this in our respective positions as professors on campuses in Canada and the United States: our students are increasingly aware of the world around them and are concerned with how their own identities shape their view of the world – and with how the world views them. We believe that studying the *comedia* can be an excellent platform for reaching these students, providing them with a structure to question and analyse the human experience. Issues of gender and race are so prevalent in the *comedia* that it is almost impossible to study even the most canonical works without touching on several points of interest to today's student. This is also true of many of the adaptations being done of these plays currently, including those discussed in this volume.

Social justice, theoretically speaking, is difficult to define. It can encompass a variety of issues, many stemming from the lack of equality given to minority groups by the group in power. Although legal justice is meant to make society fair for all, the application of blind justice can often lead to inequality for those who start with less power in the first place. Individuals, in any given place and time, may have a different concept of what is fair and just for themselves, their family, and their in-group, and various theories and systems of justice have been established and modified over time. Early on, advocates of the divine command theory argued that justice came directly from God, as one of the four cardinal virtues in Christianity, along with temperance, prudence, and fortitude. These cardinal virtues and the three theological virtues of faith, hope, and love made up the seven virtues (1 Corinthians). In the Renaissance period of Spain, Francisco de Vitoria argued in favour of natural law, understood to be inherent, universal, and endowed by nature through human reason rather than from God, as traditionally defined. In such light the law of nature was understood to exist independently of the law of specific states, religions, and so on, which in Vitoria's context legitimized the rights of the native peoples of the New World. Therefore, Vitoria denied that native peoples could be understood as slaves by nature in Aristotelian terms, but, rather, he adopted from Aquinas the Roman law concept of *ius gentium* and defended the intrinsic dignity of man in the New World. This concept of justice belongs to the background of the plays that we present in this volume, and showcases the early modern struggle to achieve the "stoic insistence on the undifferentiated humanity of all people ... as a corrective to the dominant ideology" (Long 243).

There is a long and winding road from the early modern view of justice to what we call social justice today, and today's definition of what is just, and what constitutes justice, particularly social justice, is not always agreed upon by all parties. In spite of the strides made by various rights movements, especially since the mid-twentieth century, there is still a long way to go, particularly for those whose gender, race, sexuality, and other identifying features have been used against them in previous iterations of legal justice. The idea that the "personal is political" can be traced back to the title given to a memo by Carol Hanisch when it was printed in 1970 in *Notes from the Second Year: Women's Liberation*. Although Hanisch has since claimed, in a new introduction written in 2006 (1), that the title is not her own, but rather was given to the paper by the editors, the phrase has become a fixture in feminist circles. We recognize that there are varying markers of justice, and that the time and space in which something occurs can have an effect on the level of justice each individual or group can reach or aspire to. What might have counted as a victory for social justice in 1600 will appear unjust by today's standards. Still, we believe that the plays represented in this volume, both during their time and in recent adaptations, portray groups that suffer discrimination for a variety of reasons, be it religion, gender, economics, and so on, and that the playwrights' and/or adapters' work, in ways of varying subtlety, against the prevailing inequities of their time periods. As Loretta Capeheart and Dragan Milovanovic point out in their introduction to *Social Justice: Theories, Issues, and Movements*, those who are "subject to discriminatory forms of institutionalized conceptions of justice may go to excesses for survival purposes, or may be brutalized to the extent that their behavior will be expressive" (4), in the hopes that such excess brings them justice. This is a struggle that is played out in the plays herein, to varying degrees of success. To this end, we, the co-editors, have left the more detailed analysis of the issues of social justice to the individual authors, with the understanding that the actions examined make a statement on the social situation of the agents involved, in an attempt to improve the status of a group within the norms of the setting of the play and/or its adaptation.

The *comedia* has long been seen as a potential tool to sway its audiences, and theoreticians have claimed that the theatre of early modern Spain can be seen as everything from government propaganda to subversive literature. The readings herein of the plays as they would have been seen in their own period demonstrate that there is almost always an underlying tone of irony that allows us to contextualize the critiques. Once we add the dimension of the modern adaptation, these plays can become instruments through which we can view our own time, using the sometimes hidden interpretations as a method of understanding our own experiences.

Perhaps the best example of a work that allows us to understand notions of justice from both its time period and our own is Lope de Vega's *Fuenteovejuna*. No other Spanish play so vividly embodies the power of theatre as a tool for denouncing injustice. Vaguely based on a historical event that took place in the town of Fuente Obejuna, Córdoba, at the end of the fifteenth century, it is a drama that has been utilized by a wide range of political agendas. In the midst of the Civil War, the government of the Republic chose this *comedia* to be the one shown at the Spanish Pavilion in the 1937 Paris Exposition. In the early years of the Franco era, it was adapted to be an allegory of how the "good" Spaniards were oppressed by the Republic but achieved their freedom after the war. On the seventieth anniversary of the beginning of the war, Lope's text was reworked as *Fuenteovejuna en el frente, 1936*. The play meant to bring back audiences to two different spaces of the war: the battlefront and the home front. While actors characterized as Republican militias performed at a theatre in Almagro, listeners of Radio Nacional de España could follow the development of the drama in the way that many Spaniards followed the day-to-day of the civil war. *Fuenteovejuna* has also been a favourite of Russian stages before, during, and after the 1917 Revolution. In more recent years, this *comedia* has been used to explore an array of political, social, and economic issues. *De Fuenteovejuna a Ciudad Juárez* (2008) drew a link with the numerous disappearances of women in the Mexican city of Juárez. In 2013, the New York–based company Repertorio Español transformed the town of Fuenteovejuna into a contemporary corporate environment. The list of examples could go on and on. But *Fuenteovejuna* has done much more than move an audience to reflect on a particular struggle; it has itself been a path to escape injustice. Starting in 2015, it has been produced in Spain by two companies, both of whom modernized the setting in order to focus on contemporary issues, but in very different ways. One, the Joven Compañía Nacional de Teatro Clásico (the National Youth Classical Theatre Company of Spain) has produced a version that the director described as "buscamos entender las razones que hacen que como ciudadanos repitamos una y otra vez el error de permitir ser gobernados de forma despótica [searching for the reasons behind why we repeat, as citizens, the same errors over and over again that allow us to be governed by despotic rule]" (Hernández-Simón; our trans.). Some might maintain that despotic rule ended in 1975 with the death of Franco, yet the resurgence of extreme-right politics in Spain and other parts of the world would belie the notion that this is an antiquated concept.

The other more recent version began production, directed by Pepa Gamboa, in 2016. She had been directing an adaptation of *Fuenteovejuna* which features a troupe made up almost entirely of Roma women from Portugal, most of them illiterate, who live in the shantytown of El Vacie, Seville. In an interview recorded for Canal Sur during one of the rehearsals, fifty-six-year-old actress Rocio Montero declared: "Yo cuando estoy aquí dentro me siento más grande, más poderosa, más mujer [When I'm in here I feel bigger, more powerful, more of a woman]" (Gamboa 2016; our trans.). In fact, this production emphasizes women's empowerment onstage and has helped these women gain it in real life. They are not trained actresses and being part of this project has helped them gain personal and professional confidence, an appreciation for the arts, access to resources and connections that are often outside their reach, as well as achieving higher economic status and recognition within their communities. All of which has, in return, helped them obtain more respect from their partners and from people outside their communities who are often prejudiced towards Roma women (Gamboa 2018).

Gamboa's *Fuenteovejuna* is just one obvious example of the incorporation of the modern concept of social justice in adaptations of Golden Age theatre. By using an all-female, all-*gitana* cast, the director throws light on the issues of gender inherent in the play and adds a layer of racial oppression that gives the production an even more relevant, and modern, twist. This volume seeks to explore other dramas of the period that can be portrayed in a similar light. Thus, we settled on the issues of social justice that are present in the original plays, as well as in those adaptations that bring contemporary matters to the stage. We believe that studying *comedia* through these lenses, we can show not only that the text of the *comedia* is relevant in the classroom, but that modern stagings and adaptations will resonate with audiences around the world.

This book recognizes the power of theatre in the dissemination, condemnation, and reflection on issues related to social justice in Spain during the sixteenth and seventeenth centuries. Issues of gender, class, and race are so prevalent in the *comedia* that it is almost impossible to study any given play without touching on points of social justice. These essays present an alternative to the traditional monolithic view of the *comedia* as a tool for expanding the ideology of the Catholic traditional upper classes; they instead show how plays engaged the audiences in a dialogue about abuse, injustice, and inequality. We study how adaptation of classical theatre can be a tool for achieving social justice today and how, throughout history, stagings of *comedias* have been at the service of a wide range of political agendas. The essays focused on textual analysis take into account legal, feminist, and collective bargaining theory. Those focused on contemporary performances pay attention to theatricality, performativity, adaptation, and intellectual property laws. We also reflect on how contemporary theatrical companies manage to maintain the integrity of their goals while dealing with political entities not always welcoming of their messages.

Barba has claimed that "all theatres are archaic in our times," and yet he also recognizes that there are far more theatres around us than the official chronicles care to acknowledge (16). We believe that now, more than ever, with the advent of social media and video-sharing platforms, that artists are able to create theatre and interact with the public in ways that could not have been dreamed of during the time of Lope de Vega and Calderón de la Barca. They translate this interactive component to their live performances to further connect with their audiences, allowing them to reinforce the link between sixteenth-century Spain and twenty-first-century social issues. Many of the theatre troupes discussed herein are on the margins of what Barba calls the "translucent pinnacles of the mountains of ice" that are made up of the known artists (16); some are even further beneath the surface, and without the opportunities afforded them by online networking, and small theatre festivals willing to take a chance on an unknown entity, they might never have been known to us either. But it is for precisely this reason, at this moment, that they are also able to take risks and create adaptations that speak to the issues that they and their audience members grapple with, whether it be the unjust criminal justice system that favours the rich over the poor, the humanitarian crisis facing refugees and their host countries, or small towns fighting against an actors guild for the right to portray their cultural heritage.

This book is divided into three parts, each of which focuses on an important aspect of the interpretation and adaptation of these plays. The first two parts include scholarly articles, while the third is a collection of interviews with theatre practitioners. Articles in Part I analyse a wide range of early modern plays through the lens of social justice. The authors discuss how specific plays depicted and denounced injustices of their time. This part aims to include works from different genres (tragedy, hagiography, *auto*, *loa*, historical drama, *comedia de enredo*, and short theatre), that portray a variety of social topics (gender, race, religion, class, and imperial power). Harrison Meadows reads *La serrana de la Vera* as a portrayal of the harmful consequences of gender normativity. Tania de Miguel Magro reflects on the rarity of divorce as a topic of discussion in early modern theatre, and argues that in *El descasamentero* Salas Barbadillo proposes a utopian society in which the happiness of its inhabitants supersedes any religious norms. Francisco López-Martín looks at Sor Juana's *autos* and *loas* through the lens of the conquest, reading her allegorical characters as representations of the Indigenous Other. Melissa Figueroa demonstrates that *El gran Patriarca don Juan de Ribera* uncovers how Morisco figures were used unjustly as social scapegoats, while also challenging spectators and readers, regardless of social, economic, or religious background, to view social injustices as universal. Moisés Castillo explains how in *El Gallardo español* and *La Numancia* Cervantes problematizes fame as a dehumanizing force that leads to injustice, and re-examines the construction of the enemy as a radical Other. Finally, Jaclyn Cohen-Steinberg proves that Ana Caro's seemingly traditional denouement of *El Conde Partinuplés* is actually an inversion of societal expectations of the play's character and contemporary audience.

The second part of the book centres on modern adaptations of early modern texts (for both the stage and the screen) that highlight social justice issues and questions related to performing classical theatre today. The practitioners discussed in this part of the book attempt to embody Barba's "Third Theatre," which creates an asocial theatrical society, not to separate themselves from society but to create an environment in which they can oppose what Barba calls "the sociality of injustice" (192). By taking artefacts of theatre, early modern plays, and stories that might otherwise be discarded as irrelevant, and by creating spaces for the connections between past and present, performer and spectator, these performers imbue the early modern texts with meaning that resonates with their twenty-first-century spectators. Erin Alice Cowling analyses the adaptation of Lope de Vega's *El príncipe inocente* by the Mexican company EFE TRES Teatro. She explains how the success of this adaptation in connecting with a modern audience has to do with the creation of a frame structure in which two prisoners act out the *comedia* to pass their time, ultimately inverting the traditional denouement in order to comment on present inequalities. Glenda Y. Nieto-Cuebas offers a reading of Morfeo Teatro's adaptation of *El coloquio de los perros*. She highlights how through each element of the performance (script, clothing, stage, etc.) the alienation suffered by Cervantes' seventeenth-century characters is transformed into an atemporal example of social exclusion. Mina García Jordán examines *Tratos*, by Ernesto Caballero, an adaptation of Cervantes' *El Trato de Argel*. She explores how this production promotes political activism and increases consciousness about the vicissitudes of the lives of immigrants. Charles Patterson looks at two twentieth-century adaptations of *El retablo de las maravillas* for television and film that take Cervantes' impish tricksters to the Americas: Manuel Altolaguirre's *Las maravillas* and José Sanchis Sinisterra's *El retablo de Eldorado*. Patterson reveals how each piece works as a satire of social injustices that force individuals to act out. Elena García Martín follows the campaigns of small towns in Spain, such as Fuente Obejuna, Zalamea, and Olmedo, to take back their cultural heritage and stage the historical *comedias* that bear their names. She delves into the controversial implications of the SGAE's (General Society of Spanish Authors and Editors) decision to intervene and put a stop to unauthorized productions of these plays.

The final part of the book is a series of interviews with theatre practitioners who discuss their approaches to social justice in their adaptations. Our goal is to let the reader hear the voices of individuals who work as directors, actors, professors, and translators in the United States, Spain, and Latin America. They discuss their struggles to bring early modern theatre to a contemporary audience and a sense of social responsibility, while balancing their artistic desires with the need for financial gain and concerns for political pushback.

With all three parts we, the editors, hope to have contributed in an effective manner to the call for action that Stroud issued in the plenary that we referred to above. First, we have endeavoured to link the social, economic, political, and cultural aspects of Golden Age *comedia* to today's issues by presenting essays that examine those commonalities. Second, we have engaged in a collaborative effort that merges scholars, actors, and directors from all over the world. Finally, we have attempted to show the continuing relevance of *comedia* studies, a field that we constantly fight to keep alive and well in our classrooms, our scholarship, and our passion.

PART ONE

Readings of *Comedias*

1 The Poetics of Tragedy and Justice in Vélez de Guevara's *La serrana de la Vera*

HARRISON MEADOWS

In our current age, in a world dominated by political partisanship and ideological polarization, discussions surrounding the topic of gender expression and identity have often given rise to a polemic that seems irresolvable. This reality directs us to consider alternative modes of discourse, ones that can change the course of the debate towards a more fruitful conclusion. Theatre offers just such a terrain; it provides a space to reify the parameters of the conversation by portraying characters who experience the consequences of harmful ideologies related to gender, thereby compelling audiences to reflect on specific issues that arise onstage. Out of this potential to impact popular discord over the question of gender, I offer a framework for understanding Luis Vélez de Guevara's *La serrana de la Vera* (The Mountain Woman of La Vera), one that highlights its capacity to produce transformative experiences for theatregoers and to open avenues for productive conversation. Thanks to the destabilizing force exerted on traditionalist perspectives on gender by the play's female protagonist, Gila, Vélez de Guevara's *comedia* is a unique and largely untapped resource for contemporary practitioners of socially committed theatre. I will begin this chapter by addressing the reception of the play in the cultural context of its original staging. To accomplish this task, I read the play through the lens of the early modern conceptualization of the tragic mode, which in this work delineates the matrix of signification by which the work produces its message. Put differently, tragedy underpins the social implications of the work, and forms the parameters by which readers and members of the audience are to judge Gila's actions and their consequences. This critical approach provides a fresh opportunity to advance long-standing debates in scholarship over the nature of the final scene, either as a display of justice, fittingly administered, or as the tragic end of a character due to the imposition of repressive institutional control. In this chapter, I argue for the latter, and ultimately turn my focus to discuss how Vélez de Guevara's *comedia* can inform current polemics on gender expression and identity, the evidence of which can be found in a recent translation and stage adaptations of the work that have emphasized the intensely relevant, socially charged dimensions of the play related to gender.

The audience's first encounter with Gila occurs when the villagers of Garganta La Olla, formed in a procession, interrupt the opening scene by bursting onto the stage while singing in unison. Their song tells of the renowned deeds of the protagonist, drawing from actual ballads in the popular tradition.[1] The descriptions of her exploits by other characters maintain a relatively positive tone during the first two acts; she is exceptional, but is by no means seen as a threat to the integrity of the social order. Stroud acknowledges that "at least at first, no one seems bothered by her masculinity," or is cognizant of what he describes as her "obvious homosexuality" (125, 134). The pre-eminent Vélez de Guevara scholar George Peale notes the impact of this scene on the initial reception of Gila, positing that the celebratory mood of the villagers overflows into the audience, thereby blurring theatrical space: "La prolongada entrada ... va y viene por el patio del corral mezclándose con los espectadores, siempre cantando en loor de la figurona titular [The lengthy procession snakes through the *corral* patio mixing itself among the spectators, always singing the praises of the marvellous protagonist]" ("El Acto I," 148).[2] This mood persists throughout the first two acts, which can be observed later, in Act I, when the Catholic Monarchs, Fernando and Isabel, attend the festivals taking place in the nearby town of Plasencia. Gila learns the Queen will be there, so she makes it a point to impress her, which she accomplishes by subduing a bull with her bare hands. In response to this spectacle, Isabel remarks, "Enamora / verla tan valiente y bella [Seeing her so valiant and beautiful provokes love]" (1.937–8). As Gila's character develops she pushes the boundaries of prescribed gender norms and articulates explicitly how her actions reflect a greater sense of identity. On five occasions, Gila rebukes men who either attempt to emphasize her femininity or call into question her ability to outmatch them in a challenge (1.349–52; 1.773–81; 1.888–90; 2.1576–1600; 2.1833). In each instance, her comments go beyond a description of her masculine qualities and interests towards the expression of a male gender identity. Perhaps this expression is no clearer than in her first exchange upon meeting the military captain Don Lucas, who, at the beginning of Act I, has arrived in Garganta La Olla, seeking quarters for his men. When he comments he has never met a woman like her, Gila is quick to rejoinder: "Si imagináis / que soy [mujer], os engañáis, / que soy muy hombre [If you imagine that I am a woman, you deceive yourself, for I am very much a man]" (1.350–3).³ Later, when her father agrees for her to marry the captain, Gila pleads that he rescind the agreement. She desperately wishes to avoid the social constraints imposed by wedlock and the identity crisis it would precipitate. In her view, playing a role incongruent with who she sees herself to be can lead only to significant emotional and physical turmoil. This psychological distress is reflected in subtle shifts in her language over the course of the play. As institutional pressure begins to build once her father agrees to her marriage to Don Lucas, Gila's own expression about her identity becomes less direct, more tentative. Now, upon her betrothal, this can be observed in lexical shifts, in the way she identifies herself from her first encounter with Don Lucas to the second:

> Hasta agora
> me imaginaba, padre, por las cosas
> que yo me he visto ser hombre y muy hombre,
> y agora echo de ver, pues que me tratas
> casamiento con este caballero,
> que soy mujer, que para tanto daño
> ha sido mi desdicha el desengaño. (2.1578–83)

> Until now father, I imagined myself, because of the things I have seen, as a man, and quite a man, and now I see, since you have arranged my marriage with this man, that I am a woman; such tremendous pain of my misfortune has been my disillusion.

The solidity with which she previously expressed her masculinity with the verb *ser* ("que *soy* muy hombre [that I *am* a man]" (1.353) has suddenly become a contingency beyond her control. However, she indicates that she always *imagined* herself a man ("me imaginaba"), but now she sees that she *is* a woman ("soy mujer"). Highlighting the cognitive tension building inside Gila, this scene is representative of the harmful effects of repressive institutional control on the subject that causes her image of self to begin to dissolve. Gila's father refuses her pleas to cancel the marriage agreement, and immediately the plot begins to unravel for the protagonist. On the day prior to their wedding, Gila and Lucas spend the night together, only for Gila to awaken to the reality of her lover's absence, and the consequences of his deception.⁴

After being left scorned by a false suitor, she vows to kill every man who crosses her path until she exacts revenge on the one to whom she surrendered her honour. In Act III, the audience learns, from villagers' accounts, that she has kept her word; she affirms this first-hand when she claims to have murdered two thousand men (3.3240). As punishment for her crimes, she is sentenced to death, and the Catholic Monarchs preside over her execution in the final scenes. As her lifeless body hangs from the gibbet upstage at the play's close, Fernando, the Catholic Monarch and arbiter of her sentence, proclaims her death to be an example for all of Spain: "de ejemplo sirva a España [may it serve as an example for Spain]" (3.3296). This ending has long perplexed modern readers of the text. When the king makes this proclamation, he reinforces the conspicuous exemplarity signified by Gila's violent death, and provides his audience – both the internal one present onstage and the external one beyond the fourth wall – with an authorized view on how to interpret Gila's body. At first glance, it would seem that Gila's punishment serves as a warning to deter others from the criminal act with which she was charged, namely, murder. However, a fundamental ambiguity lies just beyond Fernando's decisive pronouncement. Margaret Boyle signals this interpretive possibility of the nature of exemplarity in Vélez de Guevara's work. She concisely outlines the critical history of the text, followed by the suggestion that the message conveyed in the conclusion is more complex than Fernando's lines might suggest:

> The question of how to interpret Gila's story has frequently lent itself to analysis in terms of a cautionary tale. Giraldo as the misguided father has poorly instructed his naturally weak-minded daughter and has failed to counsel her with the advice of contemporary conduct manuals. Because he wrongfully praised her at the opening, he is punished by her death at the end. But Gila's forceful presence onstage, principally the novel staging of her violence as well as the comedic force of her excess, complicates this kind of didactic reading. (161)

Her careful reading "opens the space to consider the shifting meanings of exemplarity throughout the play, by liberating Gila from the frame of the cautionary tale" (161). The implications of her observations are far-reaching, and require further consideration as to the accuracy of her model for understanding the nature of social discourse realized by the play.

With Gila's corpse as a visible backdrop to the closing dialogue, Fernando publicly offers an authorized reading of her body as text. The implications of his proclamation of her exemplarity raises key questions that must be considered before any claim can be made about the straightforward presentation of repressive ideology on display at the end of Vélez de Guevara's work. Although upon first glance Fernando's declaration seems to serve as a clear reinstatement of the status quo, Mujica poignantly argues against this traditional reading of the play: "in spite of Maravall's and Díez Borque's observations, the political and social structures Vélez de Guevara depicts are not particularly orderly" (231). Fernando's judgment of Gila's exemplarity supports this claim to the extent that it comes off as incongruent with the dramatic tension and character development that unfolds over the course of the *comedia*. The complex forces that drive the conflict cannot be so simply resolved. Moreover, the king fails to outline a concrete moral or ethical message to be drawn from the gruesome spectacle overshadowing – in a literal and figurative sense – his monarchical authority.[5] At the moment Fernando declares that Gila will be immortalized as an example in the collective memory of Spain, he creates a dissonance between the cautionary intention of his enunciation and the affective response of the audience. This ironic space materializes as a direct, and seemingly deliberate, consequence; audiences are likely to lament Gila's tragic end. After taking pleasure in her exploits during Acts I and II, they watch her life spiral frenetically out of her own control at the opening of Act III. Put differently, the problem with reading the work as a cautionary tale is its incongruence with the development of the plot. The specific actions that give rise to Gila's final punishment commence only at the beginning of Act III, the consequence of which diminishes the dramatic force of the developments in the action and characters up to that point. The relatively brief attention given to her spree of murderous vengeance pales in comparison to the concentration on Gila's character development during the two thousand verses that precede the murder of her first victim. Even then, the scenes that depict those murders focus primarily on her final encounter with Don Lucas, the deceitful husband. In terms of the primary conflict and the economy of the plot, the action that develops onstage during the first two acts centres on the nature of Gila's prodigious masculinity, first solidified through her words and deeds to increase the dramatic effect when Don Lucas's deception shatters it. This exposition and inception of the conflict therefore renders the despicable captain's death as much an instance of poetic justice as it is a punishable crime. Assuming the play has any poetic cohesion and the final scene provides closure to the work as a self-contained unit, analyses that do not account for the forces that drive its trajectory prior to Act III fall short of a comprehensive approach to the work.

Since audiences see almost nothing of Gila the murderer, we must imagine them to be particularly shrewd to turn on her so readily. Moreover, other characters are less inclined to pass judgment on Gila as Fernando does. At the very least, Madalena, her beloved cousin, is ambivalent on the subject. She describes Gila as maintaining a certain ineffable countenance, even in the moment the executioner tightened the rope around her neck: "Bizarra quedó en el palo también [She remained something to behold on the gibbet as well]" (3.3285). Bárbara Mujica affirms Ruth Lundelius's assertion regarding the opacity of the term "bizarra," which implies exaggeration but can have positive or negative connotations (Mujica 231). Therefore, Madalena's statement depends on how one interprets it; Gila's excess is either something to exalt for its singularity or deserving of scorn for its unwavering and spectacular transgression of established norms. Queen Isabel also struggles to respond to the gruesome sight of Gila's body hanging from the stake, but in her case this uncertainty betrays an underlying sympathy for the executed protagonist. After Fernando's assessment of the punishment ("Ha sido / justo castigo [It was a just punishment]" (3.3285–6)), she reflects: "A mí me enternece el alma [It has moved my spirit]" (3.3287).

Comedia playwrights often leveraged the symbolic potency of monarchical figures to persuade baroque audiences to form a "passionate attachment to a particular version of the world" subtended in their works (Egginton, *How the World* 155). The Catholic Monarchs, venerated as iconic arbiters of social order in the ethos of Spanish national identity, proved singularly useful, as their unquestionable virtue could be exploited to smuggle a multitude of socially charged messages into plays. However, in *La serrana de la Vera*, the restoration of order signified by the conventional presence of the monarchical figures in the final scene dissolves in its equivocal finale. Rather than cohesion between the characters of Fernando and Isabel in authorizing and responding to Gila's execution, there is dissonance. Moreover, they provide only two examples of the plurality of perspectives offered by various characters in the final scene. The theatrical apparatus through which Gila's death is supposed to guide audiences to believe in its exemplarity undermines itself by acknowledging the indecipherability of her death through the range of responses given voice in Vélez de Guevara's *comedia*. That is, the playwright depicts tension in the plurality of competing reactions to Gila's death that encompass a wider spectrum of possibilities than the one expressed by the king. Isabel and Madalena emphasize their own affective responses, Fernando expresses its legal necessity, while Giraldo acknowledges his personal culpability: "Confieso que es justo pago / a mi descuido [I confess that it is the deserved price of my neglect]" (3.3258–9). These varied perspectives obstruct the presentation of a singular or privileged position on the response the final scene should elicit, which further diminishes the force of Lundelius' argument that Vélez de Guevara "carried the legend of the *serrana* to a conservative and expected end" (239). The ambiguity perceived by Boyle in her analysis offers a more accurate point of departure towards an understanding of the social implications of the *comedia*'s ending.

Early modern notions on the poetics of tragedy may offer a useful framework for explaining the function of that ambiguity and closing the gap in scholarship on the nature of Gila's exemplarity. As justification for the relevance of this approach, we know Vélez de Guevara thought of his play as a tragedy (Mujica 230). Furthermore, it is clear that the very nature of tragedy remained a hotly debated topic at the time the playwright composed *La serrana de la Vera*, the polemics of which require a brief exposition to outline the theoretical context out of which the practice of early modern tragic drama took shape. The debate centred on the lasting influence of classical tragedy as outlined in Aristotle's *Poetics*. Lope de Vega directly addresses the utility of the Aristotelean definition of tragic drama for contemporary playwriting in his famous *Arte nuevo de hacer comedias en este tiempo* (1609), while authors like López Pinciano and González de Salas offer prescriptive insights on the relevance and value of classical theatre in lengthier treatises.[6] Lope demonstrates his familiarity with Aristotle's *Poetics* throughout the *Arte nuevo*, which he apparently composed in response to criticism for his plays' "failure" to conform to the Aristotelean unities of time, space, and action. Lope's expressed ambivalence to the strict adherence of the concepts outlined in the *Poetics* evinces not only the persistence of classical drama's influence on baroque cultural production, but also the artistic liberty contemporary playwrights exercised by manipulating the Aristotelean unities to increase the entertainment value for their audiences. To best suit his dramatic purposes and the tastes of the theatre-going public, Lope often heeded classical prescriptions, while sometimes he directly undermined it. In either case, he clearly wrestles with the anxiety of influence of classical dramatic art in his own playwriting and the reception of his works.[7] *La serrana de la Vera* demonstrates a similar commitment and rejection of Aristotelean poetics. It is impossible to discern whether this aspect of the play evinces an intentional and explicit tragic poetics on the part of the playwright or is simply a function of conventional dramatic practice at the time, as outlined in the *Arte nuevo*. However, it is clear Vélez de Guevara gestures towards the defining features of tragedy but swerves away from them at critical moments. This aspect of the composition of the play serves to maximize the impact of specific scenes; it is also fundamental to the process by which the play produces its salient message. Identifying and analysing those moments where the playwright diverges from classical prescription clears new avenues for resolving the ambiguities observed in recent scholarship on the work.

Nevertheless, in one important regard, *La serrana de la Vera* exemplifies a defining characteristic of tragic theatre, going back to its classical origins. Rebecca Bushnell contends that this pervasive characteristic is ambiguity itself, which she traces back to its ritualistic origins surrounding Dionysus, "the god whose contradictions define the essence of tragic ambiguity" (3). This ambiguity, which Boyle observes as an obstruction to a reading of the play as a cautionary tale, is also the characteristic that Lundelius understands to buttress the play's repressive ideological closure. Rather than ambiguity, however, Lundelius identifies the element of Vélez de Guevara's dramaturgy more specifically as paradox, paradox which "swirled around Gila in scene after scene, replete with ambiguous social implications, until in the end the established social order was overwhelmingly reaffirmed" (237). For her, the social implications of the exposition and conflict of the plot are nullified by its resolution. This follows William Egginton's description of the "major strategy" of baroque artistic production, which would view the "ambiguous social implications" to which Lundelius refers as the dramatic representation of the persuasive, but ultimately illusory, deceptions of the world, where it seems harmless to celebrate the exploits of a figure such as Gila. However, the drama goes on to correct this notion, depicting her as a serial killer to affirm the necessity of social order, rightfully restored and faithfully depicted in the carriage of justice in the final scene (*Theater of Truth* 8).

There is validity to this reading, but as I contend above, it erases the role of the emotional impact of the final scene on audiences' reception of the play's message. Readings that argue the ending presents a straightforward reaffirmation of the status quo privilege its legal justice at the expense of the emotional force of Gila's death. Fernando's perspective, then, is the only one that can matter, thereby stripping Isabel and Madalena's reactions of all significance. Yet, their responses more accurately reflect the intensity of the scene, as individuals who attempt to come to grips with the brutal death of a person they cared for as a cousin and friend (in the case of Madalena) or deeply admired (Isabel). The Queen's comment on Gila's death evokes the inexplicable awe she felt the first time she saw her at the festivals in Plasencia: "A mi me enternece el alma [It moves my spirit]" (3.3287). Like the external audience viewing the play, they have been informed of Gila's murders, but find it impossible to resolve the dissonance created by learning the same person they had regarded so highly from first-hand experience went on to kill thousands of men. Because these murders occur in the no-space between the final two acts, they take place in a time frame that audiences must artificially construct for themselves and imagine for the characters onstage. While this could be understood simply as the effect of the pragmatic impossibility of staging two thousand deaths, the specific murders that *are* viewed by the audience are tightly woven into the development of the plot, and therefore serve a primary dramatic purpose associated with events that have transpired onstage. I would argue, in fact, that concealing these murders from view is a question of emphasis on certain elements of the popular tale, while diminishing others. Even if only as an affective rather than rational response, this yields a sense of incongruity in the symbolic algebra required to assess the justice of Gila's punishment.

This transgression of the Aristotelean unity of time produces a particular dramatic effect. Vélez de Guevara condenses Gila's crimes in order to amplify the sense of compassion for her misfortune that lingers from Don Lucas' deception at the end of Act II. We see her exact revenge in response to a violation of her honour by a Don Juan character, after which she is almost immediately executed. The juxtaposition of these events leaves the audience to make sense of how the two events are connected; meanwhile they produce incompatible emotional effects. In other instances – Tirso de Molina's *El burlador de Sevilla* being a prime example – the death of characters like Don Lucas can be seen only as poetic justice. Nevertheless, critics have rarely cast Don Lucas in the same light as other Don Juan characters of the *comedia*, even though it provides a conventional template for doing so. If moralist ideological commitments so unequivocally generate early modern audiences' approval of the death of characters like Don Juan, it should be expected that characters with analogous qualities (e.g., Don Lucas) would elicit a commensurate response. Therefore, the artificial manipulation of time between the second and third acts is far from arbitrary; by juxtaposing Gila's revenge on Don Lucas with her execution, audiences are likely to see Gila as a tragic character. As Mujica asserts, "Gila only rings true as a tragic hero if we see her, as she sees herself, as a victim of predestination set right only by death" (230). This effect is achieved, in part, at the expense of the unity of time.

Aristotelean prescription is thereby sacrificed to increase the emotional impact of Gila's death; ironically, this transgression of one tenet of classical poetic art serves to maximize another: the play's *psychagogic* force – "that is, the power, literally, to lead the minds of those in the audience" (Eden 47). In this respect, Rodríguez Cuadros identifies emotional impact and dramatic action as the inextricable building blocks that constitute tragic logic: "lo importante para esta adhesión no es atribuir la esencia de lo trágico a la acción, sino que lo que es capaz de *movilizar* la acción, es decir, las emociones trágicas mismas [For this adhesion to occur, it is not most important to attribute tragic essence to action, but rather to that which is capable of *generating* the action, that is, tragic emotions themselves]" (188, emphasis in original). Specifically, Gila's situation evokes one affective response described by Aristotle as *hamartia*. Usually translated as "tragic flaw," *hamartia* should be understood more broadly as the error made by the protagonist, and, importantly, as the forces upon her or him that influence the course of action and transform her or his fortune from good to bad. According to Eden, *hamartia* is "precisely suited to tragic fiction" because "while it is not, strictly speaking, voluntary, in that the agent does not freely choose the act with full knowledge of its particulars, neither is it, strictly speaking, involuntary, in that it is not wholly unforeseen" (46). Gila's story unravels as a result of her acquiescence to the pressures of social convention when she agrees to marry Don Lucas, and consequently "tragic events happen 'contrary to expectation yet still on account of one another'" (Aristotle, cited in Eden 46). Rather than initiating a plot sequence that leads to a happy ending, Gila's compliance with social prescription results in her loss of honour. Once deceived, however, she refuses to find herself subordinated by a system that permits the punishment of those attempting to follow its rules. The cause of Gila's rage, then, is a just one even within the bounds of baroque social ideologies, which fuels the audience's response to Gila at the end. On this level, Vélez de Guevara's stagecraft masterfully triggers this emotive reflex through the manipulation of the unity of time by juxtaposing the cause of Gila's rage (her loss of honour) and the apparent injustice of its effect (her execution), irrespective of its legality.

Of course, the murder of two thousand men deserves punishment; however, the development of the plot guides audiences to *feel* otherwise, thereby successfully accomplishing the social critique essential to Aristotelean tragedy. Vélez de Guevara accomplishes this by transgressing one convention of classical dramatic composition – the unity of time – to "harness the power [of emotion] for some socially useful end" (Eden 47). This psychagogic force compels audiences to look beyond *what* happens and persuades them to understand more precisely *why* events occur, which thereby "sharpens [the] audience's ability to judge human action" (48). Gila makes the most sense in Vélez de Guevara's dramatic telling of *La serrana de la Vera* if we celebrate her extraordinary feats towards the beginning of the play, question her haughtiness upon claiming victory over men who challenge her unsuccessfully, vilify Don Lucas for his deception, and, alongside Queen Isabel and Madalena, sit perplexed at the ambiguous exemplarity signified by her lifeless body hanging as the backdrop of the play's final scene. If we are to consider the play a tragedy, then we must look beyond what happened (i.e., Gila's murders) and ask why the events transpire as they do. This task requires that we analyse the complex events and forces that brought about what occurs, which, as I have outlined, developed long before Gila began flinging men from the precipice. It is not simply by her actions that she arrives at the gibbet. She is affected by social forces that equivocally both celebrate and seek to curb her self-identified masculinity, which renders her displays of excessive pride a comprehensible mechanism to maintain that identity. This sensitivity to the precarious nature of an identity constantly under attack leads to a greater ability to acknowledge the psychological trauma (or at least the poetic significance) entailed by her subordination to Don Lucas. We are told she kills two thousand men, but we are shown the developments that lead to the unravelling of her story, an overview which provides insight into Vélez de Guevara's tragic *poiesis*. He leverages the elements that comprise tragic fiction to guide audiences to experience the emotional impact of a character who comes undone as a result of the irresolvable tension between her masculine identity and the prescriptions of social convention. The pressure of those competing realities comes to a head, the inevitability of which exemplifies the tragic nature of the work.

In the *Poetics*, Aristotle mentions that the primary factor that distinguishes tragedy from comedy "depends on the sort of characters proper to" each (ch. 4, 1448b25). Lope de Vega acknowledges this distinction in the *Arte nuevo de hacer comedias* as well, citing Aristotle's indication that "the only thing that separates comedy and tragedy is that the one depicts humble and plebian concerns, while tragedy presents noble and regal ones" (vv. 57–60). Of course, as Lope indicates, contemporary dramatists had come to largely ignore this prescription, and *La serrana de la Vera* is no exception. However, in the case of Vélez de Guevara's *comedia*, the incorporation of members across the social spectrum serves a dramatically significant purpose that buttresses the play's tragic poetics; chiefly, diminishing the importance of Aristotelean prescription on character directly elevates the role of another facet of classical tragic *poiesis*. In this case, common affairs, not simply noble ones, must be given representation to maintain the integrity of mimesis that is critical to classical tragic drama. Essential here to the faithful imitation of nature through art is the inclusion of stories and prerogatives of a multiplicity of agents, including Gila, a peasant woman; Don Lucas, a noble soldier; and even the Catholic Monarchs, Fernando and Isabel. This plurality of agents and classes creates a space for the message to apply to society as a whole in a specific context, in contrast to the universal and timeless truths imparted by classical tragedy on ancient theatre-going audiences.

To emphasize its universality, classical theatre relied on the chorus to comment on the action of the play, thus "mediating between the heroic and fictional action depicted onstage and the sociopolitical sphere of the spectators" (Calame 229). Vélez de Guevara incorporates a chorus of his own in *La serrana de la Vera* to mediate the events that take place onstage and within the social realities of the world beyond the fourth wall. On three separate occasions in the work, characters enter singing lines taken from a ballad that popularized the tale of the mountain woman of La Vera, long before the composition of Vélez de Guevara's adaptation for the seventeenth-century stage. The first instance occurs at the beginning of the play, when Gila appears onstage for the first time. She is surrounded by a host of villagers, who sing the beginning of a well-known ballad to introduce the protagonist. Their appearance evokes the Greek chorus, entering as a faceless mass to sing in unison a song that interprets the events taking place for the audience. Moreover, they stop the action and exist outside of it; the characters onstage are not aware of the villagers' presence. Their song has an explicitly celebratory tone:

> Dios mil años nos la guarde
> la Serrana de la Vera,
> y la dé un galán amante,
> la Serrana de la Vera,
> para que con ella case,
> la Serrana de la Vera,
> ...
> ¡Quién como ella,
> la Serrana de la Vera! (1.235–40, 43–4)

May God protect for a thousand years the Serrana of La Vera, and give her a handsome lover, the Serrana of La Vera, so that he marries her, the Serrana of La Vera, ... There is no one like the Serrana of La Vera!

As a point of departure for how the audience is to receive Gila, the villagers here provide a barometer for the protagonist's status at the opening of the play. While they view her in a positive light and celebrate her deeds, their well-wishing also sows the seeds for her ultimate demise. Their hope for her path in life is one that she would never wish for herself, namely, marriage. The ideological commitments supposed by the ballad overlook their own incompatibility with the figure they celebrate, and signify the social forces to which Gila will ultimately be sacrificed. This initial overt representation of the ballad tradition as an evocation of the Greek chorus establishes the link between the two when ballads are sung throughout the play.

Later on in the play there are two other occasions when characters sing Gila's story, following in the ballad tradition. Notably, they are sung by individual characters rather than larger groups, and both occur in Act III, after Gila has already gained notoriety for the murders she has committed. The universalized perspective, depicted by the ballad sung en masse at the opening of the play, becomes fragmented and particular at its close. Mirroring the plurality of perspectives emphasized in the work's denouement is the fact that they sing different versions of the ballad.[8] The very entity that is meant to guide the audience's interpretation of the action – the tragic chorus – is pluralistic and contradictory in Vélez de Guevara's *comedia*. The chorus indeed guides the audience's reception of the work, but rather than a unified mass offering straightforward universal truths to be drawn from the plot from a privileged space beyond the dramatized world, the members of the chorus are incorporated into the action of the play as mimetic examples affected by the universalizing ideologies that drive public and personal opinion. When the first ballad/chorus is sung, there is a dissonance between its celebratory nature and the social constraints surrounding Gila's identity. Towards the end of the play, individual members of that chorus continue to sing Gila's ballads, but they highlight the plurality of its makeup and the impossibility of universalizing discourse; nevertheless, the ballads they sing vilify the same character they previously celebrated once she exposes the untenable contradictions of their collective belief. Therefore, those songs must turn her into a monster to maintain their disavowal. Remarkably, this implementation of the chorus depicts examples from which the audience – both as a representative faction of larger society and as individuals – are affected by and agents of the ideological suppositions behind the cultural world depicted by the drama. The very elements that are supposed to anchor our interpretation of *La serrana de la Vera* have the opposite effect; the privileged perspective of the king and the chorus are set on equal footing with the affective responses of two women of diverse social classes – Isabel and Madalena – and the opinion of the masses, manifested by the incorporation of the multiple versions of Gila's story from the popular ballad tradition.

The constituent elements of tragic drama prove to be malleable resources for Veléz de Guevara's dramatic purposes. As exhibited in the play text, he demonstrates a flexible approach to the unity of time, the social status of the characters, and the identity of the tragic chorus, allowing him to transform those elements into tools with a greater capacity for social commentary through mimetic representation. The playwright's *poiesis*, based on this representation, distinguishes between the means and ends of tragedy. Aristotle made prescriptions about time, action, place, and character to maximize the emotional impact within the social context of ancient Greece; these are moulded to accommodate the cultural milieu of baroque Spain in *La serrana de la Vera*. By breaking the rules of tragic drama, Vélez de Guevara better accomplishes the ultimate purpose emphasized by Aristotle in the *Poetics*. He awakens the social consciousness of contemporary audiences by moving them to compassion for a character who transgresses their collective cultural mores. However, the playwright was not immune to the same social pressures that he critiqued in the original composition of his play. As further proof that the playwright understood the disruptive potential of his work, archival research carried out by George Peale reveals that Vélez de Guevara redacted many of the scenes that would lead audiences to the interpretations I have outlined thus far. According to Peale, Vélez de Guevara sterilizes the work in the process of preparing the play for its first staging:

> The alterations diminish the psychological complexity of the play and simplify the moral issues. Rather than a tragedy, the play becomes the melodrama of a badly brought-up child who takes vengeance on two thousand men because her father failed to discipline her adequately. (Mujica 232, paraphrasing Peale 62)

Knowledge of Vélez de Guevara's self-revision leads the modern reader to a number of important conclusions. First, it confirms the realities of censorship and the repressive apparatuses that reify Maravall's assertion of the society of the Spanish baroque as a "cultura dirigida [guided culture]" (107). Nevertheless, even though Vélez de Guevara was impeded by outside forces, his revisions to *La serrana de la Vera* indicate that he was both conscious and critical of the status quo, and, furthermore, that he was profoundly aware of theatre's potential for productively engaging in social critique, if permitted the opportunity. Although it seems he was reluctant to leverage Gila's character as a means for ideological disruption, the suppressed material substantiates the artistic mindset of an author with a socially aware dramatic conscience rather than that of a devoted acolyte eager to conserve the tenets of hegemony.

It would be a mistake to assert that the ideologically destabilizing elements were or could be completely eradicated from the play. Even if Vélez de Guevara's *comedia* can be seen to fit Maravall's framework of the baroque, one in which theatre played a principal role "in the capturing of desires ... in the service of established political interests," *La serrana de la Vera* must at least be understood to exemplify what Egginton deems as the defining characteristic of baroque aesthetics: "The stage ... is the very essence of the Baroque ... Because the Baroque is theater, the theater of the Baroque offers the most vivid expression of its core; in the elements of its basic design we see the seams of its construction, and the traces of its ultimate undoing" (*Theater of Truth* 40). Theatre, in its modern form, finds its ideological efficacy by negotiating the space between reality and its representation, or, more precisely, the audience's ability to acknowledge the difference between reality and its representation in theatrical space, while still accepting theatrical representation's bearing on a perceived reality. In fact, Egginton pinpoints "this split between interior and exterior audience, and the concomitant negotiation and play between those levels, [as] perhaps the single most powerful marker of Baroque aesthetics" (*Theater of Truth* 42–3). The medium is constituted by an inherent "theatrical aporia," by which "the mediation of appearances and presence to self" suggest that appearance and reality can be mediated in the first place, and that the difference between the version of reality presented on the stage and the audience's perception of that reality ultimately and necessarily means that a third reality, the one that's *really* real, must exist elsewhere (43).

The *comedia*'s ideological function, as traditionally understood, packages the fantasy of a unified society as if it were that reality, faithfully exhibited. Inevitably, though, according to Žižek, the totalitarian project is stymied by some "fundamental blockage" that "prevents society from achieving its full identity as a closed homogeneous reality" (143). Gila represents one of those "fundamental blockages" to baroque order, which are perceived as "simple deviations, contingent deformations and degenerations of the 'normal' functioning of society... and as such abolishable through the amelioration of the system" (144). Nevertheless, characters like Gila "are necessary products of the system itself – the points at which 'truth,' the immanent antagonistic character of the system, erupts" (144). Gila's lifeless form, which remains onstage at the play's close, embodies the equivocal theatricality that pervades baroque aesthetics. While her death may persuasively guide the audience to form a "dogmatic attachment" (23) to ideologies that demand her execution to abolish the threat she posed to social order, Gila also refuses elimination. The absence signified by her death can only be perceptible through the conspicuous and visible presence of her inert body hanging from the gibbet. She remains a tragic symbol that points to the violence engendered as an inevitable cost of establishing and maintaining the ideological commitments of repressive social apparatuses.

Four hundred years after the original staging of *La serrana de la Vera*, imagining a society less inclined to police modes of conduct specific to dominant culture at any cost is as crucial as ever. The themes presented in *La serrana de la Vera* related to gender identity and sexuality surely resonate today, yet, there have been few modern productions of the play. The Compañía Nacional de Teatro Clásico staged the play in 2004 under the direction of María Ruiz, and Radio Televisión Española's created a made-for-TV version in 1994. Maybe unsurprisingly, RTVE diminished many of the same aspects Vélez de Guevara felt the need to revise for its original seventeenth-century staging. In Bárbara Mujica's estimation, "the production maintains most of the original text intact, but downplays the problematical areas," which include the intimations of homosexual desire between Gila and the Queen, the softening of Gila's masculinity, and even the suggestion of her complicity in Don Lucas' deception as "willing prey" (233). Today, "problematic" has become a term often used to describe the tacit sexism and homophobia that causes these types of omissions from the original text, rather than the nature of the content in question. Nevertheless, Mujica's point that RTVE "sanitized" the text is well taken. In September 2017, La Compañía Nacional de Extremadura de Teatro y Kabaret, a theatre company in Cáceres also known as Labotika, made no such concessions in their production of the play. According to director Marce Solís, Labotika's production sought to consider a number of themes: "educación de padres, libertad femenina, independencia, lesbianismo, protesta social, crítica de la tradición y las costumbres [parental guidance, women's rights, independence, lesbianism, social protest, criticism of traditions and customs; cited in Núñez]." The subtitle they gave their adaptation provides a succinct explanation of the presentation of Gila found in their play: "mujer libre y fiera [a free and fierce woman]." Although Labotika adapted the work "para convertirla en una divertida comedia del Siglo de Oro, sin perder un ápice la leyenda y el mito ancestral [in order to transform it into an enjoyable play from the Golden Age without losing any part of the original legend]," significant changes are not necessarily required to highlight the themes that appear in Solís' list.

In 2019, the theatre department at the University of Massachusetts at Amherst also staged a production of the play based on Harley

Erdman's recent bilingual translation, which they brought to the annual Nuevo Siglo Drama Festival at the Chamizal National Memorial Cultural Center in El Paso, Texas.[9] Erdman's introduction conveys the translator's careful attention to the dynamics of gender presentation in the work, and submits the view that the play is "constructed ... so as to make audiences sympathetic" to Gila (2). Under the direction of Gina Kaufmann, the UMass Amherst production of *Wild Thing* reflected this portrayal of Gila, allowing for the protagonist's non-binary gender expression to be the catalyst for the play's tragic turn. They reinforced this aspect visually through the design of Gila's costume; neither a doublet worn with pants nor a dress, it was simultaneously both, and as such, the protagonist's garment was impossible to decipher along the lines of traditional sartorial markers of the masculine and feminine. The impact of which Vélez de Guevara's *comedia* is capable became evident during the talkback session after the performance: an audience member commended the production for featuring a non-binary character who embodied a presence in the space of representation for those who also identify as non-binary. In performance, the intense emotional experience of observing Gila's tragic fall induces audiences to condemn the social forces that marginalize her; the UMass production succeeded in making this experience familiar, opening up a window for audiences to see much of our own world in the dramatized space of fifteenth-century Spain.

The politics that governed gender and sexuality in seventeenth-century Spain undoubtedly still have much in common with the repressive forces present in our own society. So long as gender inequality, sexual violence, and trans- and homophobia fail to be addressed, Margaret Greer's description of women in tragic drama of the Spanish baroque exemplifies the urgency plays like *La serrana de la Vera* can impart on these issues for contemporary audiences: "Women in tragedy, whether or not they submit to patriarchal law that dictates their obedience and confinement, are sacrificed to its demands" ("Spanish Golden Age Tragedy" 366). Now, as much as then, Gila offers a painful, critical reminder that ideology shapes culture at the expense of marginalizing subjects outside of its constructed, prescriptive boundaries. Gila's struggle against the fickle tides of social convention exposes the tenets of dominant ideology, which emerge as capricious and dangerous for those whose identities fall outside the borders of orthodoxy. While it is true that tragedies "are cultural artifacts embedded in the society that generated them" (Sourvinou-Inwood 7), it is also true – and vital that we acknowledge – that Gila's death remains as a socially relevant and affectively compelling tragedy.

NOTES

1 Vélez de Guevara relies heavily on popular literature in the composition of *La serrana de la Vera*. The incorporation of pre-existing ballads about the folkloric "serrana de la Vera" is an example of this; the original audiences would have been familiar with the character prior to seeing the play. In their edition of the play, Manson and Peale provide extensive notes on the idiomatic lexicon, aphorisms, and references to folk literature that the playwright drew from in the composition of the work (187–249).
2 Peale's extensive collaborative scholarship on Vélez de Guevara has been indispensable in reviving interest in the playwright, who had been long relegated to the periphery of *comedia* scholarship and practice. This chapter is in many ways a manifestation of the renewed interest in the playwright that he has sparked in recent years. His work on *La serrana de la Vera*, specifically, examines a number of its facets, including the representation of the *gracioso* character and the extensive incorporation of proverbs and ballads into its verse, and his critical edition remains essential for scholarship on the play.
3 For passages also cited by Stroud in his chapter "Homo/Hetero/Social/Sexual: Gila in Vélez de Guevara's *La serrana de la Vera*," I use his translations with minor alterations. In all other instances, including works other than *La serrana de la Vera*, the translations are my own. At the time of writing this chapter, Harley Erdman's highly anticipated translation and bilingual edition of the play, *The Mountain Girl from La Vera*, had not yet been published.
4 Although some scholars point to this sexual encounter before the wedding ceremony as evidence of Gila's complicity in her own demise, Mujica notes in *A New Anthology of Early Modern Spanish Theater* (in reference to Tirso's *El burlador de Sevilla*) that "it was considered acceptable before the Council of Trent (when the play is set) for a betrothed couple to enjoy sexual relations" (292).
5 Although Fernando's character is the primary and visible agent of political authority in the play, Isabel's lack of influence on Gila's adjudication obscures the functional dynamics of power between the Catholic Monarchs. At the very least, Isabel's deference is peculiar, provided the events take place in Castile where "Ferdinand's personal authority was sharply restricted" (Elliot 57). J.H. Elliot acknowledges Ferdinand took on a greater role in the governance of Castile over time (61), but it is also true that Isabel remained "a ruling queen who governed along with her husband, and both were responsible for the policies that were undertaken in their realms – often independently and at times at cross-purposes" (Silleras-Fernández 157). Neither of these perspectives on the historical figure of Isabel explain the representation of the Catholic Queen in Vélez de Guevara's *comedia*.

As Barbara Weissgerber explains, the figure of Isabel has experienced significant transformation in the cultural imagination of the peninsula over the centuries since the historical figure lived and reigned. Even during the queen's lifetime, the bulk of literary production sought to "express and mystify the threat to masculine subjectivity that the female monarch and her patriarchal political program represent" (Weissgerber xv). "The cultural anomaly of female sovereignty itself" embodied by Isabel became inscribed into a patriarchal historical narrative, over the course of which the complexities of her authority diminish while Fernando's increased. Scholars will disagree on the representation of the docile Isabel in *La serrana de la Vera*; she is either the product of the playwright's passive replication of a century-long nullification of the queen's implied threat to male power in the Iberian collective conscience, or a means by which he further emphasizes, and criticizes, the unshakeable patriarchal status quo at the expense of historical accuracy.

6 Lope's short poetic reflection on the applicability (or lack thereof) of Aristotle in the *Arte nuevo* is markedly different from the more serious and extended volumes by López Pinciano (*Philosophia Antigua Poética*) and González de Salas (*Nueva idea de la tragedia antigua*). Nevertheless, all are indicative of the tendency of Spanish playwrights who "procedieron a seleccionar las teorías de acuerdo con un sentido pragmático y, sobre todo en el género trágico, 'confrontando la tradición con la experiencia, las tradiciones de la antigüedad con la práctica de su propia época' [proceeded to select theories in accordance with a sense of pragmatism and, especially in the case of tragedy, 'confronted tradition with experience, traditions from antiquity with practices of their own time']" (Newels, cited in Rodríguez Cuadros 185).

7 See Harold Bloom, *The Anxiety of Influence*, which explores the impact of influence on authorship as a critical framework for understanding the nature of artistic innovation.

8 For information on the many versions of the "La serrana de la Vera" tale in the ballad tradition, see Piñero and Atero's "El romance de *La serrana de la Vera*."

9 I attended this performance, which took place on 10 April 2019.

2 Utopian Divorce: *El descasamentero* by Salas Barbadillo

TANIA DE MIGUEL MAGRO

One of the topics often analysed in connection to women's access to social justice is that of marriage. Article 16 of the Universal Declaration of Human Rights recognizes the right of an individual to enter into a contract of marriage without limitations as to race, nationality, or religion, provided that the spouses are free to fully consent. Although this article also states that spouses are "entitled to equal rights as to marriage, during marriage and *at its dissolution*" (emphasis mine), the United Nations does not recognize divorce as a right. In fact, while divorce is common across Europe, not even the European Union recognizes divorce to be a human right.[1]

In seventeenth-century Catholic Spain, divorce, as we understand it today, was impossible. What they called divorce was closer to our modern concept of separation, and even this was extremely rare. In this chapter I analyse the only theatrical piece of the period that openly and explicitly advocates for divorce: *El descasamentero* by Jerónimo de Salas Barbadillo. It could be argued that *El juez de los divorcios* (hereafter *El juez*), the piece that inspired *El descasamentero*, is also a defence of divorce. Nonetheless, Cervantes is more ambiguous than Salas and does not discuss alternatives to the sacrament of marriage. Salas considers divorce a desirable practice that brings justice and happiness to individual citizens and society as a whole. Accordingly, he depicts a tribunal that simplifies the process for obtaining a divorce. In order to safely transmit such a controversial (and heretical) idea, Salas takes advantage of the possibilities offered by two literary genres that distance his proposal from the actual circumstances of the reader: the utopic narratives and the burlesque theatre. Salas inverts what the church and state stipulated regarding marriage, thus revealing that real justice is impossible to achieve under the status quo. He demonstrates that the restrictions of the Catholic Church and the Spanish legal system did nothing to ensure justice, but rather brought distress and disorder. According to Salas, justice and law, as practised at the time, were antagonistic. In *El descasamentero* he presents a utopic tribunal that reconciles both elements.

Divorce, as a topic, is completely absent from the *comedia*, even though marriage is a structurally crucial element for the genre. Most dramas end with the announcement of one or more wedding arrangements that somehow resolve the conflicts previously presented, thus resulting in social harmony. Personal relations between the spouses are irrelevant, except when they lead to a real or suspected case of dishonour, as in *El castigo sin venganza* or *El médico de su honra*.² I am not arguing, like Antonio Maravall did, that all *comedias* follow the pattern order-chaos-order, and that they reflect and promote aristocratic, imperial, and Catholic values. Nor do I imply a wedding is always a happy ending, or that such marriages are unproblematic. I am just highlighting the fact that, in the *comedia*, marriage tends to be presented as a resolution and the end point of action. Furthermore, I believe that if we find affirmations of any kind of social justice in the *comedias*, it is precisely because they do not always respond to a monolithic ideology.

In *Subject Stages: Marriage, Theatre, and the Law in Early Modern Spain*, María M. Carrión demonstrates how both theatres and courtrooms became stages in which non-conforming views on marriage were represented. On the stage, she argues, State and Man did not always rule over Stage and Woman; thus it is possible to uncover "subject positions that playfully produced scenes of what the Law considered intangible, invisible, or negligible in marriage" (8). Carrión does an exceptional work locating and analysing discordant scenes. Additionally, her research inadvertently reveals what the *comedias* lack, that is, open marital quarrels or debates about divorce. This absence makes sense. The topic of divorce was taboo in the *comedia*, as in any other serious literary genre, because of the sacramental nature of marriage and the Catholic prohibition against divorce. Addressing divorce could be easily considered an attack on Catholic doctrine in favour of Protestantism.

The struggles of married couples are, though, among the most common themes in the short interludes. Love, respect, and faithfulness do not make for good slapstick comedy; instead, the *entremeses* are packed with scenes of cheating, quarrels, practical jokes, defamation, and violence. In the *entremeses* a wedding is not a happy ending, but an impediment to achieving happiness. Mary Gaylord Randel aptly defines the opposite ways in which the *comedia* and the *entremés* approach marriage: "Marriage, for the *comedia* and for most societies the great symbol of wholeness, harmony and order, becomes in the *entremés* the figure of disintegration, dissonance, separation, living death" (89). Given the burlesque nature of the genre, and that most couples in the *entremeses* are miserable, one would expect the *entremeses* to be an acceptable space for bringing up the idea of divorce as a possible solution. Nonetheless, as far as I can tell, there are only two theatrical pieces that openly talk about divorce: *El juez* and *El descasamentero*. Considering how many *entremeses* display marital troubles, it is safe to say that authors purposely avoided talking about divorce. It is important to point out how exceptional these two pieces are, not only in topic but in form. They are much longer than the typical *entremés* and they favor narration over action. More important, as I will later discuss, they were meant to be read, not performed.

El descasamentero was published with the subtitle "comedia doméstica [domestic comedy]," (my trans.), but its structure and content resemble those of an *entremés*, not a *comedia*. It is written in prose, it has only one act, and it fits the *entremesil* subgenres of the satirical tribunal and the "desfile de locos [parade of madmen]" (my trans.). Additionally, its characters often refer to themselves and their actions as appropriate for an *entremés*. In this sense, *El descasamentero* seems to be somewhere in between an *entremés* and a *comedia burlesca*. For the purpose of my analysis, generic classification, either as *entremés*, *comedia burlesca*, or *comedia doméstica*, is irrelevant, because what interests me about the piece is an element common to those three genres: the burlesque style.

Before embarking on arguments about why divorce was deemed improper for the stage (while seemingly more controversial matters such as homosexuality were not), it is necessary to review some historical facts about marriage and divorce practices. Marriage was first and foremost a sacrament. On 11 November 1563, the members of the Synod of Trent, under Pope Pius IV, met to talk about the sacrament of matrimony. Their conclusions were compiled in *The Canons and Decrees of the Sacred and Oecumenical Council of Trent* (hereafter *The Canons*). *The Canons* described matrimony as a divine bond "perpetual and indissoluble" (194);[3] thus divorce and the right to remarry were impossible. Nevertheless, the church could grant an annulment, a ruling which did not give spouses permission to break the vows but rather certified that such vows were not valid and that the spouses were not married in the eyes of God.[4] All in all, annulment was pretty rare.[5]

The dispositions of Trent directly influenced the Spanish civil codes. A year after the publication of *The Canons*, a *cédula real* "royal writ" declared that all decisions from Trent were to be considered binding law in the Iberian Peninsula. *The Canons* were thereafter widely distributed and there was a consistent effort to put its regulations into effect. In 1567 King Philip II ordered the creation of a single unifying legal document for the

Peninsula, the *Nueva Recopilación*, which explicitly accepted the dispositions of the *Canons*, not leaving any room for dissolution of marriages, although it assented to the possibility of requesting a divorce. A divorce, which fell under civil jurisdiction, only granted the spouses separation, *quoad thorum et mensam* (that is, the right to live in separate houses), but not the right to remarry. As it is the case with annulments, there is no comprehensive data for the entire Peninsula, but it is safe to say that petitions for divorce were extremely rare, and actual divorces even less common.[6]

Obtaining a divorce may have been extremely infrequent and the right to remarry totally impossible, but marital quarrels and couples wishing to separate were, one would imagine, as common as in any other time. Then, how is it that the *entremeses*, which continually present domestic fights, avoid the topic? We cannot find the answer in morality, because *entremeses* and other forms of burlesque theatre present all kinds of transgressions and often glorify infidelity and crime. It is not by chance that moralists considered interludes the most dangerous element of the theatrical spectacles. I believe the taboo is the result of the need to silence dissent in a way that was not necessary with other "crimes" for which there was a social consensus. For example, there was no harm in telling jokes about cross-dressers or homosexuals, because there was a generalized agreement about sodomy: it was a sin, an abomination. There were obviously those who secretly differed from this line of thought, but in any case, there was no room for the public defence of homosexuality as a choice. Given this social consensus, jokes made at the expense of the sexually deviant Other were not read as legitimation of the sin. Similarly, it was fine to laugh at the expense of the cuckolded husband, as long as he was a nobody who lacked the social and moral authority to reclaim the faithfulness of his wife, who was always more clever and sympathetic than he.

But things were not so clear-cut when it came to divorce. Divorce was a dangerous topic, particularly after its approval by Protestant authorities. In Catholic countries, according to religious and civil laws, marriage could not be dissolved, but not everyone was willing to adhere to the law. Until Trent, the rules for contracting and dissolving marriage were not as strict and, despite the church's efforts to eradicate traditional practices of marriage (such as secret nuptials and mutually agreed-on separations), they persisted, particularly in rural areas. Couples were more worried about practical matters than sacramental ties. So not only did unhappy spouses walk away, acting against Catholic dogma, their neighbours and friends often supported their actions.[7] What made the defence of divorce onstage particularly dangerous was not that divorce per se was prohibited, but that just defending the idea was considered heresy, as established by *The Canons*: "If any one saith, that on account of heresy, or irksome cohabitation, or the affected absence of one of the parties, the bond of matrimony may be dissolved; let him be anathema" (194). Therefore, saying that breaking the bonds of wedlock was a higher sin than the act of leaving the conjugal household. This might be why the only two *entremeses* that directly confront divorce were not staged. I will come back to this later.

El descasamentero is part of *Fiestas de la boda de la incasable malcasada* (Celebrations of the Wedding of an Un-marriageable, Ill-married Lady) (my trans.; hereafter *Fiestas*), which was published in 1622. The structure of *Fiestas* vaguely reminds us of Boccacio and the Italian Renaissance collections of short stories linked by a frame. Unlike those compendia of novellas, *Fiestas* includes pieces belonging to a diversity of genres and its frame is quite lengthy and developed, in fact, a novella in and of itself. It has been argued that the book is an amalgam that lacks any coherence or thematic unity. Despite the asymmetrical quality of its elements, there is an overarching theme that links all the parts: love, and marriage in particular, leads to unhappiness. The book mixes serious and comic genres, prose and verse, narrative and drama, but it is in the theatrical form (always burlesque) that Salas finds the proper venue to denounce a society moved by falseness and greed, and it is also in the theatre that subaltern voices find a space to justify themselves. *El descasamentero* is not just a parade of laughable characters, but the stage in which to articulate dissident points of view. In other words, Salas considers comic theatre as the preferred genre to portray social injustice and to facilitate the delivery of alternative social models.

The opening words of *Fiestas* present marriage as a sad event:

Los injustos festines de las bodas de una incasable malcasada refiero, que puede tanto la fuerza de una perversa costumbre que al estado del casamiento, que se había de solemnizar con lágrimas, escandalizamos con agoreras alegrías, siendo aquel gozo violento y breve presagio de su tormento eterno. (1)[8]

I retell the unjust festivities of the wedding of an un-marriageable ill-married woman, because the strength of a perverse custom is so powerful that the state of marriage, which should be solemnized with tears, we scandalize with prophetic happiness, when that joy is a violent and brief omen of its eternal torment.[9]

Salas maintains that his book is to serve as advice to capricious, disdainful ladies who, judging themselves too good for any man, end up waiting too long and marrying "el más indigno [the least worthy]" (1). Salas at once urges such ladies not to wait too long to marry and tells them that their marital lives will be unhappy because all marriages are "pendencias [quarrels]" (1). Salas also addresses "todos los que están en esperanza de ser maridistas [all who are hopeful to become husbands]" (2), listing for them the negative aspects of wedlock. The book, thus, demonstrates that the most basic component of social structure, marriage, is troublesome. The supposed harmony of Christian marriage is in reality a form of torment from which one cannot escape.

After the sarcastic tone of the preliminary introduction, the narration begins. For the first forty pages or so, the story develops like any other romantic novel (jealousy, courtship, changes of identity, love letters, etc.). Two cousins, Luis and Fernando, are in love with the noble, beautiful, rich, and very intelligent Dorotea. Tired of waiting, Fernando marries another woman, and Dorotea and Luis are invited to the wedding. On the way to the celebration, Dorotea confesses to her mother that she has decided to enter a convent, but at the event she meets two brothers who also court her: Lope (young, handsome, and intelligent) and Sebastián (older, stupid, and deformed). To everyone's surprise, she decides to marry Sebastián, because, as she later confesses to a friend, he is so simple that she will be able to control him. The original description of Dorotea matches that of other *mujeres esquivas* of the *comedia* such as Diana in *El desdén con el desdén* and Ana in *No puede ser* (both by Agustín Moreto), but the resolution of her conflict differs greatly. Diana and Ana end up accepting their positions and are happily married, but Dorotea's wedding is the beginning of her suffering. She becomes a victim of her own pride, but also a victim of a society which does not offer her any options. For her intellectual superiority to flourish (and the narrator makes it clear that she is indeed intellectually superior to any man), she needs to condemn her body, either locking it in a convent or submitting it to the touch of her disgusting husband. Moreover, her marriage does not close the drama, but literally opens it, because the celebration of the wedding becomes the stage for the representation of other dramas.

Even when Dorotea initially thinks that she will be free if she marries Sebastián, because he is an idiot unable to control anyone, she is, in the eyes of the law and others, irremediably subjected to him. Her initial desire to remain single derives from her yearning to avoid the limitations placed on her by virtue of her sex. Unable to escape social and familial pressures, she opts for choosing a weak husband, which she believes frees her. It is only after the wedding takes place, and while attending the performance of *El descasamentero*, that she realizes that she has made a terrible mistake. Georgina Dopico Black explains that by becoming a wife a woman became "a subject in the eyes of the church and the state, acting for the first time as her (legal) self, giving a word (a word with specific legal, economic, and religious repercussions) to her husband before the presence of both civil and ecclesiastical authorities" (5–6). Dorotea is for the first time a subject able to make a decision about her life in the moment of consenting to marry, but at such a moment she is fully subjected to her husband, with no option to change her mind. Her freedom to choose a husband condemns her to lose all other freedoms. This kind of loss, *El descasamentero* demonstrates, happens to both men and women, who upon entering wedlock renounce individual desires and happiness.

The second, and longest, part of the book includes all the pieces staged during a party in honour of the nuptials of Sebastián and Dorotea. A very jealous Luis hires an itinerant theatrical company to perform two *comedias* (although they will end up performing some more), the first of which is *El descasamentero*. Luis understands the plays he has selected may raise suspicions, and he takes the necessary precautions not to be associated with it, revealing his understanding of how threatening theatre can be. By commissioning the plays, Luis becomes the only person daring to voice what is obvious: that Dorotea will be miserable, that Sebastián has been deceived into believing that she loves him, and that either Lope or himself would have been better-suited husbands for her. Nevertheless, no one opposes the marriage because the disdainful lady has finally fulfilled her duty: entering into wedlock with a man of her same station. If this were a *comedia*, the wedding would have made for a proper happy ending. But Luis is willing to question the idea of whether any marriage is better than no marriage. Luis, like the characters of *El descasamentero*, values personal happiness over the social and legal requirements of marriage, including remaining in it despite the circumstances. He questions social assumptions by reverting to the well-established conventions of the *comedia*. Ironically, the first part of the frame story ends like any *comedia* or novella, with a wedding, but it opens the door to a series of burlesque pieces that, like *entremeses*, occupy the space between the acts. "Real life" does not resemble a *comedia*, in which all problems can be resolved with a wedding. The problems of the spouses do not end with the wedding, as in an *entremés*, they rather start at that point. Salas is playing with the reader's expectations and demonstrating how absurd they are, and he does so by employing a genre, the *entremés*, that has a tradition of inverting the clichés of the *comedia* and rejecting the social norms that it depicts.

Salas follows the structure of *El juez*, but there is one main difference between the pieces. Salas does not situate his divorce court in contemporary Madrid, but in an extemporal Parnassus, a place in which divorce is not only possible but even desirable and easy to obtain. The setting creates one layer of separation between the action and the readers. While Cervantes just presents the perils of unhappy marriages, Salas designs a utopian space, free from the rules of the church and the state, in which the law does not constrain citizens, but rather frees them. After the publication of Thomas More's *Utopia*, utopias became a staple of early modern thought and literature. Given how dangerous it could have been to openly defend divorce, Salas decides to employ the utopic model, because, as Chris Ferns explains, utopias are the ideal genre to question social injustices: "Rather than a monolithic ideal, whose unquestionable superiority to existing society is taken for granted, utopia becomes more a matter of exploring possibilities, indicating new directions" (x). This is exactly how Salas generates his utopic tribunal. His opposition to the indissolubility of marriage is accompanied by a presentation of an alternative path; utopic and burlesque, yes, but a path, something that was not envisioned by *El juez*. I will not enter the debate of whether Cervantes defends or opposes divorce, or on how to interpret the final song: "más vale el peor concierto / que no el divorcio mejor [the worst agreement is better than the best divorce]" (110; my trans.). Regardless of how we read *El juez*, it is undeniable that Cervantes does not present an alternative legal frame to the one operating at his time. *El juez* simply reveals a disjunction between the expectations of marriage and the reality of it. *El descasamentero*, on the other hand, by placing the action in a fictional time and space, offers a suitable substitute system.

The theatrical form, as well as the dialogic structure of early modern utopias, permits the inclusion of contradictory points of view, although it is true that most utopic narratives reinforce one dominant perspective and minimize the weight of dissenting voices. Likewise, in *El descasamentero* most characters consider divorce to be beneficial and such a standpoint is rendered as "truth," but there is a small space reserved for pondering the possible negative effects of facilitating access to divorce. The Ministro (prosecutor) explains:

> [Germano] viene a tratar el remedio de aquellos que por su elección se metieron en el daño, con que de aquí adelante será mayor el número de estos perdidos sabiendo que es daño que tiene remedio, y tan fácil. De modo que con esta comisión, a mi parecer, más venimos a destruir el mundo que a mejoralle. (46)

[Germano] comes to find the remedy for those who got in trouble because of their choices; therefore, from now on the number of these lost souls will be greater, knowing that there is a remedy to their troubles, and one so easy. Thus, with this enterprise, it seems to me, we are more likely to destroy than improve the world.

The Ministro often argues with Lucino, a defence lawyer who is convinced that the tribunal will benefit humanity, because Lucino himself had an unhappy marriage, which he describes as worse than being condemned to the galleys. Regardless of his initial reservations, the Ministro collaborates with the goals of the tribunal and agrees with granting each of the divorces.

As is common with any utopia, *El descasamentero* draws obvious connections between the fictional space and the world of its readers. Therefore, although the court is placed in a pre-Christian space, the work abounds in religious terminology and rituals, which serve to legitimize the premise of divorce as just, while criticizing aspects of Catholic doctrine. All characters understand the sacred dimension of the enterprise and hence use religious imagery to talk about Germano and his tribunal. For example, the first plaintiff, Dorotea (not to be mistaken with the Dorotea of the frame story), enters the scene asking: "¿No es esta la casa de la piedad? ¿No es éste el tribunal donde se ejercitan misericordias? [Isn't this the house of mercy? Isn't this the tribunal in which charity is practised?]" (48). Words and expressions such as "misericordia," "caridad," "socorro del alma," and "piedad" abound in reference to Germano and his tribunal, while marriage is defined using terminology that equates it with hell or punishment: "martirio" (martyrdom), "infierno" (hell), "galeras" (galleys), or "encierro" (prison).

Germano, who is directly appointed by Apollo, embodies many of the attributes and virtues of a good Catholic priest, although his duties are the inverse of those of a priest. While on earth Christian priests receive from God through the sacrament of priesthood the power to sanction marriages, on this Parnassus it is Apollo who uses his divine power to grant Germano a divorce. Like a priest, Germano is a faithful servant who acts as the representative of God's desires on earth. Upon receiving his charge, he proclaims: "Apolo me alumbre el entendimiento para que acierte en materias tan difíciles y, pues soy su comisario, en mi causa mire por la suya [May Apollo illuminate my judgment so I will get it right in such difficult cases, and, because I am his commissioner, in my cause may I look after his]" (46). He also shows the fear of God. Germano's assignment is described in religious terms: "comisión tan piadosa, que este es oficio que quiere ejercitarse con caridad, despenando liberalmente a los que ha muchos años que padecen en el martirio del casamiento [such a pious commission that this is a service that must be executed with charity, liberally consoling those who have been suffering the martyrdom of marriage for many years]" (46). In fact, though the word *divorcio* is used throughout the piece, what Germano is able to grant is closer to an annulment, as it allows spouses to remarry.

Apollo's divine justice is the result of reversing the sacramental dimension of Catholic matrimony. As the piece evolves, it becomes clear that real justice (the one Apollo brings) can be achieved only by contradicting the canonical and civil laws that rule on earth. The first request for divorce is presented by Dorotea, who consented to marry her husband under the condition that he would allow her to freely go about, as stipulated in their prenuptial agreement. She lived happily until her parents died, at which point the husband became a tyrant. She is petitioning either for divorce or for enforcement of the the prenuptial agreement.

Germano admits that the lawsuit is justified and calls for the presence of the *casamentero* Roberto, who performed the wedding and was witness to the signing of the prenuptial agreement. He ratifies what Dorotea said. Dorotea's husband accepts the charges, and both request an annulment. They both claim that they were married against their will, which was one of the few circumstances that could lead to a church annulment at the time. For the purposes of the Parnassian court, such a detail is irrelevant. As Germano declares, they have already established enough causation when declaring that they have been together for ten years "sin gusto [without pleasure]" (52), and thus their marriage is dissolved.

The second plaintiff, Fabio, also manifests religious reverence for the judge. His case equates marriage with damnation and divorce with salvation. He has spent one month in marital "hell" and claims that if he remains in wedlock he will "volvereme a desesperarme [be driven to despair]" (52). *Desesperarse* had at the time the connotation of committing suicide.[10] A divorce, therefore, would save Fabio from eternal damnation, which is the Catholic fate for those who commit suicide. In *El descasamentero*, hell is not the space of divine punishment but of worldly suffering, and divorce is not a sin but a path to heaven. Moreover, we are to infer, by prohibiting divorce the Catholic Church is damning individuals to hell, whether in this life or the next.

In Parnassus, marriages are performed by *casamenteros* (matchmakers), who embody everything that is wrong with the Catholic conception of marriage. Matchmakers add to the duties of an earthly matchmaker that of officiating at weddings. They act, accordingly, as priests. *Casamenteros* are the only characters to promote marriage; they follow the mandates of the Catholic Church, espousing the benefits of married life, and assert the superiority of marriage over single life. Matchmakers, though, are presented as greedy villains who contradict the wishes of Apollo. They are devilish creatures blamed for "la mayor parte de la perdición del mundo [the major part of the world's downfall]" (49). It is not hard to see here a veiled criticism of Catholicism and its insistence on imposing marriage on everyone.

In *El descasamentero*, Germano creates only one new law. This one single piece of legislation contrasts with the many limitations established by *The Canons* and operates as a direct questioning of the Catholic discipline of clerical celibacy. Once again, Salas employs a burlesque approach to protect himself from the potential accusation of being pro-Protestant in this matter. Germano decrees that all matchmakers must themselves be married: "para que conociendo con la experiencia lo que en semejante estado se padece, case a los que se pusieren en sus manos con más piedad, que esta consistirá en dar a las bodas poca prisa [because knowing from experience how much one suffers in such state, he will wed those who come to him with more mercy, which will consist of not rushing the weddings]" (60). *El descasamentero* reveals how illogical it is that, according to Catholic doctrine, those who are to perform weddings are themselves not allowed to be married.

Salas chooses to embed the dialogue with religious terminology in order to legitimize the alternative presented by this divorce court. Here divorce is not a sin; it does not break divine rules. Divorce is sanctioned by God as testimony of his mercy, and those who obtain it experience the blessing of happiness. In constructing his argument, Salas employs a religious discourse that locates divorce within the realm of that which is appropriate and desirable for the faithful. The use of Catholic verbiage serves to present divorce as an act of justice in line with Christian mercy, unlike the church's actual restrictions on divorce. *El descasamentero* maintains that a merciful God would allow divorce. Instead of directly condemning church prohibitions, Salas, through his characters, uses religious terms to praise divorce. After obtaining the divorce, Dorotea exclaims: "¡Qué grande juez tenemos! Bien se le ve que viene de la mano de Apolo, pues ejercita a un mismo tiempo justicia y misericordia [What a great judge we have! It is easy to see that his justice comes from the hand of Apollo, because he exercises at once both justice and mercy]" (52). Germano inverts Catholic dogma when he declares that the spouses who remained so long together against their will were not virtuous, but martyrs. He then promises to have their names written in the martyrology of the married. In the Catholic tradition a martyr is someone who died in defence of the Christian faith and hence went to heaven. In Salas' Parnassus, a martyr is someone whose marital life is like death and who obtains salvation through divorce.

In addition to demonstrating the injustices derived from the restrictions placed by the church, Salas targets the Spanish legal system and the negative role of civil courts. Civil law appears as a block to both individual happiness and the proper functioning of the country. Germano's divorce court is utopic not only because it can grant annulments, but because it is free from the problems of the contemporary Spanish judicial system. Richard Kagan has demonstrated that lawsuits increased in Castile during the sixteenth century, decreasing again in the second half of the seventeenth century. *Fiestas*, then, was written at the height of the "Golden Age of Litigation," as he calls it (*A Golden Age*). While processes in Castile were lengthy and expensive, in *El descasamentero* all cases are speedily resolved and fees do not seem to be a burden to any of the plaintiffs. Furthermore, Germano does not follow a procedure based on adjustment to a written law, as Spanish courts did, but rather he applies logic in order to properly administer justice as needed in each situation. According to Kagan, with the proliferation of legalistic documents and the centralization of laws, the outcome of lawsuits depended on which party was able to bring up arguments that adhered to the letter of the law, not on any kind of objective sense of justice (*Lawsuits* 22 3). Therefore, the function of the judge was not to decide whose actions were right or wrong, as it was the case in the medieval dispute tradition, but to sanction whose case fit the law.[11]

In addition to highlighting the injustices of civil and religious laws, Salas subverts contemporary manuals of conduct for women. Handbooks such as Juan Luis Vives' *Institutio foeminae christianae*, Luis de León's *La perfecta casada*, and Erasmus' *Encomium Matrimonii* (to name the most popular ones) advised "good women" to put up with everything and obey their husbands. Wives were made responsible for any frictions in the relationship, and so they were the ones expected to be patient and make any necessary adjustments. They were also to find their own happiness and fulfilment in pleasing their masters. Handbooks offered countless advice in how to achieve this goal (everything from how to dress to how to accept his beatings), but there is not one single word about when to leave or break the relationship. It is simply not an option. Contrary to this view, in *El descasamentero* none of the women are judged for not being good wives. Even in the cases in which women are the ones to blame for the lack of marital bliss (which is clearly the case with one of the couples), they are not expected to change their ways.

At the beginning of the piece, Germano's tribunal, not unlike contemporary courts, is predisposed to treat men and women differently. Before any plaintiff arrives, the prosecutor assumes that the court will be a noisy space: "Tribunal donde han de ser oídas mujeres, y mujeres malcasada[s], estruendo espera y tumultuosos escándalos [A court in which women, and ill-married women, are to be heard awaits uproar and tumultuous scandals]" (45). Germano proposes the use of muzzles, but he is reminded that he should not close the mouth of anyone seeking justice. Germano is not shy to show his prejudices and biases when he affirms that to shout, as women do, is not to seek justice and that, because women are always shouting, "tienen mal pleito, de suerte que ellas traen en el modo con que la piden la condenación de su causa [they have a bad case, because the way they bring it up leads to a negative sentence]" (45). Nevertheless, throughout the *entremés* women will have their voices heard and the members of the court will often admit to having been unfair.

Regardless of isolated insults to women in general and the introduction of a bizarre wife who is obsessed with dogs, *El descasamentero* presents an array of positive female characters that challenge common negative opinions. Later on Lucino describes the first plaintiff as a woman with hair so blond that it is "un hermoso testigo de su necedad [a beautiful witness to her foolishness]" (47). The blond woman soon demonstrates that she is intelligent and sensible, and as such she is praised by the members of the court, who recognize their mistake in assuming her hair was a sign of ignorance. The last woman to appear in court is an intellectual who impresses Germano so much that he orders a portrait of her to be made. Her case (like the one of Dorotea in the frame story and the blond woman) shows the unhappiness of spouses with different intellectual levels and interests – a radically modern take on marriage. Most literature of the time claims that the success of a marriage rests on the equality of the spouses, meaning equality in social status, purity of bloodline, and/or wealth. But in *Fiestas* equality means intellectual equality, or at least a balanced level of interest in learning. Salas incorporates three examples of women who are more literate and intellectually gifted than their partners, resulting in each case in an agonizing marriage. Ultimately, Germano's rulings go beyond granting divorces; his desire to bring justice extends to assuring the well-being and happiness of the litigants, both men and women. Contrary to the norm in early modern tribunals, justice, for Germano, is not gender bound; both men and women can bring forward their cases and defend their positions.

A proper interpretation of *El descasamentero* is possible only when reading it in the context of the framing story. The relation between performance and frame is highlighted by the selection of characters. The first plaintiff in the play, the blond woman, is called Dorotea, like the lady in the frame story. Both Doroteas have high ambitions and are admired by many. The fate of the Dorotea in the *entremés* foreshadows that of the other Dorotea, reinforcing the idea of theatre as a stage for voicing forbidden or inappropriate opinions – which is what *El descasamentero* does in relation to divorce. Luis could not tell his beloved that she had made a mistake by marrying Sebastián, but arranges for the performance of a theatrical piece in which a character by her same name faces the consequences of entering a marriage in which the bride is intellectually superior to the groom.

The utility of theatre as a space for denouncing social problems becomes obvious, when, after all the pieces had been performed at the wedding, the narrator returns to the frame story, giving a meticulous description of how the internal audience reacted to the spectacle:

> Con rostro desdeñoso y semblante turbado oyeron los novios la representación de estas fábulas. Don Luis reprendió en público a los criados ... pero en secreto les rindió risueñas gracias y mandó que enviasen bien satisfechos a los ministros de la obra burladora y picante. No quisiera don Lope que esto hubiera sucedido así, porque como el más agraviado, era siempre el más sospechoso para cualquiera venganza y temía en su opinión tan malos atributos. Mirábanse los circunstantes a los rostros y con mucha pena violentaban la risa ... Para poderlo hacer con mayor libertad, poco a poco y sordamente se fueron despidiendo las visitas y tras ellas, más quejosos que agradecidos, caminaron a su posada los novios, donde dando a entender doña Dorotea que no venía buena, se retiró a la cama. (133)

> With disdainful face and disturbed countenance, the bride and groom listened to the performance of these fables. Don Luis publicly reprimanded the servants ... but secretly he gave them cheerful thanks and ordered that those taking part in the mocking and spicy play be sent away well compensated. Don Lope would not have wanted this to happen that way, because being the most offended, he was always the most suspicious if someone wanted to take revenge, and he feared such attribution would taint his reputation. The spectators looked at each other's faces and, with a lot of difficulty, they contained their laughter ... In order to be able to laugh more freely, little by little and silently, the bride and groom started saying goodbye to the guests and, following them, more dissatisfied than

thankful, they walked to their lodgings, where Doña Dorotea led others to believe that she was not feeling well, and went to bed.

The narrator expresses how different audiences process the same play differently depending on personal circumstances. While the bride and groom feel ashamed and insulted, and Don Lope fears others will assume he had planned everything, Luis and the rest of the guests find the play amusing, but hide their feelings. The effect of the play extends past its duration and has direct consequences for Dorotea, who is so uncomfortable that she decides to go back "a la casa de sus padres y abuelos, donde era fuerza que todos la tratasen con respeto igual, encubriendo en el ánimo lo que sentían en el entendimiento [to the house of her parents and grandparents, where all will be forced to treat her with equal respect, hiding in their mood what they felt in their minds]" (134). After witnessing an insulting performance, she chooses to live in an environment in which everyone is performing the role that she wants to see, acknowledging the power of performance both to denounce and protect. The consequences on *El descasamentero* cannot be erased; Dorotea has been defamed, but the privileged position of her family will shield her from public humiliation. Dorotea takes advantage of her status, but she also understands that the damage done to her by the play is stronger than her position. She might be able to live as if she were the happy bride of a *comedia*, but everyone knows she is the disgraced wife of an *entremés*. Theatre is shown to be the proper venue to attack those otherwise untouchable because of their rank.

In *Fiestas*, the reaction of the guests at the wedding speaks to the private reader of the transcendental value of theatre and comedy. Ferns argues that one of the characteristics of utopian narratives is that they invite "readers into active participation in the text, rather than relegating them to the status of passive observers" (23). Reading in private became more common in the early modern period. At that time, traditional practices of oral transmission, such as listening to a reading (as Don Quixote did at the inns) or attending a performance, started to overlap with individual silent reading, which, according to George Mariscal "was a crucial step in the construction of the individual as an entity separate from the community" (68). The seventeenth century is still a moment of transition, in which "the subject could not be conceived of as separate from social relations" (Mariscal 73). Salas reproduces this mixed experience by creating a text intended for solitary reading that resonates with the public experience of attending performances like the one described. Salas is at once directing his controversial message to a smaller educated audience and is forcing such readers to consider how others may feel when confronted with the same play. The reader who laughs at the jokes of *El descasamentero* is compelled to contemplate the thesis from a serious angle when he learns of the specific consequences of the play for the characters of the frame story.

Today we have movies derived from bestsellers and novelizations of popular films, but reading a book and watching movies are, for the most part, both solitary experiences. Cinema is increasingly consumed at home, not in movie theatres, and even there the expectation of silence makes the experience a private one. Furthermore, a novel based on a movie is not a script of the movie, and a book and its corresponding film are intentionally different. The book and the movie need to be different because the way in which they are consumed is so similar. In seventeenth-century Spain, the person reading *El descasamentero* was someone accustomed to attending similar theatrical performances. He or she might be reviving the environment, but experiencing it from a completely different perspective, a much more subjective one. This early modern solitary reader has the awareness of reading a piece similar to those meant for public consumption and public scrutiny, but is also aware of the particular way in which he or she is approaching the text.

Cervantes had already verbalized how the experiences of reading a play and witnessing one are not equivalent. In *Adjunta al Parnaso*, published a year earlier than *Ocho comedias y ocho entremeses nunca representados*, a character named Miguel, an alter ego of Cervantes, claims that he has several theatrical pieces to give to the press, in clear reference to the preparation of *Ocho comedias*. Miguel says he wants to put his theatre in print "para que se vea de espacio lo que pasa apriesa y se disimula, o no se entiende, cuando las [obras] representan [so one can slowly perceive what happens fast and is concealed or not understood when [plays] are staged]" (183; my trans.). Cervantes recognizes the peculiarities of solitary reading and affirms that it is necessary to carefully read his pieces, because there is more in them than in the plays others compose for the stage.

We know that *El juez* was not staged, but we cannot be sure that the version that came to us was the one originally written for the stage, or even if it was actually conceived for the stage. In the case of *El descasamentero*, it is certain that it was not written for the stage. Cervantes and Salas understand the potential of the *entremés* as a means to convey a controversial message, but they are also aware of the risks of taking this message to a public stage. They rely on the popularity of the theatrical form and the possibilities it offers, but instead create pieces to be read in private by a more selective audience.

El juez and *El descasamentero* could only exist because of the popularity of theatrical performances at the time. The success of Lope de Vega's formula created a market for printed versions of the spectacles and for the creation of literary pieces that evoked the theatrical ambience. By choosing this theatrical form to convey the message, rather than other burlesque genres, Cervantes and Salas are inviting the reader, even when reading in solitude, to experience the text as if he or she were attending a performance. This imagined performance enriches the disruptive nature of the text, as the reader, now turned into viewer, confronts the experience of addressing a taboo while in the company of others, thus provoking a state of unease similar to the one experienced by the characters of *Fiestas*.

More than simply reading *El descasamentero* as a defence of the right to divorce, I argue that Salas wants to demonstrate that theatre and utopias can be spaces to fight for social justice and to envision a more just alternative. Both genres permit the use of distancing techniques that make the message seem less dangerous. Salas attacks the irrational and unjust definition of marriage as a lifelong bond. He unveils the problems caused by the current limitations on divorce and how easy it would be to resolve such difficulties, and in doing so he questions the entire social structure. Marriage was considered the foundation of society. The image of the family as a metaphor for the social and political structure of the nation was a constant across Europe in the early modern period. Particularly in Catholic countries, the permanence of marriage reflected the immutability and solidity of society. Salas demonstrates that the most basic element of society, as he knew it, was unjust. He reiterates that the unhappiness of a couple damages the entire country. If marriage is the original building block of society, the institution of marriage must be just, or the whole nation would be built upon an injustice. The well-being of the spouses is a prerequisite of social harmony. This Aristotelian consideration of harmony as primordial for the nation can only be achieved if divorce is a feasible option. Modern divorce courts take into consideration only the consequences that continuing or ending an unhappy marriage may have on the immediate family (spouses and children). They do not dwell on the repercussions that each individual separation could have on the rest of the country, nor should they. Curiously enough, the influence of divorce on the social fabric tends to be addressed only by those who opposed divorce on religious principles. Salas, though, was a man of his time who approached the rights of individuals from the perspective of the community. Individual justice must also serve social justice. The right to divorce is, according to Salas, a necessity to achieving social harmony and greater justice.

NOTES

1 Grégor Puppinck explains that "On 10th January 2017, the European Court of Human Rights reminded, by the *Babiarz v. Poland* (n° 1955/10) decision, that the European Convention on Human Rights does not impose legalization of divorce nor does it contain an individual right to divorce. On 22nd November 2016, the same judges had unanimously made the same conclusion to the *Andrzej PIOTROWSKI v. Poland* case (n° 8923/12) ... Both cases question the refusal of the Polish jurisdiction to grant divorce to unfaithful husbands."
2 Even in the few exceptions to this, like *Los malcasados de Valencia* by Guillén de Castro, the everyday lives of married individuals are overlooked.
3 Page numbers correspond to Waterworth's translation.
4 An annulment was possible, for example, when one of the parties was not single upon entering into the marriage, when parties were unaware of their blood relationship at the time of the wedding, or when one person had married without knowing the spouse was of the same sex.
5 While we do not have exact numbers for the Peninsula, local data gives us a hint on the rarity of the event. For example, Javier Lorenzo Pinar counts a total of eight petitions for annulment during the entire sixteenth century in the diocese of Zamora-Toro (82).
6 Antonio Gil Ambrona gives the following numbers: in the diocesan tribunal of Pamplona, 1 case every 10 years between 1511 and 1580, 2.3 per year between 1621 and 1630, and 1.75 per year between 1651 and 1700; in the diocesan tribunal of Barcelona, 1 case per year between 1300 and 1350, and an average of 3 per year between 1600 and 1650; and in the diocesan tribunal of Cádiz, 1.8 cases per year between 1700 and 1750 (10). Edward Behrend-Martinez identifies 91 cases in the dioceses of Calahorra and La Calzada between 1652 and 1715. The only requests for divorce that had any hope of succeeding were those in which the life of the wife was in danger due to repeated, unjustified, and severe punishments received from the husband. In those instances, and even before any legal process started, the woman was put in *secuestro* (sent to a convent or to the house of some relatives at the expense of the husband) for her safety. In theory *secuestros* were a temporary safety measure, but the legal machine was so slow that, in practice, most claims never reached a resolution and the *secuestro* became a permanent situation that worked as a *de facto* separation. In the case of Barcelona studied by Gil Ambrona, 70 per cent of cases were interrupted after ordering the "secuestro" (15). The same can be said for 68 per cent of the cases studied by Lorenzo Pinar from Zamora in the sixteenth century (84).
7 The matrimony of Cervantes is an example of how individuals navigated the prohibition. After only two years of marriage, he left his wife and

moved to Toledo. Before doing so, he signed a document leaving her all his belongings and the promise of all his earnings thereafter. Daniel Eisenberg considers this document a pact between the spouses that would allow him to leave her without the fear of being accused of abandonment (149). This privately reached agreement was not a divorce, but had the same practical result (minus the cost and headache of the trial).

8 I have modernized spelling and punctuation in all quotes from *Fiestas*. Page numbers correspond to folios in the original printing.

9 All translations from *Fiestas* are mine.

10 According to Covarrubias: "desesperarse es matarse de cualquiera manera por despecho [to despair is to commit suicide in any way out of spite]" (my trans.).

11 The main problem with enforcing the *Nueva Recopilación* was that the king did not declare it to be "the" ruling law nor did he derogate any previous codes, creating a milieu of often contradicting precepts, allowing clever lawyers to pick and choose the code that better suited their clients. Additionally those living in regions or social groups protected by *Fueros* (charters) could claim to be exempted from obeying the royal precepts. There was also an overlap between canon and civil law, particularly in issues concerning marriage. The entire legal system "was so ambiguous, confused, and misleading that it did little to promote just and equitable decisions" (*Lawsuits* 23).

3 The Voice of the Voiceless: Towards Equality and Social Justice in Sor Juana's *El divino Narciso*[1]

FRANCISCO LÓPEZ-MARTÍN

Any discussion of social justice during the seventeenth century is challenging, since social justice as a concept was not formally recognized or discussed until the emergence of the Enlightenment in the late eighteenth century. Although the concept of social justice can be approached politically, religiously, or sociologically, this discussion draws on the ideas of the political philosopher John Rawls, who stated in *A Theory of Justice* that "[e]ach person possesses an inviolability founded on justice that even the welfare of society as a whole cannot override. For this reason, justice denies that the loss of freedom for some is made right by a greater good shared by others" (3–4). Rawls believes in a society that guarantees freedom of thought and freedom of speech. However, this definition of social justice could not prevail in the world of the seventeenth century owing to the overriding belief in distributive justice, a system in which every person had a role in life, assigned by God, and in which humans should not be treated equally until the afterlife. During this period, certain groups and individuals challenged the concept of distributive justice and denounced their societies in order to defend equality. This chapter focuses on Sor Juana's use of religious representations in her theatrical works to address the ruling audience in Madrid. I will thus analyse how a Mexican author and nun, in a veiled illustration of the concerns of a colonial society unable to dialogue with the hegemonic power, challenged the established discourse of distributive justice in search of an egalitarian society based on free will.

Juana de Asbaje, better known as Sor Juana Inés de la Cruz, has been a frequent subject of analysis, with a particular focus on her more challenging writings, such as *Carta Atenagórica* and *La Respuesta a Sr. Filotea de la Cruz*, as well as her lyrical production. The voice of Sor Juana is distinctive in all her literary works, including her religious theatre. In the three *autos* written by Sor Juana, together with their corresponding *loas*, the Mexican nun expresses a scathing critique of the conquest of America, with the intention that her voice be heard in Madrid. *El mártir del sacramento* deals with the theme of the Plus Ultra, and of America as the New World, in contrast to Europe as the Old World. *El divino Narciso* explores the concept of just war, while *El cetro de José* shows us a more humane vision of the Native American. These writings, particularly in their stylistic and aesthetic content, condemn inequality, in particular the unequal treatment of the indigenous peoples of the New World by the Spanish Crown and its American representatives. These themes of inequality and injustice were best understood by the real actors: the oppressed peoples and the authorities that subjugated them. To appreciate the significance of Sor Juana's condemnation, one must develop an understanding of social justice and its opposite, social injustice, in the seventeenth-century context.

The Subaltern "Space of Difference"

The encounter between Spain and America culminated with European control of the American territories and efforts to convert its Native peoples. The conquest also generated chronic instability on both sides of the Atlantic, causing an increase in indigenous resistance, which was often quickly silenced by armed force. Initiatives by the European episteme to establish mutual understanding failed owing to the absence of a common language and points of reference. The imposition of this European episteme on the Aztec and Inca peoples relegated the latter groups to a subordinate role with, in the best view, a minimal influence on European thought. Gayatri Spivak claims that "subaltern is not just a classy word for oppressed, for [the] Other, for somebody who's not getting a piece of the pie ... In post-colonial terms, everything that has limited or no access to the cultural imperialism is subaltern – a space of difference" (de Kock 45). The hegemonic power by definition is expansive and requires the Othered group to occupy a position of inferiority.

In her three *autos*, Sor Juana fights in this subaltern "space of difference," seeking the equal rights claimed a century earlier by several Christian humanists who criticized the legitimacy of the conquest of America, supporting more egalitarian treatment of indigenous people.[2] These calls for better relations between the colonizers and colonized seem to contradict the widely held belief in the inevitability of unequal distribution of roles in life – that is, distributive justice.

Aristotle's concept of distributive justice is the original source for theories about the roles that humans must occupy on earth, but it was Saint Thomas Aquinas, writing in the thirteenth century, who explained the concept of distributive justice for the people of the seventeenth century. He justified the distribution of roles and goods according to merit, while leaving equality for the afterlife. This rigid religious and social system is manifested in the *autos* and other literary works of the seventeenth century. For instance, in *El gran teatro del mundo*, Calderón summarizes the concept of distributive justice:

POBRE: En la comedia de hoy,
yo el papel de Pobre hago;
no hago de Labrador. (906–8)

BEGGAR: In this particular play today, I have the beggar's part, and not the worker's.

In this play, Beggar accepts the role imposed on him in life, knowing well that his suffering as a beggar will be taken into account and rewarded when he is judged by God in the afterlife.

As a humanist familiar with classical philosophical writings and the thought of Aquinas about justice in the world and its compensation in the afterlife, Sor Juana knew that the latter led to equality only from an otherworldly point of view. She confronted this view of justice and tried to correct it. She ascribed dignity to the image of the Native American, confronting the Spanish conquerors and magnifying the indigenous peoples' pride in their own traditions and gods. She gave voice and strength to the Creole claims for equal treatment in both New and Old Worlds, and promoted respect for Creole beliefs and traditions. Jon Beasley-Murray rightly observes that "[s]ubalternity marks hegemony's limit" (2) and is isolated from the structures of representation. In the encounter between Spain and America, the armed forces and hegemonic Christian evangelizing discourse transform and incorporate pre-Columbian cultures. These colonial influences also isolate any subaltern resistance from official representation, and, according to David Solodkow, "el subalterno colonial – el indígena, el esclavo africano – no puede hablar o expresarse en el ámbito letrado colonial. Quizás sea mejor decir que el subalterno colonial habla allí donde su voz es silenciada o interpretada por el letrado [The colonial subaltern – the indigenous, the African slave – cannot speak or express himself in the colonial legal sphere. Perhaps it is better to say that the colonial subaltern speaks where his voice is silenced or interpreted by the literate]" (141). Rather than keeping silent, Sor Juana denounces the unequal relationship between the inhabitants of the Iberian Peninsula and its colonies and exercises the role of translator of the silenced voice of the subaltern. Her mission is to criticize all types of injustice, defending the rights of the disenfranchised and those who cannot speak. She communicates this criticism masterfully in her *autos* and *loas*, aided by the rhetorical and representative resources acquired from the poetry of Lope de Vega, Quevedo, and Góngora.³

The *Auto* and the *Loa*

The baroque *auto* presents a world of abstract values, culminating with a moral teaching in which the communion between man and God takes place. It is at the same time a tool of religious indoctrination and a cathartic spectacle. Moral teaching and the religious indoctrination are fundamental to Sor Juana's criticism of the conquest's validity and the dominant role that the church occupied as a structure promoting inequality. Moreover, through the use of the sacramental *auto*, Sor Juana could reach a public in Spain that would otherwise be inaccessible.

Autos played an important role in colonial Mexico. According to Louise M. Burkhart,

> Preconquest Nahua religion featured elaborate ceremonies that brought gods and sacred narratives to life. Priests dressed sacrificial victims in clothing, adornments, and face paint that did not simply resemble a given deity but actually *assembled* the god out of the constituent parts ... The closest thing Europe had to the Aztec temple rituals was religious theater ... Each drama told a story, with a beginning and an end, drawn from the Bible or saints' legends or illustrating a point of moral teaching. (5)

The Spanish religious orders, the Franciscans, Dominicans, and Augustinians, quickly understood the interest of indigenous people in religious representations of their beliefs. They recognized the *auto* as an effective instrument of persuasion and indoctrination through imagery. In time, the ritual character of the *auto* gradually replaced the function of the Aztec sacrifices.⁴ The ritualistic space filled by the *auto sacramental* is defined in the words of Veronica Grossi as:

> espacio de ascenso, alianza, competencia y enfrentamiento entre las autoridades eclesiásticas y civiles; entre las autoridades metropolitanas y coloniales; entre mecenas y escritores. La representación escenifica el imperio del convencimiento retórico y político: el proyecto de conversión evangelizadora enmascara y posibilita a su vez el violento proyecto imperial de conquista material y cultural de las Américas. (7)

> space for promotion, alliance, competition, and confrontation between the ecclesiastical and civil authorities; between the metropolitan and colonial

authorities; between patrons and writers. The representation stages the empire of rhetorical and political conviction: the project of evangelizing conversion masks and makes possible the violent imperial project of material and cultural conquest of the Americas.

Sor Juana uses the *loas* and their corresponding *autos*[5] as means of denouncing social injustices: the assimilation of cultures by Spanish hegemony and the suppression of difference. Through allegory, the religious scholar wishes to show Madrid's public the reality of a land distorted by conquest. However, this criticism of the conquest and the colonizing process does not present itself as direct confrontation but rather is carried out in a hidden way.

To comprehend the profound meaning of Sor Juana's *auto*[6] the reader must first understand the *loa*. According to Patterson, "the introductory *loas* to these three *autos* deal with Indigenous cultures and other New World themes in a manner that questions the Spanish imperial project" (460). But how exactly do Sor Juana's *autos* and *loas* respond to questions about inequality and justice? The *auto*, conceived by the Council of Trent as part of the pedagogical system in the fight against the Reformation, is a genre that does not allow different points of view. Instead, it aims to instil a specific set of values through extended allegory and the use of metaphorical characters. Allegory is without a doubt the most appropriate form of representation to communicate the abstract. This original form of communication, also used by ancient American civilizations in mural paintings, outdoor sculptures, and religious rites, transforms abstract ideas and concepts into visible concrete figures. This technique produces direct knowledge in the spectator without resorting to textual descriptions. Allegory concretized in this way minimizes the distortion of sensory perception, facilitating the transmission of a didactic and evangelizing message.

These extended metaphors serve as vehicles for a general critique of America's colonization and the role of the church in that conquest. Sor Juana proposes a solution to this conflict: equal treatment of indigenous religious rites, such as the offering of food to the god Huitzilopochtli by the Indians and the offering of the Eucharist at mass by the Catholics. In three *autos* and corresponding *loas*, she argues that establishing the equality of all people will inevitably lead to equal rights in all aspects of life, true equality between those arriving from the Iberian Peninsula and the *criollos* of New Spain. As Patterson explains:

> while it may have once made sense for only *peninsulares* to receive the most important government jobs, this policy should change to include *criollos*. While it may have once made sense for indigenous cultures to be

repressed, they should now be recognized as predecessors of the Catholic faith. (466)

Sor Juana presents her criticism of the church's hegemonic role in the conquest at three different levels: the philosophical-theological, the textual, and the representational. As Méndez Plancarte points out, Sor Juana displays the philosophical-theological views prevalent in 1690 when she writes the *Carta atenagórica* and *La Respuesta* at the request of Bishop Manuel Fernández de Santa Cruz. In these works, she criticizes the thesis of the Portuguese Jesuit Antonio de Vieira regarding the most important aspect of Christ at the end of his life. Vieira states that the greatest quality Christ had was his love for humankind, while Sor Juana maintains otherwise: what really matters are "beneficios negativos; esto es, los beneficios que nos deja de hacer porque sabe lo mal que hemos de corresponder [negative benefits; that is, the benefits that he does not provide for us because he knows the evil way that we will respond]" (*Carta atenagórica y Repuesta* 30). In other words, we might expect God to resolve human problems based on his love for us. However, instead of pursuing what might reflect his nature and infinite love, God chooses not to intervene, in an act of supreme love that is extremely difficult for him, according to Sor Juana. With this statement, she asserts the importance of human free will, a free will in contrast with the concept of distributive justice, one that makes us responsible for our acts and capable of change.

In the *loa* for the *auto El mártir del sacramento*, Sor Juana explores this same Thomistic question, comparing the importance of the Eucharist as sacrament and the death of Christ.[7] Two students discuss whether the most important act of Christ is to have died for us, as Saint Augustine maintains, or to have instituted the sacrament of the Eucharist, following the Thomistic thesis. This argument involves careful articulation and theological focus. That is, the end goals of the respective arguments are distinct, and distinct items are compared. Regarding this issue, Sor Juana maintains an eclectic position by introducing the figure of a third student, Sor Juana's alter ego. This third figure tries to unite the two theses by eliminating the boundaries between them. The three characters' discussion of this controversy and the need for a conciliatory position reflect the importance of human interpretation of theological and philosophical questions, which opens the possibility of a conversation about free will. This approach prepared the public for a critique of the church's role during the conquest.

This presentation of two sides in a controversy and its resolution through a third character can also be seen in the *loa* for *El divino Narciso*, which is in the form of a dialogue about the need for free will. This *loa* depicts the way in which the God of the Seeds, the essence of the true God, is syncretized with Christ. It further establishes that the Eucharist

> ... es el mayor
> beneficio, en quien se cifran
> todos los otros, pues lo es
> el de conservar la vida. (47–50)

> ... the gift from which all gifts proceed, our fields rich with golden maize, the source of life through daily bread. (Peters and Domeier 5)

Verónica Grossi comments:

> En la loa y en el auto apreciamos una síntesis de la tesis tomística y agustiniana ... Más que incoherencia filosófica, estas interpretaciones divergentes ponen al descubierto el carácter relativo de toda la argumentación teológica, humana. Las verdades que construye la escritura son máscaras retóricas provisionales que persuaden por su admirable sutileza e ingeniosidad y que conducen a través del reconocimiento público a un espacio de poder mundano. (551)

> In the *loa* and the *auto* we appreciate a synthesis of the Thomistic and Augustinian theses ... More than philosophical incoherence, these divergent interpretations reveal the relative character of all theological, human argumentation. The truths that writing constructs are provisional rhetorical masks that persuade through their admirable subtlety and ingenuity and lead to public recognition of a worldly power space.

At the same time this *loa* presents the revindication of America and the need for free will. The indigenous subject takes refuge in the space of personal freedom, giving value to the theological concept of free will:

> AMÉRICA: [P]ues aunque lloro cautiva
>   mi libertad, ¡mi albedrío
>   con libertad más crecida
>   adorará mis Deidades!
>
> ....
>
> OCCIDENTE: [Q]ue no hay fuerza ni violencia
>   que a la voluntad impida
>   sus libres operaciones. (233–6; 240–2)

> AMERICA: A weeping captive, I may mourn for liberty, yet my will grows beyond these bonds; my heart is free, and I will worship my own gods! ...
>
> THE WEST: [T]hat violence cannot devour my will, nor force constrain its right. (Peters and Domeier 19, 21)

If America and The West make use of God's greatest gift (that is, free will) to combat Religion, what does this allegorical character actually represent? For Sor Juana, Religion is none other than an integral part of the hegemonic discourse that seeks to assimilate the American people into the Spanish socio-cultural system. The character of The West displays the arbitrary and propagandistic nature of the *auto* as well as the ambiguities of rhetorical and theological discourse. This propagandistic nature is not surprising, since the *auto* coincides with the agreement made during the Council of Trent.

Meanwhile, the objective of the character Religion and of the *loa* itself is not to serve God but to create a space for human impulses. This space reveals to the public the instrumental role of religion during the period of the conquest: to provide a rhetoric that validated violent acts for a specific group of people, hence reinforcing inequality. The unmasking of religion's true motives culminates with a comparison between the Christian Eucharist and the Aztec *teocualo* rite, dislocating the latter and thus beginning the process of assimilation.[8] As these examples demonstrate, Sor Juana's theatrical works clarify the importance of point of view and the logic of discourse when it comes to understanding Christian truth, which is always a partial truth. More important, her public engagement with theological issues as a Mexican nun places her in the space of resistance against the hegemonic power, in both social and ecclesiastical spheres. She is in a dangerous position.

Sor Juana is aware of the risk she runs by publicly expressing her thoughts. To avoid reprisals, she states in both the *Carta atenagórica* and in the *Loa of El divino Narciso* that what she writes is not the product of her daring invention but of due obedience, implying that she was writing under the orders of her bishop or at the request of the Viceroy Doña María Luisa Manrique de Lara y Gonzaga. As Veronica Grossi explains, in these works "Sor Juana nos demuestra que las verdades divinas y principios doctrinales, expresados a través del lenguaje humano, son producto de la interpretación, la cual nunca es absoluta ni inmutable [Sor Juana shows us that divine truths and doctrinal principles, expressed through human language, are the product of interpretation, which is never absolute or immutable]" (546). In this way, she establishes the theoretical basis for her criticism and vindication of the Creole discourse.

In 1690 the *auto* for *El divino Narciso* was published for the first time in Mexico, in a loose-leaf format. This *loa* and Sor Juana's *auto* diverge from this static conception of allegory and become rhetorical instruments exposing different and controversial truths. *El divino Narciso* presents the theme of salvation through allegorical personifications like those of other *autos*, but unlike other *autos*, its personifications allow enormous scope for interpretation, all the while exercising their roles at a superficial level. In this religious play the different characters clearly define the European Christian world and pre-Columbian cultures. Fervour and Religion represent the hegemonic power, espousing war and evangelization. On the other side, America and The West are associated with the Mexican people. America reflects the Aztec pre-Columbian civilization, while The West represents the Creole subject who participates in both ancient tradition and new reality. The word *West*, usually used to represent the European continent, is defined differently in this work: it is the genesis of the American people who share both traditions. Thus, The West acquires an allegorical meaning, coming not from tradition but from social convention imposed by Sor Juana. Allegory in this case ceases to represent the immutable world of God and becomes a representative mechanism at the service of discourse. Here The West represents the confluence between the European tradition and the new reality in Mexico; it also serves a specific discourse in which Sor Juana exposes the historical importance of the Aztec indigenous culture and, at the same time, criticizes the way in which the conquest played out. To this end, she contrasts the characters America and The West, and the indigenous people who adore Huitzilopochtli, the God of Seeds, with Catholic Religion and Fervour, who represent European characters. Because The West is represented as indigenous, it gives the impression that, along with Europe, America is considered part of The West. This comparison reinforces the idea of equality between *criollos* and people from Spain.

In terms of the didactic value of the work, clashes between the two civilizations and the massacre of Native Americans by Spanish troops could be considered in a negative way. However, they familiarize us with the Nahua *teocualo* ceremony, where God was consumed. To accomplish this, the Nahua mixed flour and human blood to prepare a statue of Huitzilopochtli, which they later ate as a symbol of the god's death and the sharing of his strength with the entire indigenous population. In the *loa*, this event is assimilated by Catholic Religion and Fervor into the Eucharistic mystery. Sor Juana in turn uses this rite to teach the Catholic religion to the indigenous people. For this reason, at the end of the *loa*, Catholic Religion and Fervour decide to present the *auto El divino Narciso* with indigenous characters as apprentice spectators.

Interestingly, this is not the only example of the functionality of the discourse in question. Analysis of the character of Religion unveils further aspects of representation in the discourse. Faced with the violent determination of Fervor wishing to convert America and The West through force, Religion intervenes as a saviour of the indigenous people:

> RELIGIÓN: Sí, porque haberla vencido
> le tocó a tu valentía,
> pero a mi piedad le toca
> el conservarle la vida:
> porque vencerla por fuerza
> te tocó; mas el rendirla
> con razón, me toca a mí,
> con suavidad persuasiva. (210–17)
>
>> RELIGION: America has been subdued because your valor won the strife, but now my mercy intervenes in order to preserve her life. It was your part to conquer her by force with military might; mine is to gently make her yield, persuading her by reason's light. (Peters and Domeier 19)

Thus, America understands this intervention of Religion as a manipulation, which in turn leads to confrontation:

> AMÉRICA: Si el pedir que yo no muera
> y el mostrarte compasiva,
> es porque esperas de mí
> que me vencerás, altiva,
> como antes con corporales,
> después con intelectivas
> armas, estás engañada. (226–32)
>
>> AMERICA: If your petition for my life and show of Christian charity are motivated by the hope that you, at last, will conquer me, defeating my integrity with verbal steel where bullets failed, then you are sadly self-deceived. (Peters and Domeier 19)

Thus, although Religion appears as a conciliatory element in the service of God, it actually reveals the same attitude as Zeal, approving its own violent actions and using the circumstances to render the Indians with "persuasive gentleness" (217). But America does not yield to the hegemonic power, nor does it allow itself to be deceived by the rhetorical discourse of Religion.

After analysing these two different characters, The West and Religion, it is clear that Sor Juana is using allegory as a tool to reflect contradictory meanings, presenting two distinct discourses to the public. In this discourse, The West reflects a world in which Aztec and European traditions are intertwined. At the same time, it creates a discourse in which Religion represents the hegemonic European power that cannibalizes the Aztec culture. Sor Juana continues this critique in the *loa*. As indicated above, Sor Juana's *loas* give us the keys to interpret their corresponding *autos*, and therefore we must understand *El divino Narciso* in the American context.

The classical myth of Narcissus, narrated by Ovid (*Metamorphoses* III, 341–510), is well known.[9] Echo, a nymph, was punished by Juno when she learned that Echo had covered up her husband's infidelities. As punishment, she lost the ability to speak for herself; she was only able to repeat the last words of whatever she had heard. Narcissus was a young man of great beauty. The fortune teller Tiresias predicted that Narcissus' habit of gazing on his own image in a mirror would be his downfall. When Echo discovered the beauty of Narcissus, she became entranced and confessed her love to him through the animals of the forest. Meanwhile, Narcissus fell in love with himself after contemplating his own reflection while drinking at the spring. When trying to reach the figure he saw from the shore, he fell into the water and drowned, whereupon the gods transformed Narcissus into a white flower.

Sor Juana builds her *auto* on this myth. However, just as she assigns new meanings to different allegorical characters in her *loa*, the *auto* profoundly modifies the Narcissus myth to create a new allegory, which shows the manipulation that makes the discourse referential, as was seen in the *loa*. As an example of this variation, the values that the playwright attributes to Echo are those that Ovid imputes to Narcissus in his *Metamorphoses*: "era tan dura la soberbia que había en su tierna belleza que ningún joven, ninguna muchacha lo pudo tocar nunca [but in that slender form was pride so cold that no youth, no maiden touched his heart]" (*Metamorfosis* III, v. 355; *Metamorphoses* III, v. 355). This is possible, as Benjamin explains, because "[t]he allegory of the seventeenth century is not a convention of expression, but expression of convention. At the same time expression of authority, which is secret in accordance with the dignity of its origin, but public in accordance with the extent of its validity" (175). Allegory is an instrument of hegemony that Sor Juana converts to a mechanism for resistance. The religious character of the *auto* is a catalyst for the adaptation of the myth to convey the message she seeks to transmit.

In this *auto* Narcissus represents the allegorical image of Christ, who sacrifices himself for humankind, reflecting his own image; at the same time he remains in the form of "blanca Flor [a white flower]" (Sor Juana 2063; Peters and Domeier 183), thus representing the host. Meanwhile Echo, accompanied by Pride and Self-Love, symbolizes the sins of men, and Human Nature symbolizes indigenous people, a representation of the pure man who, together with Grace, becomes Adam. This free interpretation of the original text of the Narcissus and Echo myth, which transcends the traditional view understanding of the myth, allows for other new interpretations, given that the educated spectator of the time may well view the work as one of Christian mysticism, identifying Christ allegorically with Narcissus. From this represesentation the spectator thus may arrive at the conclusion that God becomes man and dies to save him after seeing him in the waters of the fountain. It is man whom he sees because Nature is behind him and it is his own image that is reflected in the fountain – he has been created in his own image and likeness:

> Viendo en el hombre su imagen
> se enamoró de Sí mismo,
> su propia similitud
> fue Su amoroso atractivo.   (2020–3)

[I]n human imperfection, [he] fell in love with her. His likeness called from Him, such passionate desire. (Peters and Domeier 181)

This interpretation is reinforced by the image with which the *loa* of the *teocualo* leaves us, and by the comparison of Narcissus' metamorphosis with the sacred host and Eucharistic food.

From a representational perspective, this *loa* and *auto* express the indigenous repudiation of the conquest and the imposition of an unknown God that the Mexican people do not understand. In this distribution of roles, Narcissus represents salvation, Human Nature the subaltern subject (indigenous and Creole), and Echo the hegemonic power. Echo's role is apparent in these verses: "Todo, bello Narciso, / sujeto a mi dictamen, / son posesiones mías [All these, lovely Narcissus, / are mine to order as I wish, / for they are my possessions]" (Sor Juana 796–8; Peters and Domeier 88, 91). Thus, when Narcissus approaches the fountain, Human Nature and Grace are at a distance, in a peripheral position. Sor Juana indicates this by means of the stage direction in scene VIII. "Llegan las dos a la Fuente; pónese la Naturaleza entre las ramas, y con ella la Gracia, de manera que parezca que se miran; y sale por otra parte Narciso, con una honda, como pastor, y canta el último verso de (cada una de) las coplas, y lo demás representa [The two [enter and] come to the fountain. [Then Human] Nature and Grace position themselves in the thicket in such a way that they appear to be looking at each other; Narcissus approaches from the other side, dressed as a shepherd, carrying a sling; he sings the last line of each stanza, acting out the rest]" (Sor Juana 1132; Peters and Domeier 111). Human Nature therefore takes the role of a spectator, like the audience members. Human Nature is at the periphery in this scene and cannot actively intervene. Sor Juana forces the audience in Madrid to assume a subaltern role, sharing the same perspective as Human Nature.

Through this setting, she explodes the absolute, static value of the *auto* through a theme that provides an argument for her *Loa* and manipulates the traditional interpretation of the myth. By making the peripheral character break into the development of the classical myth, she presents the possibility that the indigenous population might be included, enriching and transforming the western episteme. Since the indigenous culture inspired the argument of the *auto*, Sor Juana creates an important claim for the Mexican people, since *El divino Narciso* was commissioned by the Countess of Paredes de Nava and Marquesa de la Laguna to be performed in the Spanish court, according to the frontispiece of the princeps edition of this *auto*. Thus, Sor Juana was sure that her message would reach the Crown.

The allegory also demonstrates the importance of equating the rites of the Nahuatl and Graeco-Roman traditions when considering their referents from the European point of view. It is addressed to the Spanish ruling class, as indicated at the end of the *loa*, and serves to educate its audience on the importance of indigenous culture, the gratuitous violence of the conquest, and the pride shown by the Aztec peoples regarding their traditions as well as their understandable reticence towards an unknown religion. The *auto*, therefore, fulfils a catechetical but inverted function. It illustrates the epistemic violence of evangelization for the Catholic public and at the same time exposes the Aztec rite of *teocualo*, thus presenting a vision of commutative justice in place of the distributive justice Sor Juana condemned.

In conclusion, Sor Juana is in a unique position to defend equality for the indigenous and Creole peoples of Mexico. She accomplishes this in three distinct ways. On a philosophical-theological level, she re-vendicates the value of free will as the ultimate act of love given by God to humankind. At the textual level, Sor Juana incorporates the discussion of free will in her *autos* to critique the church and its role in the conquest. She also shows the partiality of Christian theological discourse and the instrumental value of allegory against unjust authority or hegemony as seen in the *auto*. Sor Juana employs the same rhetorical resources normally used in the *autos* to build a discourse of resistance that she incorporates within its catechetical structure and supports with allegory. In this discourse, Sor Juana establishes a reciprocal relationship between the *teocualo* and Christian rites, creating an equal ground where Aztecs and Spaniards can live in harmony. Finally, at the representational level, Sor Juana controlled the message, which she conveyed to an audience in Spain that needed to be retaught about the Spanish Conquest, exposing a space of inequality in which Echo represents the sins of humankind. Thus, this discourse was no longer a reflection of the divine world but rather of a less pure and a more human and unjust one.

NOTES

1 For future reference, all translations without citation are mine.
2 Francisco de Vitoria in his *Relecciones del estado, de los indios y del derecho de la guerra* opens a debate throughout Europe about the causes of just war, referring to its legal and theological aspects; *The Inca Garcilaso in Comentarios reales de los incas* (p. 36) exposes the seriousness and complexity of the Inca empire demanding the same fair treatment given to other empires. See also Pedro de Valencia's *Consideraciones de Pedro de Valencia, su coronista, sobre las enfermedades y salud del reino* (ff. 103–117), which argues that the king should leave the American lands, since they are not economically sustainable.
3 "En la capital, la actividad de sor Juana se sentía en todas partes: componía los villancicos que se cantaban en las festividades religiosas de las catedrales de Méjico, Puebla y Oajaca; ayudaba a los necesitados en sus empeños; hacía peticiones de indultos para condenados a muerte; acudía a certámenes poéticos; escribía loas y poemas para celebrar los cumpleaños del rey, de los virreyes o familiares, o ensalzaba en su poesía victorias alcanzadas por ellos [In the capital, Sor Juana's activity was everywhere: she composed the carols that were sung in the religious festivities of the cathedrals of Mexico, Puebla, and Oaxaca; she helped the needy in their endeavours; she made petitions for pardons of death row prisoners; she attended poetic contests; she wrote *loas* and poems to celebrate the birthdays of the king, viceroys, or family members, or she extolled in her poetry victories they achieved]" (Sabàt de Rivers 17).
4 *El juicio final*, represented in 1533 in Tlatelolco, is the first theatrical production in the Nahuatl language (Burkhart 3).

5 "Es evidente que el auto corresponde a un nivel de representación englobado en la loa, en la medida que los personajes de la loa terminan siendo los espectadores inmediatos del auto. El auto corresponde, entonces, a un nivel intratextual con respecto a la loa y nos encontramos frente a la utilización del recurso del 'teatro dentro del teatro' [It is clear that the *auto* corresponds to a level of representation encompassed in the *loa*, to the extent that the characters of the *loa* end up as the immediate spectators of the *auto*. The *auto* corresponds, then, at an intertextual level with respect to the *loa*, and we find ourselves faced with using the resource of 'theater within the theater']" (Zanelli 184).
6 Charles Patterson mentions various critical approaches to Sor Juana's *autos* and distinguishes "those few critics who read the *loas* and the *autos* together as cohesive units, which is how I believe Sor Juana intended for them to be viewed" (461).
7 According to Patterson, in this *loa* Columbus' arrival in America is the catalyst for the rupture of reality as it was known: "In other words, just as Columbus corrected the error of ancient geographers, Thomas Aquinas corrected the errors of a previous theologian. In this way, Sor Juana privileges the new over the old" (463). Finally, Sor Juana explains in the *loa* how, after the discovery of America, the colonization and evangelization of conquered territories would continue and "reveal the New World's potential to eclipse the Old in the same way that Spain had come to eclipse Rome" (463).
8 According to Lee A. Daniel, "Christ and His followers always overcome in the staged conflict, and the Holy Eucharist is maintained as mankind's way to salvation, if he chooses to accept it" (111).
9 "Gracias a Abreu Gómez y a su repertorio de las obras de la biblioteca de sor Juana, se sabe que ella leyó las *Metamorfosis*. Partir de este hecho lleva a la fuente verosímil de la inspiración de sor Juana, y nos induce a que hagamos una lectura *isócrona* del *Divino Narciso* [Thanks to Abreu Gómez and to his repertoire of the works of Sor Juana's library, it is known that she read the *Metamorphoses*. This fact leads to the credible source about Sor Juana's inspiration, and induces us to do an *isochronic* reading of the *Divine Narcissus*]" (Palmieri 214).

4 Staging Strikes, Depicting Merchants, and the Morisco Problem in Valencia

MELISSA FIGUEROA

Gaspar Aguilar's *El gran Patriarca don Juan de Ribera* (1616) pays tribute to the archbishop of Valencia, his reforms to the Catholic Church, and his role in the evangelization of Moriscos during the sixteenth and seventeenth centuries in Spain.[1] The play was conceived during a time of intense spiritual devotion in Valencia, as seen in the popularity of religious literature, civic pride for local saints, and public reaction over the death of Juan de Ribera (1532–1611).[2] Published in *Norte de la poesía española*, the play was one of the first works, along with poems, biographies, and testimonials, advocating for Juan de Ribera's canonization. Despite its focus on the canonization of the religious reformer, *El gran Patriarca* deals with political, economic, and social issues that go beyond the expectations of the hagiographic genre. By recounting the challenges faced by Juan de Ribera, Aguilar contributes to an idealization of the character and, to some extent, displaces the criticism against him through the representation of scenes of daily life in Valencia. The staging of day-to-day situations stresses factors that contributed to the failure to convert Moriscos, such as the problems faced by workers in the agricultural sector and the challenges experienced by merchants in an indebted national economy.

In this chapter, I argue that in staging economic inequality and depicting merchants in a socio-economic system based on debt, Gaspar Aguilar highlights audiences' obsession with blaming Moriscos during the time of their expulsion, and indirectly contradicts the official propaganda by showing how economic factors affected religious conversion. In doing so, the play aims to create an awareness of poor labour conditions and unequal compensation of workers in a society that increasingly relied on credit. In this sense, I argue that the *comedia* indirectly does justice to Moriscos, recognizing them as scapegoats of social unrest, but also confronts audiences with problems that afflict them regardless of their religious affiliation. I thus present a nuanced view of the expulsion of the Moriscos as an uncontested political decision and illustrate, as Trevor Dadson has shown with the propaganda during the reign of Philip III (2), that there were subtle ways to express criticism or disagreement in theatre regardless of its connection to the hegemonic ideology of the state.

As one of the most influential religious leaders of the sixteenth century, Don Juan de Ribera was in charge of reforming the Spanish Church according to the tenets of the Council of Trent. After studying at the University of Salamanca, he was ordained priest (1557) and was appointed as bishop of Badajoz (1562). Later, he was appointed as archbishop of Valencia (1599) and as viceroy of Valencia (1602). In the kingdom of Valencia, he founded the Royal Seminary of the Corpus Christi in an attempt to reduce the number of uneducated clergymen.[3] In spite of these positive reforms, Don Juan de Ribera is best known for his support for the expulsion of the Moriscos.

The expulsion was proclaimed during the reign of Philip III to put an end to a long struggle with Islam in the Peninsula. It was promoted by the Duke of Lerma, Francisco de Sandoval y Rojas. Aside from its religious motives, the expulsion restored the pride of a nation after coming to an uneven agreement with the Netherlands that forced Spain to concede to free overseas trade during the next twelve years. The decision to expel the Moriscos was not unanimous, and several noblemen accompanied their Morisco servants to the designated ports. A process that lasted from 1609 to 1614, the expulsion had serious social and economic consequences. Although the expulsion was announced in 1609, Juan de Ribera had proposed expulsion as early as 1582. His support for the banishment turned into an obstacle for his canonization despite the fact that, as Francisco Márquez Villanueva has demonstrated, the decision took the patriarch by surprise ("El problema morisco" 226–32). In fact, Pope Benedict XIV declared in 1756 that the advice given by Ribera to Philip III should not be taken into account in the process to declare him as a saint. Although Ribera was beatified in 1796, he was not canonized until 1960.[4]

The play recreates events associated with the life and death of Juan de Ribera. The story begins with the failed attempts of a young woman, Leonora, to seduce Juan de Ribera while he is still the bishop of Badajoz. Despite her unsuccessful overtures towards the bishop, she has two other suitors, an unnamed citizen and Roberto, who soon engage in a duel. Roberto stabs the citizen and the pious Ribera shows compassion towards the dying man and administers confession. While Juan de Ribera is invested in helping others, several workers go on strike, demanding better salaries, and a merchant pays a worker to attend mass on his behalf. Given his commitment to transform the clergy, Juan de Ribera is declared archbishop of Valencia and is honoured with the title of patriarch. In his new diocese, he cures sick people, condemns criminals, and advocates for the poor. After being threatened by Roberto, the patriarch converts him to Christianity and tries unsuccessfully to preach to Moriscos. At the end, these New Christians are expelled from the kingdom of Valencia, and Juan de Ribera dies surrounded by people, lights, and flowers. Thus, the *comedia* can be read as an informal gesture of canonization that reflects the social and political life of seventeenth-century Valencia.

Although Moriscos do not appear until the third act, their characterization allows Aguilar to address controversial debates that flourished during the period in order to support or condemn the expulsion in Valencia, that is, the successes – and failures – of the initiatives to convert Moriscos and the consequences of expelling them. This historical background illustrates the centrality of this kingdom in the religious reform promoted by Juan de Ribera, and demonstrates that this region suffered more than any other from the expulsion of the Moriscos. The depopulation of towns, the rise of wages, and the effects of an indebted society had many negative consequences and, as I attempt to demonstrate in this chapter, the playwright was aware that Moriscos were not the only ones to blame for the economic stagnation of Valencia.[5] In effect, the only scene in which Moriscos appear onstage depicts them as lacking in understanding and respect for religious matters rather than as enemies of the state plotting insurrections, like those of the anonymous *Los moriscos de Hornachos* (1609?) and Pedro Calderón de la Barca's *Amar después de la muerte* (1633). Aguilar's concern with the consequences of economic profit and the emergence of capitalism during the period is evident in two more plays, also published in *Norte de la poesía española*, that raise questions on the relationship between nobility and bourgeoisie: *El mercader amante* (The Merchant Lover) and *La fuerza del interés* (The Strength of Interest).[6] Whereas the former stages the story of Belisario, a merchant who pretends to be poor to test the fidelity of Labinia and Lidora, the latter illustrates how Grisanto uses the monetary resources of Marquess Ludovico to conquer Emilia. In both cases, Aguilar illustrates how money affects human relationships and destabilizes the power of nobility.

In *El gran Patriarca*, this concern appears in the scenes of disgruntled workers on strike and of a Jewish merchant who relies heavily on debt. Intertwined with the expulsion of the Moriscos, the emphasis on economic inequality and social justice contextualizes the effects of the expulsion in an indirect manner. Indeed, the expulsion of the Moriscos, which never appears represented on stage and is mentioned only at the end of the third act, gives coherence and unity to the play.[7] At first glance, the scenes of disgruntled workers and the Jewish merchant do not seem to fit within the main objective of the play; they do little to highlight the virtuous attributes or the good deeds of Juan de Ribera. In fact, Josep Lluís Sirera notes that the play is an atypical example within the hagiographic genre: "Éste nos brinda un espléndido y atípico ejemplar de obra hagiográfica [He offers us a splendid and atypical example of an hagiographic work]" (221). However, interpreted in the context of seventeenth-century Valencia, these scenes take on a different meaning as they address debates regarding the expulsion.

On Labour Conditions and Economic Inequality

In the first act of *El gran Patriarca*, several Christian workers complain about their poor labour conditions and the unfair compensation. After discussing their precarious situation, some of these peasants refuse to work until they are guaranteed specific payment while others defend their right to work regardless of their wage. They return to work after the employers agree to pay the requested wage. This disparity between work and payment highlights the wealth gap of the period. Although the protest is not labelled a "strike," a nautical term that first appeared in eighteenth-century England, its staging can shed light on poor labour conditions and the ways people had mobilized against economic inequality and social injustice prior to the Industrial Revolution.

At the beginning of the scene, Aguilar focuses on the abuses of the employers and insists on the point of view of the workers who are taken advantage of by the employers. The workers do not engage in deceit with their employers. Rather, they are portrayed as ordinary men able and willing to work; this is reinforced in the stage directions as the characters enter the scene carrying a hoe and one of the workers expresses his impatience for the late arrival of the employers. One of the *jornaleros* (workers), Vermejo, complains that he does not earn enough money to feed his children despite the fact that he rents his labour for the entire day for three *blancas*. As a currency of low value, the allusion to a *blanca* puts emphasis on the disparity between work and remuneration. This exploitation is emphasized again in the allusions to the blood, sweat, and tears of the poor who are deceived by those in power. Due to the long hours of labour, another worker, Machado, claims that the days are never-ending. In response, Berruga uses a powerful image to summarize the workers' exploitation by those who hire them for less money than they deserve: "Sanguijuelas que se beben la sangre de los pobres [leeches that suck people's blood]" (254).[8] As the workers complain about their labour conditions, Berruga proposes that they refuse to work for no less than three *reales*. Based on the monetary reforms of the Catholic Monarchs, the *real* would have been the equivalent of 68 *blancas*. Therefore, taken in the literal sense, the request by the workers is substantial.

Given that workers get hired directly by their employers, without a middleman, the emphasis on three parties in recent collective bargaining theory, as proposed by Orley Ashenfelter and George E. Johnson, cannot be useful in explaining this negotiation process. Direct negotiation between workers and employers can easily result in exploitation since workers do not have representation and, because of their need for income, they are at the mercy of the people doing the hiring. This illustrates John R. Hicks' argument that posits that the majority of actual strikes are doubtless the result of faulty negotiation (146). The decision of Aguilar to not include the names of the employers points not only to a desire to present the situation as a generalized problem, but also to emphasize that the workers do not know with whom they are negotiating since they are hired on a daily basis. In fact, the lack of knowledge of the workers is reinforced by the employers. Berruga asserts that the employers are convinced that workers are fools and that they can even hire them without any pay: "confiados están los labradores / en que los jornaleros son tan bobos / que les llevan baratos y aún de balde [the employers are convinced that workers are fools; they hire them with low wages and even without a salary]" (254).

From the beginning of the conversation, the call to strike is doomed to fail. The dissension among the workers does not allow for any compromise before their grievances are presented to those in charge. Some workers resort to violence, often in the form of in-fighting among members of the same faction. Machado opposes the proposal, stating that he will ask for less and he will pay to be hired if necessary:

¡Qué pena o qué vinagre!
Yo iré por dos y medio,
y si esto es mucho
iré por dos reales solamente,
y si esto es mucho,
iré por uno y medio,
y si me pareciere iré de balde,

y si de balde les parezco caro,
yo pagaré también porque me lleven. (254)

What a shame or what vinegar! I will go for two and a half, and, if this is too much, I will go for only two *reales*, and, if this is much, I will go for one and a half, and, if I like, I will go for nothing, and, if going for nothing seems expensive to them, I will pay them to be hired.

The desperate competition for work, to the extent of paying to get hired, speaks to the challenges of this job market. Machado's statement unveils the lack of solidarity among workers in times of need and the identification with the interests of those in power. Indeed, the process of negotiation begins with the workers, who must agree in selecting the specific amount that they will request of employers.

After presenting the workers' point of view, Aguilar offers the employers' perspectives. The comments of the *labradores* (farmers) confirm the criticism of the workers as it reveals their ambition and their reluctance to pay an adequate sum of money. Aguilar is extremely careful in presenting the employers as rich peasants instead of as nobles; he thus avoids losing the favour of possible patrons and protectors. Juan José Sánchez Escobar reminds us of Aguilar's dependence on the nobility in his profession: "su dedicación exclusiva a la literatura desde un planteamiento de ésta como medio de subsistencia lo convierte en un asalariado de la nobleza [his exclusive dedication to literature as a means of subsistence turns him into a mercenary of nobility]" (126). The employers refer to the oversupply of workers as cheap labour: "hay infinitos [They are infinite in number]" (255). This surplus of workers creates low wages and decreases the chances of getting hired. In the context of the expulsion of the Moriscos, Aguilar is hinting at the depopulation of the kingdom. The repopulation of the areas previously occupied by Moriscos was not an easy process for Old Christians, and the Crown had to extend the time limit on the initial offerings of lands. Henri Lapeyre affirms that the "expulsion des Morisques fut, pour le royaume de Valence, une sorte de cataclysme qui bouleversa la géographie humaine du pays [The expulsion of Moriscos was, for the kingdom of Valencia, a sort of cataclysm that affected the country's human geography]" (19). Juan R. Torres Morera suggests that the expelled community represented 35 per cent of the population (122), and, according to James G. Casey, this event was a hit to the economy as Valencia lost one-third of its manpower (6). In this regard, the statement of the infinite amount of men available for work is significant. Since the scene of the strike appears chronologically before the allusion to the banishment of the Moriscos, it is possible that the playwright was interested in contrasting the earlier surplus of workers to the deficit under present conditions.[9] The allusion to the infinite number of men available for work is an exaggeration; however, audiences of the period could easily identify this as a joke or covert criticism because they were dealing with the repopulation of abandoned areas at the time that the play was written. In other words, Aguilar places the strike scene before alluding to the banishment at the end of the play to highlight that there are not an infinite number of workers, a situation that resulted from the migration of Moriscos from Spain.

As soon as the workers discuss their salary with the potential employers, Berruga demands three *reales* for his services and a mustard seed. Polido and Vermejo refuse to work for less than that amount. Again, in the context of the expulsion, the rise of wages was problematic since employers' production costs were higher than their profits. According to Casey, agricultural wages rose steeply, yet farmers could not get enough from the sale of the grain to compensate for the production costs (70). In this sense, the plea of the workers in Aguilar's play is consistent with the economic situation of Valencia at the beginning of the seventeenth century, and reflects the fear of workers' reactions after the expulsion. The people in power were afraid that workers would rebel against the *señores* to keep the depopulated lands, so much so that Tulio Halperin Donghi calls the first period of the expulsion "la euforia del pueblo bajo [the euphoria of lower class]" (249). Taking this into consideration, Berruga's demand of a seed of mustard in addition to the *reales* is significant for two reasons. On the one hand, he asks for a seed that would cost a lot to the *labradores*, as it costs more to produce grains than to sell them. On the other hand, he asks for a seed that will allow him to plant his own farm and, consequently, become a *labrador* in the future. Thus, the scene of the strike can be read as a warning for lords and labourers to improve the working conditions in the agricultural sector. In any case, after the expulsion, Moriscos could not be blamed for the rise of wages. On the contrary, this rise can be interpreted as one negative consequence of expelling those who could work for less.

In a clever turn, the employers try to negotiate salaries with the employees one by one to diminish their power of negotiation, but the workers soon learn that it is through collective bargaining that they can claim the real value of their work. For instance, when asked at what price he is willing to work, Vermejo says that he is not worth less than others: "Lo mesmo; ¿soy menos que los otros por ventura? [The same. Am I lesser than the others?]" (256). The *labradores* want to pay less money, but the *jornaleros* do not accept the offer. The employers realize that workers have a pact and that it is unlikely that they will be hired for less than they agree to earn. Only this time do employers decide to pay the amount requested; however, this temporary concession should not be understood as an act of compassion by the employers. The *labradores* grant the workers' wishes because they know that they can easily exploit them again in the future: "Que les demos gusto / ya que habemos salido, que otro día / ellos nos le darán a costa suya [Let's please them since we are here, and, another day, they will have to please us at their expense]" (256). By showing that the workers' demands are granted, the playwright suggests that it is only through collective bargaining that they could earn more benefits and better labour conditions, at least temporarily.

Reflecting on the purpose of the strike scene, Sirera identifies a structural logic. In his view, Aguilar highlights the sainthood of Juan de Ribera and his habit of giving alms to help feed the workers. Sirera argues that Aguilar also wanted to show the everyday reality of peasant conflicts after the expulsion of the Moriscos: "En todo caso, seis años después de la expulsión de los moriscos, hasta 1609 la mano de obra servil que había sostenido la economía señorial valenciana, se nos habla aquí de terratenientes y jornaleros como realidades habituales del campo español [In any case, six years after the expulsion of Moriscos, until 1609 the workforce that had supported the Valencian economy, landowners and day labourers are presented as usual realities of the Spanish countryside]" ("Mercaderes" 359). By choosing to stage the life of Juan de Ribera, the playwright was aware that he chose to draw attention to the main promoter of the expulsion of the Moriscos. However, Aguilar was not oblivious that doing so would illustrate the economic struggles of the Valencian kingdom as well.

On Debt Economy and Wealth Distribution

Aguilar also addresses economic challenges and social problems through the Jewish merchant Enrico. The scene at Enrico's store emphasizes features of seventeenth-century Valencia that highlight the dangers of a debt-based economy at the time of the expulsion. In a previous essay ("La expulsion"), I suggested that the playwright wants to show that the Moriscos are not the only ones experiencing difficulties in a society that makes it hard to earn a living and be a good Christian at the same time. In effect, a Christian *jornalero*, Leoncio, receives a salary for attending mass on behalf of Enrico, but after being reprimanded by Juan de Ribera, he returns the payment. By showing the rentability of devotional practices, Aguilar illustrates how poor labour conditions affect devotion and demonstrates that the challenges of conversion are not due only to religious factors. On the one hand, the long workday interrupts religious observance. On the other, attending mass turns into an economic transaction (34–6). Aguilar wants to show that Christian workers and Jewish merchants experienced the same challenges that Moriscos did. In all these cases, people had to choose between carrying out their work duties or fulfilling their obligations to the Catholic Church. Curiously, the playwright waits to show the case of the Moriscos until the last act when Boamit refuses to enter church by alluding to his labour duties: "Luego vuelvo yo también / que me he dejado en la viña / la azada [I have to leave too since I forgot the hoe at the vineyard]" (274). Boamit's refusal to attend mass on the grounds of the need to work is based on the same logic that drives the workers' reason for not going to church. Curiously, this is the second allusion to a hoe in a play that uses minimal props. As I already mentioned, in the first act, Machado, Polido, Berruga, and Vermejo enter the stage carrying a hoe and neglect to attend mass after being hired for the day. Thus, the hoe turns into a symbol of how work interferes with religious duties.

The merchant's statements focus on the effects of an indebted society before the expulsion of the Moriscos. After having a vision of Juan de Ribera, Enrico converts to Christianity and decides to distribute his wealth among the poor: "Y así quiero repartir / entre los pobres mi hacienda / después que la mal ganada / a cuya es la restituya [I want to distribute my wealth among the poor since it has been not well earned and must be restored]" (260). The sense of restitution in Enrico's statement hints at Aguilar's commitment to those in a disadvantaged position due to economic inequality. However, this false optimism can be problematic. As a use of wealth based on debt, the good deed of Enrico does nothing to improve the economy. Before his conversion, Enrico asks his servant if he has collected the money from his debtors. Recognizing that his master might not collect the debt, his servant states that it is better not to lend money. In response, Enrico defends his choice of lending and the never-ending desire to acquire more money: "No fiar es no vender / y eso es no apagar la sed/ que de ganar tengo yo [To not lend is to not sell, and this is not to satisfy the thirst/that I have for winning]" (258).

The debts of the *señores* and the spread of *censales* – loans to be paid in perpetuity – contributed to the economic decline of Valencia. Thus, Aguilar is interested in convincing the audience that Moriscos were not the only ones to blame for economic stagnation, and that nobles and merchants played a part in the accumulation of debt. Casey notes that "the first proposals for getting rid of the Moriscos began to be mooted around 1580 in government circles, and gathered strength with every year, as the weakness of the Moriscos' erstwhile protectors, the senyors, became apparent" (122). In other words, the seigneurial borrowing and the accusations against Moriscos intensified in the same period. The expulsion worsened the problem because the *señores* could not use Moriscos to borrow more money and could not collect the money they lent to those who had been expelled. Halperin Donghi affirms that creditors accused the *señores* of using the expulsion as a pretext for not making payments, when clearly the poor financial situation was not created by the expulsion: "De modo que por parte de los censalistas los señores eran acusados de utilizar la expulsión para resolver una situación que la expulsión no había creado, que de todas maneras estaba destinada a hacer crisis [Thus, from the census traders' perspectives the *señores* were accused of using the expulsion to solve a situation that was not created by it and that in any case was destined to create a crisis]" (253). Interestingly, this critic offers the example of the Duke of Gandía, Carlos de Borja. The duke, a noble with a substantial number of Morisco servants and the first to accompany them to the maritime ports, was almost bankrupted before 1609 for debts incurred in Italy. In other words, he was almost financially ruined before the banishment.[10]

The scene at the store is key to understanding the economic decline of Valencia, a decline that was largely driven by the importation of luxury goods from other parts of Europe. The types of commodities that Enrico aims to sell, such as fabrics and porcelain flasks or pitchers from Milan, suggest the profits to be derived from importing goods, thus reducing the likelihood of producing or exporting on a large scale products from Spain. In this sense, Enrico is no different from the *labradores* who take advantage of workers; he gains from the debts of customers and sells what he does not produce. By showing Enrico's store, Aguilar intends to remind the audience that economic problems go beyond the agricultural sector. In putting the burden of debt in the hands of Enrico, the playwright upholds the stereotypical view of Jews as moneylenderst. At the same time, he avoids mentioning the nobles and Moriscos who played a role in moneylending. While the scene of the disgruntled farmers emphasizes workers' complicity with their own exploitation in order to satisfy basic needs such as food and shelter, the scene at Enrico's store focuses on the profits to be made by selling commodities that only wealthy people can afford within a debt-ridden society. Aguilar makes a similar critique in *La fuerza del interés* when the wealthy marquess Ludovico buys an entire store from a jeweller to impress Emilia. The commodities mentioned in the scene – fine silk from

China, fabrics from Italy, and beautiful porcelain from America – hint to a global economy that affected the production and consumption of commodities in Spain. In this regard, Moriscos are not the only ones upsetting the economy in Valencia.

Moriscos became the scapegoat for the problems of the kingdom. In *El gran Patriarca*, Aguilar illustrates how Old Christians took financial advantage of Moriscos. At the beginning of the third act, Aguilar, in order to draw attention to the role of Juan de Ribera, focuses on the reluctance of Moriscos to embrace Christianity. The sheriff announces the fee that must be paid for not taking the holy water or making the sign of the cross: "Cualquiera que entre en la iglesia / sin tomar agua bendita / y santiguarse en la frente/ pagará un par de gallinas [Anyone who enters church without taking holy water or crossing the forehead will pay several chickens]" (275). Instead of asking for repentance, the *alguacil* demands a payment. Whereas Enrico is willing to pay someone to attend mass on his behalf, the Moriscos must pay a penalty for not embracing Christianity. Although this scene takes place before the expulsion mentioned in the same act, it is easy to draw connections with the accusations made at the time against Old Christians. During the expulsion, some Old Christians took possession of the material goods left behind by the Moriscos. Aguilar seems to be critical of this practice. In his epic poem *Expulsión de los moros de España*, he condemns how the town of Valencia was enriched by the property of the expelled Moriscos: "Los ricos pobres y los pobres ricos [The rich poor and the poor rich]" (358).[11] Without denying the challenges of converting Moriscos, Aguilar reminds us that, despite being blamed for the problems of the kingdom, they generated profits for Old Christians.

Aguilar's depictions of strikes and merchants are ways to address the debates on the expulsion without showing all its aspects or alienating his patrons. The connection between the scene of the strike and the portrayal of Enrico's store shows that the play is more organized than it seems and that it deals with the issue of the expulsion from a radically different perspective than that of the apologists. As Luis Sánchez Escobar observes, "en *El gran Patriarca* Aguilar se nos revela como un extraordinario conocedor de la técnica dramática que utiliza para mostrar sus discrepancias ideológicas con respecto al sistema que posibilita la medida de la expulsión de los moriscos [in *El gran Patriarca*, Aguilar reveals himself as an extraordinary expert of dramatic technique, which he uses to show ideological discrepancies in regard to the system that makes the expulsion of Moriscos possible]" ("Gaspar Aguilar" 145). Thus, it is precisely in the scenes that seem disconnected from the rest of the play that the audience can access these ideological discrepancies.

Further Reflections

In this chapter, I argue that Gaspar Aguilar highlights his audience's obsession with blaming New Christians during the time of their expulsion and indirectly contradicts the official propaganda by showing how economic factors affected religious conversion. In doing so, he focuses on economic inequality and social injustice by staging a strike. To the best of my knowledge, scenes of strikes are rare in Spanish early modern theatre or, at least, difficult to identify in that playwrights did not use modern sociological terms to depict these types of conflicts. In the play, the strike allows us to hear the voices of the exploited or those at the mercy of employers because of their need to earn a living within a context of intense debate regarding the expulsion of the Moriscos. In this sense, the play speaks to a contemporary audience in two important ways. First, the recent influx of immigrants from North Africa to Spain forces us to look back to the seventeenth century and to rethink their current presence as a kind of a "return of the repressed." Departing from Assia Djebar's reading of Cervantes' Zoraida in *Don Quijote de la Mancha* as metaphor for Algerian female writers, William Childers emphasizes the vacillation between belonging and not belonging in Spanish society: "What strikes us today as mysterious about Zoraida is her uncanny vacillation between belonging and not belonging to Spanish society. More than a foreigner, she is that which had become *estranged* from European civilization, and has now returned" (93). This vacillation can be applied both to Moriscos in the seventeenth century and non-European immigrants in the twentieth and twenty-first centuries. In both situations, the practices and the limits of integration reveal perceptions of both groups as an internal colony within the nation. This growing presence of North African migrants shows that the expulsion did not entirely erase their existence on Spanish soil. In Childers' own words, "The expulsion of the Moriscos no longer marks the 'definitive' absence of the Muslim minority" (171).

Second, contemporary audiences face labour exploitation, high-interest loans, and job scarcity. They can identify with the disgruntled workers who demand better labour conditions and higher salaries. In this regard, Aguilar's play proves to be extremely relevant to modern times. Perhaps Juan de Ribera is a prototype for the political figure in need of image polishing in the wake of controversial decisions. The expulsion could be replaced by a ban on immigrants or new policies regarding migration. The *labradores* could be CEOs more interested in profits than in workers' rights. In addition, Enrico's store could sell iPhones, iPads, or Kindles, manufactured around the world and assembled in China, then sold at high-profit margins. Moreover, witnessing such a strike onstage might move today's theatregoers into action to fight for social justice and economic equality.

The possibility of adapting the play to the challenges of modern society aligns with the new form of theatre proposed by Augusto Boal in his *Theater of the Oppressed*. According to Boal, the purpose of the poetics of the oppressed is "to change the people – spectators, passive beings in the theatrical phenomenon – into subjects, into actors, transformers of the dramatic action" (122). Although Aguilar's play does not conform to the style and motives that defined the theatre of the oppressed, one can see glimpses of how it can move spectators to transform, if not the dramatic action, at least the course of their working lives, and to understand the discourses that blame them as workers in precarious conditions. Spectators could see a reflection of their own struggles and recognize themselves as potential employees suffering from the exploitation of those in power. In a sense, the the play's effect is similar to those of the workers' theatre in the United States at the beginning of the twentieth century. In describing these plays, Colette Hyman posits that attending these performances offered spectators access to the labour movement: "For women and men who would not have attended a union meeting or workers' education class, attending performances of labour plays or participating in their production offered access to the labour movement, its past, its struggles, and its vision for a more just society" (2). In the same vein, *El gran patriarca* offers audiences a vision of a better society for workers and recognizes their right to negotiate better compensation. It is a call to action for social justice and economic equality that is not restricted to the hegemonic values of the period. Thus the early modern Spanish theatre of Aguilar, in addressing issues of oppression, discrimination, and violence, is more vital now than ever.

NOTES

1 In this chapter, I use the term "Morisco" to distinguish the descendants of Muslims forced to convert to Christianity at the end of the fifteenth century from the Muslims who invaded the Iberian Peninsula in the eighth century and ruled until the conquest of Granada in 1492. However, as L.P. Harvey has observed, there is an ideological bias inherent in the word. According to him, "*Moro* and *morisco* were names that *other people* had for them, not the name they used for themselves" (5). Emphasis in the original.

2 Aguilar participated in several festivals in honour of saints, such as the beatification of Fray Luis Bertrán (1608), the beatification of Tomás de

Villanueva (1619), the celebration in honour of Saint Teresa (1621), and the celebration in honour of the Immaculate Conception (1622). He wrote another hagiographic play in the context of the festivals for the beatification of Luis Bertrán.

3 Several biographies were published to advance the canonization of Juan de Ribera; these included works by authors such as Escrivá (1612), Busquets (1683), Jiménez (1798), and Boronat y Barrachina (1904). More recently, Ehlers offers a nuanced perspective of Juan de Ribera's struggles with religious reformation in Valencia. He also was given the title of "patriarch." In the Christian Church, the title is assigned to bishops in recognition of their authority over members of the congregation.

4 On the expulsion of the Moriscos and the canonization of the archbishop, see Fiume.

5 On the economic consequences of the expulsion, see the studies of Lapeyre, Halperin Donghi, Reglá, Hamilton, Magraner Rodrigo, Casey, Císcar Pallarés, Reizábal Garrigosa, and Torres Morera.

6 Aguilar also published *La suerte sin esperanza* in *Norte de la poesía española*. However, this *comedia* does not exploit the issue of economic wealth in as strong a way as the other three plays. On *El mercader amante*, see Campbell, Casa, and Cohen.

7 For the treatment of the expulsion in theatre, see Pedraza Jiménez, Marchante-Aragón, and my own article.

8 I quote from the modern edition *Poetas dramáticos valencianos* (1929). The numbers correspond to the pages. All translations from Spanish to English are mine.

9 Another option is to read the scene in a more conservative manner and argue that Aguilar was supporting the views of the apologists of the expulsion to minimize the negative consequences of the event. This is a plausible stance given the tendency of Aguilar to privilege ambiguity in most of his work. On Aguilar's ambiguity regarding the expulsion of Moriscos in his epic poem, see Magnier.

10 Aguilar was the secretary of the Duke of Gandía since 1599. This position gave him access to the perspective of the *señores*. However, it is not sufficient to explain Aguilar's ideological contradictions with nobility despite his financial dependence.

11 In order to diminish the negative impact of the expulsion, Marcelino Menéndez y Pelayo quotes this verse and labels Aguilar as a communist poet: "algo comunista poeta [a somewhat communist poet]" (633). A similar critique appears in *El mercader amante*, also published in *Norte de la poesía española*, in which the father of Labinia gets angry as the merchant Belisario loses his fortune and his servant Astolfo gets rich.

5 Notes on An Ethics of Theatricality in Cervantes: *El gallardo español* and *La Numancia*

MOISÉS R. CASTILLO

As Cervantes realized in the context of the newly born mass culture of the Catholic, imperial, Spanish state, irony expertly wielded is the best defense against the manipulation of truth by the media. Its effect was and still is to remind its audience that we are all active participants in the creation and support of a fictional world that is always in danger of being sold to us as reality.
William Egginton, "'Quijote,' Colbert and the Reality of Fiction"

In his book *Cervantès dramaturge*, Jean Canavaggio made the following claim for Cervantes' theatre: "Par-delà ses vicissitudes, la trajectoire que dessine la production dramatique cervantine fait apparaître d'emblée une constante essentielle: celle d'une réflexion sans cesse reprise et approfondie sur le statut même de la fiction. Pareille préoccupation ne saurait surprendre chez un écrivain qui a inscrit au coeur même de son oeuvre majeure le débat de la vérité et du mensonge romanesque [Beyond its vicissitudes, the path that Cervantes' drama traces makes patent one essential constant: an inquiry, taken up again and again and constantly deepened, into the very status of fiction. This concern hardly surprises us, in a writer who has inscribed in the very heart of his major work the debate between truth and novelistic invention]" (35; my trans.).

In light of this reflection, the idea that Cervantes' theatre is marked by a constant enquiry on the nature of fiction takes on motifs that are familiar to us today. Our modern or postmodern world is more baroque than ever, in so far as we are immersed in a panorama of appearances, ostentation, manipulation, and excess; it is a world driven by mass spectacles and media realities that promote an immediate and non-reflexive response, along with foment, indifference, apathy, indolence, and in some instances fake news and post-truth. Faced with this dire situation, it is necessary to pause and reflect, and to draw from

Cervantine strategies to encourage reality literacy (Castillo and Egginton, *Medialogies*). In this precise sense, Cervantes' deliberate ambiguity and irony awake and undeceive us, sharpen our critical judgment, and restore our autonomy and creativity.

Cervantes' oeuvre, as is well known, was a response to the newly born mass culture promoted by the imperial Spanish state, with Lope de Vega as its lead. In fact, Lope's new form of *comedia* exemplified the baroque spectacle that essentially bewildered and entertained the masses, moulding, in most cases, an a-critical spectator. With all this in mind, this chapter will take a closer look at the meaning behind Cervantes' stagecraft. Through an analysis of *El gallardo español* (The Valiant Spaniard, circa 1605–6), in connection with other captivity or war plays that stage different versions of "our" violent clash with the Other or Others and of the quest for fame, such us *La Numancia* (Tragedy of Numancia, circa 1583–5) or *La conquista de Jerusalén por Godofre de Bullón* (The Conquest of Jerusalem by Godfrey of Bouillon, circa 1583–5). I aim to underscore the humanistic lessons of Cervantes' theatricality and their ethical implications, which, as we shall see, open up a space for considerations of social justice.

On the one hand, in these plays in which war is thematized, the playwright problematizes a hyper-individualistic version of fame, akin to hubris; this notion of fame will be ultimately cast as counterproductive, a dehumanizing force leading to injustice. On the other hand, he re-examines critically our construction of the enemy as essentially different from us, that is, a radical Other, allowing the reader or spectator to imagine the possibility of cross-cultural commonality. Indeed, imbued with a humanistic attitude that stresses individual dignity, worth, and virtue, Cervantes upholds our shared humanity, moving towards a humanization of the adversary.

Fame is at the basis of the plot in *El gallardo español*, the first play of Cervantes' *Ocho comedias y ocho entremeses nuevos, nunca representados* (Eight Plays and Eight New Interludes, Never Performed).[1] This *comedia* of captives, in the tradition of romance Morisco (Moorish ballad) and romance *fronterizo* (frontier ballad),[2] constitutes a mixture of history and fiction, a story of valour and romance that allegedly takes place during the siege of the Spanish fortress of Oran in 1563.[3] The romantic heroine is the beautiful Moor Arlaxa, who is longing to see the famous Spanish soldier Fernando de Saavedra, famous for his heroic deeds. Arlaxa tells her guardian Alimuzel that if he brings Don Fernando to her as a captive she will marry Alimuzel. Having accepted Arlaxa's proposal, Alimuzel travels to Oran and challenges the Spaniard, only to learn that Don Fernando's superior will not permit him to accept Alimuzel's challenge. Yet, Don Fernando cannot allow such an affront to his *honra* (reputation). Against the stated wishes of his superior, he will in fact surrender to the Moorish troops in order to challenge Alimuzel to a duel and to meet Arlaxa under a secret identity, showing both extraordinary bravery and gallantry. His reckless determination to defend his reputation or fame above all else will drive him to fight his own Christian co-religionists in defence of Arlaxa. In the end, however, loyalty wins the day as Don Fernando swallows his misplaced pride and fights bravely alongside his Christian comrades once again.

Desire and fame move the plot forward. Don Fernando's fame inspires Arlaxa's determination to meet him and it is also the reason why the Spaniard disobeys his superior by accepting the challenge that will allow him to build on his reputation. Don Fernando's ego-driven version of honour as the pursuit of individual reputation or fame will ultimately be unmasked in *El gallardo español* as hubris. I agree with William A. Stapp's claim that Cervantes criticizes Don Fernando's behaviour as "inconstante [inconstant]" and "mudable" [mutable]" (129), while condemning him as a turncoat whose sole ambition is to attain personal glory, regardless of the common good: "el bien tangible ... colectivo [the tangible, collective good]" (127). Therefore, it is not a "désobéissance momentanée [momentary disobedience]" on Don Fernando's part (Canavaggio 393), or a venial sin that embellishes the heroic protagonist (Carrasco Urgoiti 578), but a "misplaced sense of honour" that ultimately drives him to desert and to place "his own interests above those of his fellow Christians" (Gethin Hughes 66, 69), a clearly unpatriotic and unheroic attitude that Cervantes boldly condemns.[4] Not surprisingly, Melanie Henry has recently attributed Don Fernando's actions to Cervantes' critical attitude towards Spanish imperialism:

> The gap which exists between audience expectation of Don Fernando, and the reality of who he is, establishes a profound sense of ambiguity. This has further repercussions if we accept *El gallardo*'s protagonist as representative of Imperial Spain, which is, therefore, as fictitious as the analogies evoked by Arlaxa and Margarita. His desire to forsake his duty and indulge his capricious nature destabilises the illusion of a glorious nation founded on absolutes ... The idea of a Spain founded on "one nation, one faith, one destiny" is, therefore, problematized by Don Fernando's arrival on stage. The early-modern audience is confronted with the uncomfortable image of a Spain whose rhetoric and reality are violently at odds. (83)

Yet, I would add that Cervantes is at the same time calling attention to the shared humanity of Muslim and Christian rivals who do not see each other as essential enemies but as fellow humans, even potential friends, who happen to profess different faiths. The dramatist makes use of available conventions in such genres or subgenres as "comedias fronterizas de moros y cristianos [frontier *comedias* of Moors and Christians]" and "romances moriscos [Moorish ballads]," while foregrounding the shared humanity of cultural others, as seen in the following exchange:

> ALIMUZEL: No es enemigo el cristiano;
> contrario, sí; que el lozano
> deseo de Arlaxa bella
> presta para esta querella
> la voz, el intento y mano.
> FERNANDO: Presto te pondré con él,
> y fía aquesto de mí,
> comedido Alimuzel;
> y aun pienso hacer por ti
> lo que un amigo fiel,
> porque la ley que divide
> nuestra amistad no me impide
> de mostrar hidalgo el pecho;
> antes, con lo que es bien hecho
> se acomoda, ajusta y mide. (vv. 1035–49)

> ALIMUZEL: The Christian is not my enemy but the man, my rival, and it is the luscious desire of beautiful Arlaxa that gives to this challenge, the voice, the intent and the hand.
> FERNANDO: Soon I will bring you this challenge, and trust me, prudent Alimuzel, that I intend to do for you what a loyal friend would, for the law [faith] that divides our friendship does not impede me from showing my noble heart, which does not stray from the true measure of what is right.

These verses seem to go beyond the typical courtesy shown in the "romances moriscos" or "comedias fronterizas" to portray both adversaries acting in accordance with virtue: "lo que es bien hecho" (what is right). Familiar notions of religious or cultural hatred or intolerance are entirely absent here. The Moor is a worthy enemy.[5] Moreover, Cervantes "does not insist on the conversion of the two Muslims, a detail he would surely not have overlooked if his concern had been to emphasize the superiority of Christianity" (Hughes 74). Thus, in Act III, Alimuzel will even use a rhetorical oxymoron to call Don Fernando an "amigo enemigo [friend(ly) enemy]" (v. 2779), underscoring, once more, not just chivalric courtesy, but their shared humanity. As a matter of fact, Cervantes stresses the human weaknesses of both Don Fernando and Alimuzel in foregrounding the Spaniard's arrogance alongside Alimuzel's own flaws.

The word *deseo* (desire) is often used in the play alongside its synonym *antojo* (whim). As Alimuzel remarks, "the luscious desire of the beautiful Arlaxa" sparks a personal conflict between male rivals, not between their respective military allegiances or religions. As seen in the rest of Cervantes' *comedias* of captives (*El trato de Argel* (The Trade of Algiers), *Los baños de Argel* (The Bagnios of Algiers), *La gran sultana doña Catalina de Oviedo* (The Great Sultana), and *La conquista de Jerusalén* (The Conquest of Jerusalem), desire and love connect the Moor and the Christian in scenes that invite us to rethink one's attitude towards the Other.[6] We are thus engaged as spectators and possibly witnesses of dramatic displays of empathy, commiseration, and understanding of the Other's vicissitudes and suffering. For instance, the Moor Arlaxa feels pity and expresses solidarity in learning about the suffering of the Christian Margarita: "Cristiana, de tu dolor / casi siento la mitad [Christian, of your pain / I almost feel half]" (vv. 2310–11). In *El trato de Argel* Muslims and Christians are presented as equally greedy; in *El gallardo español* Margarita accuses her brother of the same vice:

Vi que mi hermano aspiraba,
codicioso de mi hacienda,
a dejarme entre paredes,
medio viva y medio muerta.   (2199–202)

I saw that my grasping brother, covetous of my estate, aimed to leave me between walls, half alive and half dead.

The same can be said about positive attributes such as virtue, solidarity, and compassion. They transcend the barriers of blood and religion in scenes of dramatic – tragic at times – affirmation of our shared humanity.

Contrary to the claims of Gustavo Correa (292) or Joaquín Casalduero (27, 35), and despite what its title might seem to suggest, *El gallardo español* is anything but a patriotic celebration of Spanish gallantry, heroism, and/or honour in any familiar sense. As Stapp puts it most succinctly, "esta *comedia* no es un encomio de la gallardía española [this drama is not an encomium of Spanish gallantry]" (135). I have recently made a similar argument in discussing another Cervantine drama, *La Numancia*, which on the surface can be read as a nationalistic tragedy only to point in a much different direction under closer scrutiny ("Apocalyptic Stages").

The play recreates the last stand in the heroic uprising of the Celtiberian people of Numancia against the Roman Empire. Numancia, a Castilian city located near present-day Soria, was historically in rebellion against the power of Rome and was under siege for fourteen years (sixteen years in the play, v. 117). The tragedy recreates onstage the final siege lasting one year and seven months, led by General Publius Cornelius Scipio Aemilianus against the Numantines, resulting in the city being razed in 133 BC. So far, we have the perfect script for a good historical play, especially if we consider the tragedy's dramatic apocalyptic climax and its portrayal of the immolation of the defiant Numantines. Over time, Numancia will become, in Spain's collective imaginary, a synonym for patriotic pride, resistance, and unlimited courage. And we should not be surprised by the fact that the Celtiberians and the Spanish are identified with each other; a few years before Cervantes wrote *La Numancia*, Philip II's chronicler, Ambrosio de Morales, was already celebrating the Numantine feat as a landmark episode in the history of Spain (*Corónica general de España* [General Chronicle of Spain] 1574).[7]

Numancia is therefore a proto-Spain that becomes a foundational myth of national and imperial identity: the exemplary Numantine strength is thus projected as the source of the Habsburg dynasty's character, the courage of the lineage of kings that, going all the way back to Ferdinand, will rule the world and that Philip II now leads.

> FAME: Indicio ha dado esta no vista hazaña
> del valor que en los siglos venideros
> tendrán los hijos de la fuerte España,
> hijos de tales padres herederos. (2424–7)

> FAME: This peerless deed hath given proofs most plain what valour, in the ages yet to be shall dwell within the sons of mighty Spain, the heirs of such ancestral bravery!

The allegorical figures of the Duero River in Act I and War and Fame in Act IV all ensure that the Numantines' "único y solo [unique and sole]" (v. 2422) courage will be immortalized, and will also prophesy the fall of the Roman Empire at the hands of Attila the Hun's troops, or of Rome itself at the hands of the Spaniards in the sixteenth century.

However, the matter is not left at that since, as the literature on the subject has shown, in this play the Habsburgs are not only portrayed as the heirs to Numantine courage but also as the successors to the power of the Roman Empire. On the one hand the play seems to celebrate, without even the slightest chink in its armour, Spanish heroism and the imperial glory that goes hand in hand with a fully patriotic Cervantes (see Francisco Ynduráin, Ricardo Doménech, Joaquín Casalduero, Melveena McKendrick, Paul Lewis-Smith, Brian Stiegler, Jack Weiner, Francisco Vivar, Jordi Cortadella). And yet, on the other hand, the tragedy is fraught with signs that allegorically project a link between the Roman consul Scipio and his troops, and King Philip II and his. According to this interpretation, after the battle against the Numantines waged by this newly disciplined army led by Scipio, Rome has become militarily worthy of being a great empire, an empire that appears to have been brought back to life, "renovado [renovated]" with new spirit and splendour in the powerful Habsburg Catholic kings (Juan Bautista Avalle-Arce 254). Therefore, if the play prophesies this "renovatio et translatio imperii," this identification of Scipio–Philip II and Rome–Spain, then the Spanish Empire is portrayed as a victim (Numancia) and victimizer (Rome), which calls into question its action in search of the imperial ideal.[8]

In this political vein, some of the critics have focused on those passages of the play – ones focusing on the specific acts and motivations of the two leaders, or the involvement of the allegorical characters Guerra (War), Hambre (Famine), and Enfermedad (Sickness) in Act IV – that allegorically have the potential to evoke the battles that the Spanish Empire wages with possible historical and more contemporary Numancias; in other words, against the revolts of the Moriscos (Hermenegildo), of Flanders (King, Johnson), or of the Araucanians (King, Simerka). Also, according to Aaron Kahn, "In *La Numancia*, Cervantes's general target of criticism is Philip II's shift in imperial policy and the nearly one hundred years of Spanish incursion into America" (37).

All of this is what has led literary critic Michael Armstrong-Roche to explore the consequences of role reversal, of Spain viewed as a new Rome, and thus convincingly reveal the paradoxes that threaten the creation and defence of the imperial national identity in Cervantes' *La Numancia*. He explains: "rather than defend a triumphalist patriotic or anti-imperial critical reading of the play as has already been done very well, I am interested in drawing attention to the way the text plays those implications off one another in the light of Numancia's sixteenth-century consolidation as a proto-national myth for Spain" ("(The) *Patria* Besieged" 208). In two articles on *La Numancia* that complement each other, Armstrong-Roche thus tries to give meaning to the large number of historical referents mentioned in the literature ("Imperial Theater") as well as to the internal polyphony of the text itself ("(The) *Patria* Besieged"). In the first article, he contrasts the classical and humanistic idealization of Scipio – a model of virtues – with Cervantes' version, which addresses the repeated abuse of the rhetoric of virtue in unfair wars fuelled by a quest for fame. In the second article, he proposes a paradoxographical reading of the internal polyphony of a text that ends up mixing up the two anti-heroes, Scipio and Theogenes, and therefore Rome and Numancia, and thus celebrates – through the voices of the River Duero, Spain, and Fame – the concept of homeland and patriotic sacrifice that appears to inform Cervantes's play and, at the same time, question it – through the voice of Famine, the repeated association of suicide with homicide, the lack of consensus among the Numantines regarding "suicide," cannibalism, and the desire for fame that causes Theogenes to kill his own wife and children.

In light of these arguments, and in line with other plays in which Cervantes' vision of the Moorish or Jewish Other is portrayed (*La gran sultana, El trato de Argel, Los baños de Argel, El gallardo español, La conquista de Jerusalén*), *La Numancia* shows a deliberate ambiguity – as Johnson or Hermenegildo would say – a wavering, an ambivalence that celebrates patriotic heroism yet at the same time strongly calls into question the notion of fatherland and patriotic sacrifice, which clearly undermines the construction of national identity and imperial expansion surrounding these concepts. To be sure, this is not about defending a Cervantes who is relativistic, anti-imperialistic, or unpatriotic, but rather an author who – as I have argued elsewhere – by continuously positioning himself on both sides of the issue, or by defending opposing perspectives in the same play, is denouncing the fatuous ideals imposed by the dominant ideology, thereby calling into question all that smacks of fundamentalism or cultural essentialism.

What then are we left with? On the one hand, there is the tragedy, the end of a civilization: the Numantines' deaths are an apocalypse in the same way it is for all of those subjugated by the empire (Greer), or under "the injustice of tyrannical imperialism" (Kahn 25). On the other hand, there is praise for the qualities that make us all better – whether we are Numantines or Romans – and that the play distils: resistance in the face of adversity, dignity, charity, commiserating in the face of suffering, the search for peace, and courage.

Thus, in *La Numancia*, not only does the Roman leader Scipio have a blind desire for fame associated with victory, which brings about the total destruction of the Celtiberian people, but also, when the time comes, the Numantine chief Theogenes shows the same defect as evidenced by the last words of the leader to one of his men: "camina, que se tarda / el tiempo de morir como deseo, / ora me mate el hierro o el fuego me arda, / que gloria nuestra en cualquier muerte veo [make haste, for my desire / outruns Fate's tardy step with panting breath; / let sword devour me, or the furious fire, / I see our glory in whatever death!]" (vv. 2172–5). For denying the Roman enemy glory – a vengeance that becomes homicidal as Armstrong-Roche ("(The) *Patria* Besieged") would put it – is also an incentive to go down in history:

> TEÓGENES: Sólo se ha de mirar que el enemigo
> no alcance de nosotros triunfo y gloria:
> antes ha de servir él de testigo
> que apruebe y eternice nuestra historia;
> y si todos venís en lo que digo,
> mil siglos durará nuestra memoria:
> y es que no quede cosa aquí en Numancia
> de do el contrario pueda haber ganancia. (vv. 1418–25)

> TEÓGENES: One thing alone is needful, that the foe shall reap from us no triumph and no fame, nay, rather shall he serve, in this hour woe, as witness to immortalize our name. If now with me ye hand in hand will go, through thousand ages shall your glory flame, for nothing in Numancia shall remain which these proud foes can garner to their gain.

What is more, this glory will lead Theogenes to impulsively and unnecessarily murder his own family and then cry out, baring his soul, and beseech one of his soldiers to kill him with his own sword as if he were a "pérfido romano [perfidious Roman]" (v. 2141). This makes him the target of criticism from the character of Famine, who, several verses earlier, had stated that the desire for fame is a "strange," choreographed, and "murderous" way to seek his death for posterity and "harm" to one's own people:

> Venid: veréis que en los amados cuellos
> de tiernos hijos y mujer querida,
> Teógenes afila y prueba en ellos
> de su espada el cruel corte homicida,
> y como ya, después de muertos ellos,
> estima en poco la cansada vida,
> buscando de morir un modo estraño,
> que causó, con el suyo, más de un daño. (vv. 2048–55)

Come, you shall see how in the bosom dear of tender children and beloved wife, Theogenes sharpens and proves in them the temper of his homicidal knife, and when the deadly work is over here, so little recks he of his wearied life, he seeks for Death, by a mode strange, which causes more harm than his own. (my trans.)

Lastly, the Roman soldier Gayo Mario relays the words that Theogenes had uttered before committing suicide by way of throwing himself into the fire, words that emphasize this quest for fame: "¡Oh clara Fama, / ocupa aquí tus lenguas y tus ojos / en esta hazaña, que a cantar te llama! [O brilliant Fame, / come hither with thy countless tongues and eyes, / behold a deed it fits thee to proclaim!]" (vv. 2282–4). That desire for fame casts a pall on both Scipio and Theogenes, on both Rome and Numancia, thereby making it difficult to tell which of the two is a victim and which is a victimizer. This difficulty is made worse if, as was mentioned above, we assume the role reversal that the play prophesies and identify Scipio with Philip II.[9]

On the other hand, *La Numancia* also shows cannibalism on the part of the Numantines. That anthropophagy not only is a homicidal act of desperation that postpones certain death, but one that could be the ultimate expression of the inhuman violence (cannibalism) that imperialism – here Spain as a new-Rome – inflicts on its oppressed (Hulme 5).

To be clear, the tragic cannibalism to which the Numantines resort in their desperation and their expressed quest for immortality through fame add to the sensationalistic feel of the drama, which seems to point in the direction of the familiar Cervantine exaggeration, the kind of dramatic excess that we see at work in other plays as a means to introduce ambiguity. In so doing here, Cervantes is testing – if not openly calling into question – the concepts of fatherland, patriotic sacrifice, and imperial national identity vis-à-vis the audience.

Perhaps the best example of this ambivalence on the part of Cervantes occurs when the allegorical figure War comes onstage to say that all those who curse war, including the Numantines, are mistaken, given that in the future it will help Spain in its dominions and conquests in the same way it has helped the Romans in theirs:

pero tiempo vendrá en que yo me mude
y dañe al alto y al pequeño ayude.
....
aunque quien me maldice a veces yerra,
pues no sabe el valor desta mi mano,
sé bien que en todo el orbe de la tierra

> seré llevada del valor hispano,
> en la dulce sazón questén reinando
> un Carlos, un Filipo y un Fernando. (vv. 1982–91)

> but time will come when I shall change it all, will smite the mighty, and assist the small. ... Though he who curses me at times errs greatly, unaware of my own worth, I do know well that throughout all the land Spanish valour will prevail, at that sweet season when a Charles, a Philip, and a Ferdinand will reign. (my trans.)

What is indeed telling is the fact that it is War herself who indicates how Spain, now the heir to the Numantine "abatidos hispanos [defeated Hispanics]" (v. 1981), will at some point in the future become the successor to Roman imperial power in the monarchy of the Catholic Ferdinand and the Habsburgs. And even though their coronation is considered to be a happy or "sweet" occasion ("dulce sazón"), the consequences of war as an instrument of imperial expansion in these verses are patently clear: the place that the Numantine victims occupy vis-à-vis Rome will be the same as that of the victims of the future Spanish empire, whether they be the Moriscos, the Flemish, or the Amerindians. Once again, as so often happens in Cervantes' texts, ambiguity and conflicting messages rear their heads; this apparently positive image of the war – as moral and just expansion – will be harshly criticized if it is accompanied by the ambition or fame that Scipio and Theogenes clearly show here. Cervantes simply cannot accept the fact that what is so often merely ambition can also be portrayed as a virtue, and he, therefore – as also pointed out by Armstrong-Roche ("Imperial Theater") – believes that wars that are waged out of a desire for fame are unjust and refers to them as "bárbara arrogancia [barbarous arrogance]" (v. 2298) in the words of Scipio himself. This is also made absolutely clear in another work by Cervantes, written contemporaneously: *La conquista de Jerusalén por Godofre de Bullón*.[10]

In Act III of *La conquista*, the soldiers Charles and Fabricio, two of the protagonists involved in the first crusade of 1099, talk about their various ups and downs, and in their dialogue, one of them says he is quite happy. When Fabricio asks him what the reason for his happiness is, Charles' response is telling: "El ser esta jornada diferente / de cualquier otra, qu'ésta es santa y justa, / las demás llenas de ambición y envidia [That this war is different from any other, for this one is holy and just; the rest are full of ambition and envy]" (vv. 1335–8). Indicating that this war is "the only one that is holy and just" strikes me as an unnecessary but typically Cervantine exaggeration; it plants the seed of ambiguity and calls into question what it expresses. While perhaps not calling into question the legitimacy of this "holy war," it does cast doubt on the legitimacy of "all other wars that are full of ambition and envy." Looking at the passage from an undeceived perspective, it perhaps shows a distrust of wars and entails a self-criticism regarding the motivations behind all previous wars that Christians have waged for less laudable motives, especially those wars waged to further personal ambition and fame.

Bearing all this in mind, perhaps what Cervantes is trying to emphasize at this point in *La Numancia* is both the futility of the quest for fame, as in Roman's annihilation of a people, and the emptiness of misplaced and exaggerated patriotism (patriotic suicide) that, when imbued with a desire for fame, leads to genocide. Though Theogenes and the Numantine senate, through its decree, trumpet this genocide, many of the Numantines are deeply critical, calling it "cruel sentencia [cruel sentence]" (v. 1675), "rigor bárbaro estraño [strange barbarous rigour]" (v. 1676), and stressing that "verdugos de nosotros nuestras manos / serán, y no los pérfidos romanos [ourselves our executioners must be, / and not these Romans steeped in perfidy]" (vv. 1678–9). This horror, highlighting the lack of unanimity on the senate decree of collective suicide, is voiced by the anonymous characters Numantine 1° and 2°, and the Numantine woman, as well as the young Variato and Servio. In addition, the allegorical characters War, Famine, and Sickness take charge of narrating in graphic detail the atrocities of the people's mass self-immolation that occurs offstage.

At this point we may want to make explicit the question that drives the present essay: What kind of ethical value, or better yet, what mode of ethics are we acknowledging in (or assigning to) Cervantes' theatricality, as expressed in *El gallardo español*, *La Numancia*, and *La conquista de Jerusalén*, and in other dramas, including *El trato de Argel*, *Los baños de Argel*, and *La gran sultana*, in which cultural and religious Others play prominent roles? All these Cervantine works stress our common humanity rather than what divides and separates us from our Others, whether they be Moors, Christians, Jews, Romans, or Numantines. With its military focus and its tragic aspects, *La Numancia*, perhaps more than the others, extols such human qualities as empathy and solidarity.[11] These go above and beyond courage, even when expressed as resistance in the face of adversity and lethal power. It should be noted that the Numantine ambassadors in Act I seek justice, not independence from Rome, and justify their rebellion on a history of victimization going back to the depraved and unfair rule of the Roman consuls. The concepts of dignity and justice are also alluded to when Variato accuses

Scipio and Rome of having broken previous "pactos y conciertos [pacts and agreements]" (v. 2354; my trans.). We see a collective quest for peace, something that the Numantines emphatically stress in Act I: "pedirte, señor, la amiga mano [beg you, lord, for your friendly hand]" (v. 237), "paces [treaties]" (v. 258), and "concierto [agreement]" (v. 252; my trans.). And we see honourable actions (vv. 592, 593, 1295, 1298), along with radical expressions of solidarity. We see the self-sacrifice of a starving mother unable to nurse her child. We witness courageous and moving stories of love and friendship, as when a husband and his best friend sacrifice their lives to provide a few morsels of bread to a starving wife. We witness eloquent rejections of War, a "mal" and "dura pestilencia [evil and harsh pestilence]" (vv. 1156–8; my trans.), which appears onstage flanked by Famine and Sickness. And we sense a strong criticism of any war that is waged in pursuit of individual ambitions or personal glory.[12]

It is often in the borderland contact areas that empires, nations, and religions come into conflict and lay bare the contradictions they are based on; this is where the characters of Cervantes clearly display their precarious and complex humanity, their noble attributes and shortcomings, their hopes and fears, and their theatrical but authentic life experiences. We have seen, in *El gallardo español* and *La Numancia*, how Cervantes' dramatic craft humanizes cultural and religious Others, even when they are represented as military enemies. As political philosopher Antonio Cerella puts it, "If we believe in humanity, we must grant it to our enemy" (36). Scipio's blind desire for glory drove him to treat his Numantine adversaries as unworthy barbarians who did not even deserve the chance to meet his troops face to face in the battlefield. Instead, he carried out a cruel and dehumanizing siege that drove the Numantines to cannibalism and mass suicide. This is the blindness of empire, which, as we have seen, can be attributed to the Romans as well as the Spaniards of later centuries.[13]

Yet, Cervantes' dramas offer models of resilience, virtue, courage, and dignity. Against conventional dramatic treatment of the enemy as a radical Other, one who is essentially different from us, Cervantes' plays allow the reader or spectator to imagine the possibility of cross-cultural commonality. Today, these Cervantine lessons are echoed in Antonio Cerella's warnings against entrenched nationalism and fundamentalist discourse. We would make the point – with Cerella – that any workable notion of justice must start with the humanization of the enemy:

> When the enemy is reduced to the empty image of "collateral damage" or the "inverted icon" of the crusader to be destroyed, a frightening abyss – in

which all the legal covers sink – opens, leaving room only for naked violence and its intrinsic brutality. German jurist Carl Schmitt warned against this ideological drift. The figures of the enemies, he argued, are our existential reflections, the shaping of ourselves, the embodiment of our own question. Their dehumanization leads to the loss of our most intimate humanity. The dehumanizing mechanism rips human faces from the Others, thus transforming them into what is infinitely identical to itself and yet ontologically different, into the indefinite, abstract, and absolute Enemy of humanity: Islam, the West, America, the French, the Arabs. In this way, individual responsibilities are turned into collective ones: everyone is guilty, and no one is responsible. (35)

To conclude, in today's world, when one can witness daily the tragic results of continued social strife and senseless war, it is worth revisiting the writings of an author who was deeply scarred in mind and body by the political and military conflicts of his time. These open wounds inspired in Cervantes an unprecedented style of critical thinking, one that has the power of reaching across the centuries. Cervantes speaks to us today about the worth of human life and the horrors of warfare and captivity, and about the value of understanding, empathy, solidarity, dignity, ethics, and virtue. Faced with the struggles of our current conflict-ridden world and our own posthuman condition, we must now find the Cervantine courage to dream other worlds so that we may work to improve the one we inhabit.

NOTES

1 All quotes from *El gallardo español* and *La Numancia* come from Florencio Sevilla's Guanajuato edition. I use the translation of *La Numancia* into English by James Y. Gibson of 1885, unless noted otherwise. In the case of *El gallardo español* all translations are mine.
2 See Anne Fastrup and Mª Soledad Carrasco Urgoiti.
3 Some critics have focused on the dichotomy between fiction and truth in the play (Eric Kartchner), or how the Cervantine text juxtaposes them. Michael Gerli examines the way Cervantes subverts Aristotle's concept of verisimilitude in order to claim that the drama's purpose is "to probe the limits, possibilities, and difficulties of integrating historical and strictly imaginative (essentially mendacious) discourses" (44); "In this way, *El gallardo* offers a kind of ontological critique of theater which discloses at every step the semiotic strategies it exploits to represent the truth" (53). In the same vein, Lourdes Albuisech explores those meta-theatrical devices

used by Cervantes to expose the limits of truth through concepts such as valour (330).

4 This episode, brought to the stage by Cervantes, is based on what happened to a real soldier, Alonso Maldonado, when, in 1539, he abandoned his post to engage in a duel that would lead to his death, and on the eventual fall of the Castelnuovo fort. Jerónimo de Urrea in *Diálogo de la verdadera honra militar* (Dialogue on the True Military Honour, 1566) recounts, analyses, and condemns the soldier's conduct (Carrasco Urgoiti 579). Anne Fastrup has recently argued, "*El gallardo español* considers how the individual, in the name of his own heroism, ends up in a demonstration of fatal disobedience to the state" (363). Francisco Márquez Villanueva has called it an "impasse entre el individualismo de la caballería y una disciplina militar a la moderna [impasse between chivalric individualism and a modern military discipline]," a dilemma which leads to Don Fernando's "flagrante y quijotesca desobediencia [flagrant and quixotic disobedience]" (50–1).

5 As Abi-Ayad writes, "Cervantes rompe las barreras étnicas y religiosas para sobrevalorar la amistad, el respeto y la tolerancia [Cervantes breaks the ethnic and religious barriers in valuing friendship, respect and tolerance]" (138).

6 See my two articles, "¿Ortodoxia cervantina?" and "Espacios de ambigüedad." Anne Fastrup contends that "Cervantes' works have played and still play a decisive role in this research as a type of literature which in a low-key way resists the state's mono-cultural constructions of identity by pointing to the presence of many and mixed cultural identities in Catholic Spain" (366).

7 Part of the discussion of *La Numancia* and *La conquista de Jerusalén* is due to appear in a forthcoming essay titled "Apocalyptic Stages: Lope de Vega's *El Nuevo Mundo* and Cervantes's *La Numancia*."

8 Felipe Valencia also contends that not only would the sixteenth-century Spaniards identify with the Numantines, but with the Romans as well (100).

9 In her insightful analysis of *El trato de Argel*, Tania de Miguel Magro has corroborated that this drama shares with *La Numancia* a contradictory imperialist discourse that, while on the one hand celebrates the values of the Spanish empire, at the same time constitutes a direct attack on the imperial policies of Philip II (186).

10 I cite the critical edition by Héctor Brioso Santos of 2009. Translations from this play are mine.

11 Behind those qualities perhaps lie what A. Robert Lauer has perceived as the fundamental idea of the drama: "la patria no es aquí un territorio o una comunidad religiosa, estamental o militar, sino una unidad fraternal, desinteresada y común que inspira amor, solidaridad y sacrificio [here

patria is not a territory or a religious, stratified or military community, but rather a fraternal unity, altruistic and communal, one which inspires love, solidarity and sacrifice]" (995; my trans.).
12 Manuel García Puertas has commented on Cervantes' critique of war, especially in those instances in which the conflict is motivated by personal interest (78).
13 Zimic notes that in his theatre Cervantes speaks against "bestialidad humana" (human brutality) regardless of religious distinctions, while upholding ideals of universal peace (51).

6 Using Shame and Guilt to Impose Social Injustice in Ana Caro's *El Conde Partinuplés*

JACLYN COHEN-STEINBERG

The concepts of shame and guilt were of vital importance in Spanish Golden Age society. Having a pure bloodline, seen as a sign of honour, and maintaining honour within one's family were crucially important for Spaniards of the time. These sought-after characteristics included the ability to prove Christian ancestry, without the taint of Jewish or Muslim blood, and the ability to exhibit a respectable public image. There was a constant fear of shame in being suspected of impure blood and it is this fear "that is the essential factor in understanding the cultural and psychological structure of the *comedia*" (Mintz 2). Many Golden Age works of fiction, whether short stories, poetry, or dramas, examine the theme of honour and the complications this human value can bring. Since honour is a prevalent theme in Spanish literature, having a sense of shame, which includes restraint and lack of dishonourable conduct for fear of embarrassment, is of utmost importance as well.

Ana Caro Mallén de Soto, a female playwright of Spain's Golden Age, explores this emotion, along with guilt, in her play *El Conde Partinuplés* (1653). Writing for the public sphere of the theatre, Caro is one of many women who wrote secular plays during the sixteenth and seventeenth centuries in Spain:[1]

> In an age when moralists still denounced women's public speech and activity, these women dramatists wrote and created performable and utterable works that, whether produced on stage or not, reveal each writer's familiarity with the theatrical conventions and literary/artistic practices of the period. (Soufas, "Introduction" ix)

These secular plays show that women participated in this male-dominated arena. Caro herself received payment for the composition of two *autos sacramentales* for the Corpus Christi festivals in Seville from

1641 to 1645.[2] That fact that Caro was compensated for her work indicates that she achieved professional status as a playwright. Her ability to succeed in such a public arena, at a time when women were to remain silent and indoors, has recently sparked much scholarly interest in Caro's life and works. She has become perhaps the most famous woman playwright of Spain's Golden Age.

Ana Caro was born around 1600 in southern Spain and spent the majority of her life in Seville, one of Spain's theatrical centres. In addition to her *autos sacramentales*, she wrote two secular plays: *El conde Partinuplés* (1653) and *Valor, agravio y mujer* (n.d.). Various references in these works and "commentary from her contemporaries suggest that Caro's *comedias* may have been performed or at least circulated in manuscript form among literary circles" (Soufas, "Ana Caro Mallén de Soto" 133).[3] She was in the court of the Count Duke of Olivares and was praised by her fellow playwrights María de Zayas, Luis Vélez de Guevara, Castillo Solórzano, and Matos Fragoso. Despite this high visibility, there is little information available about her life and nothing more is known after 1653. Scholars believe that she may have been a plague victim, "during the terrible epidemic that struck Seville from 1649–1652" (133).

Caro's connections, along with her capacity to write for such a public arena, gave her a power that other women of her time did not have. She was able to convert the male-dominated genre of the theatre into something new. Her works, for example, depict the influence of various male canonical writers of her time, most notably Tirso de Molina. His writings, when compared to Ana Caro's, bring to light the fact that she is "una transformadora de materiales literarios que opera a través de la imitación de modelos [a transformer of literary materials who writes through imitating models]" (Luna 14).[4] In doing this, Caro ends her plays with conventional marriages, yet her focus throughout her works differs greatly from that of the dominant discourse. As Lola Luna explains, "Ana Caro se adhiere a los valores y estructuras de la sociedad patriarcal de su época, creando al mismo tiempo una inversión de roles y ensayando una cierta reorientación en la posición de las mujeres en la sociedad [Ana Caro adheres to the values and structures of the patriarchal society of her time, creating all at once an inversion of roles and a testing of a certain reorientation of a woman's position in society]" (31–2). Caro's originality, then, lies in her ability to depict strong female characters who subvert gender roles and who argue for a change of status for women. In utilizing traditional models, as Caro does in *El Conde Partinuplés*, the focus of this chapter, she still manages to argue against the societal expectations of chastity, silence, and restraint placed on women. The work provides a critique of the concept of shame for both men and women and emphasizes the need for reform in male behaviour in order for women to succeed. The men who surround Rosaura, the main protagonist, hold her to impossible standards, believing that their ideas maintain justice within their society, while, in reality, they create social injustice for Rosaura. I aim to prove that these men use shame and guilt (a concept that did not exist in the modern sense at the time)[5] to ultimately force Rosaura to marry, an act that is unjust for her. The males' shameless actions also cause them to assume that the women should feel guilt even if they are not to blame. Caro strives to argue against these injustices towards women.

El Conde Partinuplés is a reworking of the anonymous French romance *Portonopeus de Blois* (1188), but Caro makes significant changes.[6] Caro presents a male character (Count Partinuplés), who, at the end of the play, remains unrepentant of his sins against Empress Rosaura. She is a ruler who fulfils her societal role as leader to her people, but does not receive equal social justice in return. "Social justice is concerned not in the narrow focus of what is just for the individual alone, but what is just for the social whole" (Capeheart and Milovanovic 2); Rosaura believes that as a fair ruler she is providing justice for her people. She states:

> ... saldré a defender valiente,
> de estos Reinos la corona
> y aun ofreceré la vida
> con resolución heroica porque vosotros gocéis
> la parte que en ésa os toca,
> pacíficos y contentos.   (Caro 83)

> ... I will go out and valiantly defend this crown and these kingdoms and I will even offer my life with heroic resolution so that you all enjoy the life that is yours, peaceful and happy.

She will fight for her kingdom with her own life and concerns herself only with what will allow her people to live in peace. Her vassals, on the other hand, seem to be plotting a mutiny against her; she declares, "Motín injusto, tened: /¿dónde vais? [Unjust mutiny, you have: where are you going?]" (82). Rosaura then becomes angry, but continues to listen to her council members despite this injustice. The men around Rosaura do not grant her equality because this mutiny arises from the fact that their empress does not currently have a husband. They believe that her marriage will lead to justice and benefit society as a whole, even if it goes against what their leader desires. Clauso, one of the councilmen, declares: "Cásese o pierda estos Reinos [She must marry or lose these kingdoms]" (81). Caro's focus in the play, therefore, is on the treasonous conduct of these men and on how their actions hurt Rosaura. Caro, like other women writers of the seventeenth century, emphasizes the female character and her efforts in an attempt to achieve the goal of: "exposing the social and moral disorder – private and public – caused by the failure of the males to develop both the so-called male virtues (reason, bravery) and the female ones (temperance, mercy), and thus their failure to preserve stability in the hierarchical cultural system" (Soufas, *Dramas of Distinction* 42). Caro, therefore, uses Rosaura to highlight men's failures and show that their lack of restraint, and therefore shame, causes her to suffer social injustice.

Rosaura is the ruler of Constantinople, yet, as seen above, she is not deemed fit to govern because she is a woman and is unmarried. Rosaura is strong-willed and, owing to her governing responsibilities, has begun to adopt various male attributes. She becomes furious and asks what the mutiny is about:

> Decidme qué es, porque yo,
> atrevida y fervorosa,
> con vosotros, imitando
> las ilustres Amazonas,
> saldré a defender valiente,
> destos Reinos la corona.   (Caro 82–3)

> Tell me what this is because I, daring and fervent, with you, imitating the illustrious Amazons, will go out and valiantly defend this crown and these kingdoms.

Rosaura will resort to violence if necessary to protect her kingdom, and even compares herself to the famous Amazon women warriors, who in Golden Age Spain are the models of the *mujer varonil*, or masculine woman.[7] This declaration of battling for the kingdom is acceptable for a man, yet inappropriate for a woman. As Julian Pitt-Rivers shows in his definitions of honour and shame with respect to Mediterranean societies, honour is the value of a person in one's own eyes, but also in the eyes of one's society. Honour "is his estimation of his own worth, his *claim* to pride, but it is also the acknowledgement of that claim, his excellence recognized by society, his *right* to pride" (Pitt-Rivers 21). Honour derives from reputation and bloodlines and inspires proper conduct. Honour becomes linked with shame when "a woman is dishonoured, loses her *vergüenza* [shame], with the tainting of her sexual purity, but a man does not" (42). These conditions oblige a man to defend his honour and that of his family, while the woman must preserve her innocence. For a woman, honour is synonymous with shame. This is the only case where honour and shame become equal:

> Shame, no longer equivalent to honour, as shyness, blushing and timidity is thought to be proper to women, even though it no longer constitutes virtue, while honour, no longer equivalent to shame, becomes an exclusively male attribute as the concern for precedence and the willingness to offend another man. (42)

This shows that, when the terms honour and shame are not equated, they contain qualities specific to each sex. Honour is a male attribute while shame is a female one. These roles cannot be reversed because, as Pitt-Rivers further points out, "for a man, to show timidity or blush is likely to make him an object of ridicule, while a woman who takes to physical violence or attempts to usurp the male prerogative of authority or, very much more so, sexual freedom, forfeits her shame" (42). Therefore, Rosaura, just by being in a position of authority, forfeits her sense of shame and puts her honour in jeopardy. In addition, she calls upon the Amazon warriors to defend her right to her kingdom, thus adding to her shame. Her vassals have triggered her downfall within only a few pages of the play.

In the previous quote, Rosaura also describes herself as "atrevida" (daring), which according to Sebastián de Covarrubias y Orozco in his dictionary, the *Tesoro de la lengua castellana o española,* published in 1611, coincides with the definition of a *desvergonzado* (someone with little shame). The entry for *desvergüenza* shows the importance of this term and of avoiding the qualities it represents: "poca vergüenza, desmesura, atrevimiento, poco respeto. *Desvergonzado,* el mal criado, atrevido. *Desvergonzadamente,* libremente. *Desvergonzarse,* atreverse [little shame, lack of moderation, nerve, little respect. *Desvergonzado,* the ill-mannered, daring. *Desvergonzadamente,* freely. *Desvergonzarse,* to dare]" (Covarrubias 421). In other words, a *desvergonzado* is someone who is shameless and has no morals. A person who acts shamelessly is one who lives freely without following the rules, while one who causes himself to lose shame gives up an honourable life. The term is often used in reference to women who have lost their chastity and to anyone thought to be a heretic or a gypsy. A shameless individual no longer has honour because he or she lacks respect and courtesy. Honour, according to Covarrubias, is the same as *honra,* which means "reverencia, cortesía que se hace a la virtud [reverence, courtesy towards virtue]" (644). The *Diccionario de Autoridades* (1726) goes further to state that *honra* "significa también pundonor, eftimación y buena fama ... Se toma también por la integridad virginal en las mugeres [also signifies modesty, respect and a good reputation ... It also refers to the virginal integrity of women]" (RAE, "Honra"). One with little respect, a *desvergüenza*, does not strive for virtue and is therefore not honourable. On the other hand, someone with *vergüenza*, or shame, is full of honour because he or she is virtuous: "como vergonzoso el que de cualquiera cosa que a su parecer no haya hecho con la decencia debida se pone colorado y le llamamos *vergonzoso*, indicio de virtud y modestia [the shameful one is he who owing to something he feels that he has not done with the decency required becomes red in the face; we call him shameful, which indicates virtue and modesty]" (Covarrubias 960). Rosaura, in calling herself *atrevida*, fits this definition of someone with little shame and no morals. She must behave this way in order to please the men around her, and this will lead only to her detriment, since in the end, she must obey her council's demands in order to keep her lands. Her single status, along with the adoption of male qualities mentioned above, is ultimately unacceptable and can only be dispelled by her having a partner. Arcenio, another member of the committee of ministers, even blames Rosaura for causing the mutiny by not having yet married.[8]

Marriage is the only way for Rosaura to keep her territories, her social privileges, her leadership, and, in the end, to remain an honourable woman. Gabriela Carrión discusses this theme in a different context with a different Rosaura, the main character in Calderon's *La vida es sueño*: "Like many heroines before and after her, Rosaura seeks marriage as a means of legitimizing her place in society" (xi–xii). Caro, in her work, instead focuses on the men, who use marriage to legitimize their empress' place as their ruler, rather than on the woman seeking this institution herself. They threaten her with a division of lands and with bodily harm. They also declare that she is being unjust by not marrying. Emilio, one of her councilmen, declares:

Cásate pues, que no es justo,
que dejes pasar la aurora
de tu edad tierna, aguardando
a que de tu sol se ponga.
Esta es inviolable ley.   (Caro 84)

Get married; since it is not fair that you allow the dawning of your young age to pass, waiting out that brightness from the sun. This is an inviolable law.

These men, swayed by their emotions, advocate social injustice: "it [emotion] begins when an outcome or event does not conform to one's expectations or goals" (Cropanzano 64). For the men, Rosaura refusing to take advantage of her youthful beauty goes against their expectations. Russell Cropanzano goes further to say that emotion is deeply tied to social justice: "To decide that an injustice has occurred, one must adduce additional evidence, such as the violation of a moral standard" (64). A moral standard can be tied to a moral or "self-conscious" emotion, which includes shame, guilt, embarrassment, and pride.[9] Rosaura's refusal to marry and to follow society's law goes against her sense of shame because she is not following the rules of an honourable woman of her time. Therefore, in violating this moral standard, the men around Rosaura feel that there has been a miscarriage of justice. They can now use the expectations of shame in Golden Age society to force Rosaura to right this wrong and restore social justice to the kingdom.

The men's mutiny causes Rosaura to become extremely angry and impatient with the shameless actions of her people: "¡Hay tan grande atrevimiento! [There is such great audacity!]" (Caro 95), yet she has no choice but to obey. Her subjects demand that she marry quickly, and thus "[s]he becomes the objectified courtly *dama*, gazed upon by the entire court and scrutinized as to her physical attractiveness from the male perspective ... Even royal office does not change the cultural demands upon woman for containment in the institution of marriage" (Soufas, *Dramas of Distinction* 47). Rosaura's identity as a woman and the conditions expected of her sex take precedence over her status as a ruler. Left with no other options, she recruits the help of Aldora, her cousin, who is also a necromancer. The two women decide that Rosaura will have a year to marry a suitable man and if she does not, the council will then decide the fate of the land.

The council approves this agreement, even after Rosaura declares that her future husband will aid in her demise. Years earlier, her father had consulted the stars and learned that any husband for his daughter will only trick her and cause harm to both her kingdom and herself. In other words, the husband's actions would cause the downfall of the woman and lead to an unjust ending for the protagonist, both for her personally and for the good of the society as a whole. Lola Luna also declares that a negative aspect to Rosaura's marriage would signify her disempowerment and political and social disorder.[10] Emilio states,

> Yo te aconsejo, yo justo:
> tú, Emperatriz, mira ahora
> si te importa el libre estado
> o si el casarte te importa.   (Caro 85)

I will give you advice, I, who am just: you, Empress, decide now, if what's important to you is free choice or marriage.

Here, Emilio, as the voice of justice, asks Rosaura to sacrifice her own happiness for the social good. He is implicitly asking her to think about her vassals rather than herself. He uses guilt as a means to achieve his ultimate goal. As Bernard Williams shows in his book *Shame and Necessity*, guilt and shame are two very different things. He expounds on the differences between these two emotions in ancient Greek culture, yet these distinctions are present in Spain as well. Shame is more narcissistic than guilt in that the viewer's gaze will draw the subject's attention to himself or herself (22). Shame involves a personal shortcoming, some unhappiness within oneself. Guilt on the other hand, draws attention to the victim and turns its focus to those whom were wronged. What can arouse a feeling of guilt is "an act or omission of a sort that typically elicits from other people anger, resentment, or indignation" (89). Emilio, again, feels that the empire is being wronged by Rosaura's refusal to marry, and therefore wants her to draw her attention to the victim (the state). The men around Rosaura are also angry and resentful, and they hope, ultimately, that these emotions will cause guilt in the empress.

Ana Caro justifies Rosaura's single status by essentially saying that any husband she chooses would be to her detriment, yet the playwright must ultimately submit to societal norms and provide her character with a husband. The path that Rosaura takes to secure this husband, though, is very different from that of the traditional female character who is pursued by a male suitor and must passively accept his advances. Rosaura cannot have free choice in deciding not to marry; yet she has the ability to choose her own mate among those who are eligible. Rosaura speaks with her cousin Aldora:

Quisiera yo, prima mía,
ver y conocer primero
estos caballeros que mis vasallos me han propuesto,
y si de alguno me agrada
el arte, presencia e ingenio,
saberle la condición,
y verle el alma hacia dentro ...   (Caro 91)

I would like, Cousin, to see and know these men that my vassals have chosen for me first, and if any of them please me with their art, presence, and wit, to know their conditions, and see their internal souls ...

The empress does not simply want to marry in order to keep her honourable status, but rather needs to be assured that her husband will be worthy of her kingdom. Rosaura, at this point, chooses reason, a quality traditionally attributed to men, over emotion.[11]

This ability to rationalize her decisions diminishes throughout the play. She becomes afraid that she will not find a suitable husband after her cousin Aldora tells her that she cannot truly see into men's hearts. The solution for Aldora is to use her magic to gaze upon the men while they are in their palaces. Rosaura's curiosity takes over and she becomes anxious to observe her suitors: "sabes que las mujeres / pecamos en el extremo / de curiosas [you know that us women sin to the extreme because we are curious]" (Caro 93). Here, Caro seems to be strengthening the traditional views of women with regard to sin and guilt, that is, that they are more prone to sin because they are more emotional and thus cannot resist temptation. These views go back to the story of Adam and Eve: Eve could not resist temptation and ate from the Tree of Knowledge of Good and Evil, bringing sin and chaos into the world. The Spanish Inquisition during the sixteenth and seventeenth centuries forced many women thought to be heretics or *conversos* to confess their sins, thereby demonstrating guilt. Confessors' manuals were were in wide circulation, representing a new focus on the confession of sin after the reforms of the Council of Trent (1545–63). During the Reformation there was a shift in emphasis "away from the field of objective social relations and into a field of interiorized discipline for the individual" (Bossy 21). French historian Jean Delumeau highlights this shift in his book, *Sin and Fear*:

> the more zealous men of the church and the ones most concerned to Christianize the masses undertook an intensive program of orienting people's minds toward guilt. They did so by relentlessly emphasizing the different categories of offenses, as well as the ontological seriousness of sin. (198)[12]

This guilt forced worshippers to contemplate their sins and suffer internal shame and embarrassment for their actions. Ana Caro reflects upon these well-established ideas, prevalent during her time, and places the guilt with the woman. In doing this, though, the playwright is also emphasizing a reversal of gender roles because the woman is looking upon the men instead of the other way around.[13]

The above quote also shows that women are unable to contain their emotions; in this case the empress is unable to control her curiosity. This also seems to strengthen traditional arguments found in the texts of Juan Luis Vives and Fray Luis de León, for example, yet again Rosaura uses her emotions to gaze upon the men, rather than the other way around. Juan Luis Vives and Fray Luis de León discuss women's emotions and how they must be controlled in order to avoid shameful situations. Juan Luis Vives, a Renaissance scholar and humanist, published *De institutione feminae Christianae* (The Education of a Christian Woman) in 1524. This text, written to advise the Christian woman on proper behaviour, declares that all vice is shameful and places great emphasis on the importance of feminine chastity for the avoidance of sin:

> the unchaste woman is a sea and storehouse of all evils. The inseparable companions of chastity are a sense of propriety and modest behavior. Chastity (*pudicitia*) seems to be derived from shame (*pudor*), so that one who has no sense of shame cannot be chaste. Chastity is a kind of veil placed over our face, for when nature and reason covered the corrupt body and the sinful flesh because of the shame caused by the first sin but left the face open and free of the coverings that we wear, they did not deny its cloak, namely, shame. (Vives 116)

A woman has a sense of shame so that she does not submit to temptation or emotion and forfeit her chastity. According to Vives, chastity, together with shame, acts as a veil. The humanist's emphasis is on the emotion's visual aspects: a female's virtues and vices are written on her face. The author goes on to say: "The lord curses an unchaste woman, saying, 'Your brow has become that of a prostitute, you have lost all shame'" (Vives 117).

Fray Luis de León, an Augustinian friar, also discusses a woman's uncontrollable emotions and their relationship to shame. He published *La perfecta casada* (The Perfect Wife) in 1583 as an instruction manual for newly married women. In it he asserts that wives must follow certain rules within a marriage, the most important of which are to remain chaste and to serve their husbands. Being "honesta," or chaste, is what makes a woman a human being, because without this quality, she "no es ya mujer, sino alevosa ramera y vilísimo cieno, y basura la más hedionda de todas y la más despreciada [is no longer a woman, but rather an arrogant prostitute and is like vile mud and dirt the most foul-smelling of all and the most hated]" (90). In order for a woman to remain chaste she must feel a sense of shame, which will keep her from doing something dishonourable. This shame, also combined with guilt, is imposed by society as a means of bodily control. Georgina Dopico Black, in her reading of *La perfecta casada*, sees the text itself as a body that is guilty of the same faults it attributes to the imperfect wife: one outcome of this paradox is the untenable position it accords the historical woman who must live by the manual's strictures. Within a social and textual economy that clearly privileges the notion of proper place, she is relegated to a place that is always necessarily improper (56). The woman, therefore, must behave properly yet, even in doing so, her society will never truly see her as perfect. Ana Caro uses these traditional models, but does so to show that the woman, at least temporarily, is in control. Rosaura cannot tame her curiosity, yet she is able to determine, based on only a glance, which male suitor is best. Since shame involves a personal shortcoming or some unhappiness within oneself, the experience of shame can be connected with sight and with the idea of others "seeing" your personal flaws (Williams 89). Rosaura can, therefore, see each man's imperfections and can impose shame upon him by criticizing those weaknesses. Rosaura, then, plays the role of a man who can judge the opposite sex but not be judged in return. This quality, as found in a woman, will lead to her downfall.

Rosaura observes and judges the images of four princes presented to her magically by Aldora. Of all of the suitors, Aldora declares that the prince of France, Partinuplés, is the most desirable because he is noble, modest, and courageous. Rosaura agrees, but is mainly interested because he is engaged to her cousin, Lisbella, and is therefore unavailable. Partinuplés and Lisbella exhibit, respectively, the qualities of a gentleman and honourable woman with strong senses of shame and honour, and Rosaura represents the exact opposite. She is shameless, perhaps because her position as ruler has forced her to adopt the male role of authority. Owing to this, she exhibits the qualities of a man in a position of power who has no regard for the rules of courtship. She decides to pursue the French prince and remains determined to marry him: "Yo lo difícil intento, / lo fácil es para todos [I will try that which is difficult, that which is easy is for everyone else]" (Caro 97). Rosaura, since she is forced to marry, desires the best man available even if he is not easy to win and if her actions go against societal norms. The expectations of the men around her have caused her to become shameless and to disregard common courtesy. As Julio Caro Baroja explains in his definitions of shame and shamelessness, someone who is without shame has a general lack of respect for laws and institutions. He first defines the term *vergüenza*, or shame, by looking at its Latin root, *verecundia*, which "shows itself not only as chastity and modesty, as the blush which lewd speech brings to the face, but also as respect for parents and elders, which prevents one from doing certain things in their presence, and as humility, reserve and respect for the laws and their representatives" (87). *Inverecundia*, on the other hand, is immodesty in sexual matters and disdain of laws and institutions. In Spanish, this attitude can be expressed with the term *sinvergüenza*, or a shameless one. Caro Baroja also expounds on the various uses of the Spanish word for shame, with one example being the expression *darle vergüenza* (to put to shame) or literally "to give someone shame." Rosaura, by disregarding the social norms of her time whereby she would not be allowed to pursue an engaged man, is acting as a *sinvergüenza*. Her status as a shameless woman increases throughout the play as she thinks of nothing else but pursuing Partinuplés until the end. If her council had not forced her to marry, Rosaura would have never attained this dishonourable status.

In order to make Rosaura known to the prince in the first place, Aldora places an alluring painting of the empress in Partinuplés' view. Partinuplés is instantly captivated by the woman in the painting and soon deserts his fiancée for her. The prince has now dishonoured an honourable woman and his only motive is to find the woman in the painting. Aldora conjures a beast for Partinuplés to follow into the forest. He is then faced with the spirit of the same woman in the picture. The spirit tells the prince to search for her, which he then does, in the company of his servant, Gaulín. Rosaura approaches Partinuplés in the dark once the men arrive at her castle and tells him that he is forbidden to see her. The prince is filled with curiosity and sadness:

> Pues, ¿por qué,
> cuando me tenéis rendido
> en vuestro poder y estáis
> satisfecha de lo dicho,
> me negáis vuestra hermosura?   (Caro 127)

> Why, when you have me submissive to your power and are satisfied with what I say, do you deny me your beauty?

At this point, it is Partinuplés who is curious and cannot control his emotions. The woman has complete control and the man is irrational, and here Caro reverses traditional gender roles. Rosaura's response to Partinuplés' plea is that she expects him to obey her. Here Rosaura is daring and is exhibiting traditional male qualities: two aspects that continue her status as a shameless woman.

In denying Partinuplés, a man, to gaze upon her and forcing him to do as she pleases, Rosaura is also imposing shame upon him. Pitt-Rivers shows that the term *avergonzado* (shamed) is negative in meaning because one is forced to recognize that one has accepted humiliation (43). Shame becomes equivalent to dishonour because it is imposed from the outside. When shame and dishonour are equated in the term "shamed," the result is a decline in the aspiration to status (honour) as well as a recognition of loss of position (Pitt-Rivers 43). The count must accept the humiliation of not fulfilling his desires and not being allowed to court his lady in the traditional manner as an honourable gentleman. Now, as a shamed and dishonoured man, he must actively seek to regain his honour by marrying the source of his dishonour. Caro also changes the traditional discourse here by placing a man in this role instead of the traditional scorned woman who does likewise. Both Partinuplés and Rosaura have become shameless through their actions and must be restored to honourable status. Rosaura's request to remain unseen is a test to establish whether or not the prince is worthy of her. His success or failure will determine if he is able to regain his honour. Partinuplés suppresses his curiosity and even declares that an imagined beauty is enough for him. Gaulín cannot accept this and fears that there is something wrong with the woman since she does not want to reveal herself: "siempre la discreta es fea / y siempre es necia la hermosa [the discrete woman is always ugly and the foolish woman is always beautiful]" (Caro 141). Caro, through the voice of the servant, criticizes the institution of shame, in the form of discretion, in her society. A woman is expected to be discreet, exhibit restraint, and be out of public view, but even if she fulfils these expectations she is still judged harshly. In Caro's society it is impossible for a woman to achieve true justice and equality, even one with as much power as Rosaura. Women cannot succeed while these ideas persist.

This situation is exacerbated when Partinuplés, weary from waiting for Rosaura's permission, gazes upon her while she sleeps. He has now dishonoured her by visiting her privately when they are not married and by not following her orders. Partinuplés wants to approach her and Gaulín again shows his disregard for a woman's honour: "Acaba ya; / ¿no es mujer y tú eres hombre? [Stop already; isn't she a woman and you a man?]" (Caro 155). Gaulín does not worry about Rosaura's request, nor is he afraid of a woman's revenge. He believes that the woman has no power precisely because she is a woman. Also, Partinuplés has decided at this point to forfeit any honour he may still have. He is aware of his sin: "¡Gran yerro intento, pasiones! ... ¿es posible que yo ... / falte a mis obligaciones / por lisonjear mi gusto? [I am making a great mistake, my passions! ... is it possible that I go against my obligations in order to give in to my pleasure?]" (155–6). Partinuplés, again, becomes irrational and battles with his obligation as a man to preserve a woman's honour. By not respecting Rosaura's request and succumbing to lust and pleasure, Partinuplés willingly sins and gazes upon her. Rosaura awakens extremely angry: "¿qué atrevimiento?

[What audacity?]" (157) and immediately sentences him to imprisonment and death. Rosaura now shames the prince by calling his actions an "atrevimiento" because his gaze has resulted in her dishonour. Her honour is her life, and therefore, as Frederick A. De Armas declares, "for a moment, Rosaura did lose her life metaphorically" (185). Partinuplés' sin causes the social downfall of the woman.

Rosaura's dishonour causes her to react emotionally and lose any sense of judgment she may still possess. She rushes to punish Partinuplés, and here "Caro dramatizes the ideological threat that being seen poses to a woman but insists ... on punishing the male observer rather than the observed woman" (Soufas, *Dramas of Distinction* 55). Partinuplés' imprisonment, while making him fear for his own life, does not cause him to apologize for his actions. He instead blames Gaulín for his downfall and calls him *atrevido*, never accepting his own guilt. Aldora arrives to free the men and the count asks about Rosaura: "¿Ella está ya arrepentida? [Is she now /remorseful?]" (Caro 165). As mentioned previously, a term for guilt in the modern sense, or the term *culpabilidad*, is not found (to my knowledge) in any Spanish dictionary in the Golden Age. Guilt at the time was defined in the *Tesoro Lexicográfico*, which mentions Covarrubias' definition: "a la culpa responde la pena [to guilt corresponds punishment]" (Gaya 687)[14] and extends its entries to include "culpable [blame-worthy, guilty, culpable]" and "culpar [to blame]." In order to show that this feeling of guilt did in fact exist in Caro's text, I turn instead to terms such as *arrepentimiento*,[15] or remorse. Covarrubias' definition of *arrepentida* is: "la mujer perdida que, conociendo su yerro, se arrepiente y se vuelve a Dios [the lost woman who, recognizing her mistake, regrets it and returns to God]" (122). In the previous quote, therefore, Partinuplés believes that the woman has wronged him because she has in some way lost her way to God. He expects Rosaura to feel guilty even though he is the one who has dishonoured her. The man's shamelessness, expressed previously by Rosaura when she identifies his actions as an "atrevimiento" after he gazes upon her, leads to feelings of guilt in the woman, emotions expected of her.

Partinuplés' actions have now dishonoured the woman and the only solution is for her to marry him. The play ends with their wedding and with Partinuplés' kingdom in France being given to Lisbella in restitution for her unhappiness. The prince, therefore, enters the marriage without anything to offer his bride. Lisbella, on the other hand, inherits her own kingdom, yet, like Rosaura, she cannot rule as an unmarried woman. Lisbella is considered to be dishonoured because of both her single status and her rejection by Partinuplés. Lisbella has also become a warrior woman in her quest to reclaim Partinuplés. She enters Rosaura's kingdom dressed with a sword and helmet, and states:

> ... verá ... Rosaura
> como, valerosa aspiro
> a destruir sus Imperios,
> si no me entrega a mi primo. (Caro 161)

> Rosaura will see how valiantly I aspire to destroy her empire if she does not give me my cousin.

She is thus considered to be a shameless woman as well. Lisbella cannot rule and bring true social justice to her people unless she marries, and therefore a wedding is arranged between her and Roberto of Transylvania, one of Rosaura's previous suitors. Lisbella cannot argue against the decision and, therefore, when asked what her answer is, she simply states: "Que obedezco [That I obey]" (172). The woman must follow the rules of her society and ultimately submit to the demands of the majority. Even the necromancer is married off, showing that

> Neither magic nor the realm of the fantastic has been portrayed as adequate to overcome the prohibitions to female social autonomy or freedom from male-identified status within the dramatic conventions accessible to Caro. Empresses, queens, and enchantresses must all marry. (Soufas, *Repetitive Patterns* 102)

Caro ends her play with a re-establishment of every character's honourable status, thereby eliminating guilt.

Although marriage is a traditional conclusion in many Golden Age *comedias*, the final marriages in Caro's text seem unsatisfactory and to represent a form of social injustice. There is no indication that Rosaura is a poor leader on her own or that she is not mindful of the greater good, yet male-dominated society forces her to marry a man who could potentially cause the downfall of her kingdom. Her father's prognostication that her future husband will commit acts against her is of no importance to her council, a group of men whose primary concern is the control of a powerful single woman. The text does not describe whether or not Partinuplés will eventually dishonour his future wife, yet his previous dismissal and shaming of Lisbella show that he can readily flaut social rules. His ability to cast shame upon women in the past suggests a bleak future for the empress. In the end, Rosaura's marriage seems to be a punishment for guilt. Her guilt, from the viewpoint of her vassals and the men around her, stems from her desire to remain single. She is also guilty of adopting the male role of power, therefore forfeiting her shame. Her assuming power is unacceptable because she is a woman, and the men around her punish her based solely on her gender. They resort to forms of social injustice and promote inequality to achieve what they believe to be just for their society. Rosaura's ultimate penance is to marry. Her single status is equal to being shameless and dishonourable, and is therefore unacceptable. Caro criticizes this idea, not through a radical twist in the plot at the end, but instead by emphasizing Rosaura's marriage to a man who is dismissive and unrepentant of his previous actions. He instead emphasizes the need for her to feel guilt and to repent for her unfair treatment towards him. Caro uses the traditional concepts of shame and guilt, or remorse, to show that women cannot succeed in this environment. Rosaura's marriage to Partinuplés, along with the behaviour of the other men around her, is responsible for her downfall.

Rosaura, a strong, independent woman who in the end must submit to patriarchal society, resembles a *desvergüenza* because she does not conform to traditional expectations of marriage and children. On many occasions she also adopts male qualities, which causes her to forfeit her shame. We also see these qualities in Lisbella, another female character that Caro uses to emphasize that the institution of shame hurts all women. In addition, Rosaura's husband expects her to feel guilt, and her marriage is a punishment for refusal to conform to societal standards. Caro provides an impossible future for her female characters. Women must be discreet and have a strong sense of shame and restraint, yet even Rosaura, an honourable ruler committed to social justice and service to her people, cannot thrive in a male-dominated society. Until men achieve a sense of social equality with regard to gender and exhibit the same level of self-control that is expected of women, women will suffer. Rosaura's guilt, along with her shameless status in being a single woman, is absolved through marriage, yet her penance will continue for the rest of her life.

NOTES

1 For more information on this topic see Valerie Hegstrom, "Women and the Secular Theater," in *Engendering the Early Modern Stage: Women Playwrights in the Spanish Empire*, ed. Valerie Hegstrom and Amy R. Williamsen (New Orleans: UP of the South, 1999).
2 For details on Ana Caro's life, see Lola Luna's introduction in her edition of *Valor, agravio y mujer*.

3   Teresa Scott Soufas also mentions in her introduction that both of these secular plays exist in seventeenth- and eighteenth-century manuscript form as well as in printed editions. *El Conde Partinuplés* was printed in a collection entitled *Laurel de comedias*, which also contained plays by Pedro Calderón de la Barca. The only seventeenth-century form of *Valor, agravio y mujer* exists as a handwritten manuscript and is housed in the *Biblioteca Nacional* in Madrid.
4   All of the English translations in this chapter are mine unless otherwise specified.
5   For modern definitions of guilt, I refer those of twentieth-century thinkers such as Sigmund Freud, Friedrich Nietzsche, and Karl Jaspers. For a general overview of their theories see Herbert Morris' *Guilt and Shame* (1971).
6   In the original tale, the young heiress, Melior, chooses Partonopeus as her suitor and forbids him to look upon her. When he does not obey, he is banished and proceeds to undergo a period of trial and repentance. He becomes a "mature knight, worthy of Melior and of the throne," according to Judith A. Whitenack, "Ana Caro's *Partinuplés* and the Chivalric Tradition," in *Engendering the Early Modern Stage* (61). Caro's version differs greatly, mainly in the fact that Partinuplés never shows true repentance, but instead expects the woman to feel guilt for his sins. Caro also provides three rival suitors for Rosaura and omits the large battle scenes found in the original romance. For more information on these distinctions, see María José Delgado's doctoral thesis: "*Valor, agravio y mujer* y *El conde Partinuplés*: Una edición crítica," University of Arizona, 1993, and Judith A. Whitenack's article mentioned above.
7   For an extensive study about the *mujer varonil* see Melveena McKendrick's *Women and Society in the Spanish Drama of the Golden Age: A Study of the Mujer varonil*, Cambridge UP, 1974.
8   Arcenio is apologizing to Rosaura for his sin of participating in the mutiny, yet he blames her in the same sentence. He states, "Gran Señora, / bellísima Emperatriz, / nuestro delito perdona, / que tú sola eres la causa [Great Lady, beautiful Empress, please excuse our crime, you solely are the cause]" (Caro 83).
9   For recent research on the moral emotions see the article entitled *The Four Moral Emotions*, by Ilana Simons, in *Psychology Today Online* (https://www.psychologytoday.com/ca/blog/the-literary-mind/200911/the-four-moral-emotions).
10 Luna discusses the negative aspects of Rosaura's marriage in a footnote to line 90 of the text (Caro 85n).
11 The theory of the humours, popular during the Golden Age, asserted that women were cold and moist, and therefore more emotional.

12 Guilt was focused on the rejection of the flesh spanning from an immodest kiss all the way to incest, sodomy, and bestiality.
13 Soufas, in *Dramas of Distinction*, declares that Aldora is able to "reverse the pattern of the male gaze and its female object" when she provides the images of the suitors (51).
14 Each dictionary entry is a compilation of definitions from different dictionaries of the time. Covarrubias' text was the most utilized in Spain. The *Tesoro lexicográfico* was completed only up through the letter E.
15 Covarrubias' definition of *arrepentirse* is as follows: "Pesarle a uno de lo que ha dicho o hecho [Weigh down on someone something he/she has said or done]."

PART TWO

Adaptations

7 A Social Justice Framing of the *Comedia*: EFE TRES Teatro's *El príncipe ynocente* Adaptation

ERIN ALICE COWLING

Lope de Vega is perhaps the best known and most prolific author of Spanish Golden Age *comedias*. His 1609 treatise *Arte nuevo de hacer comedias* solidified his place as the father of the early modern theatre, and many of his plays, particularly those written afterwards, have earned canonical status, being performed and taught throughout the almost five centuries since his death. Plays like *Fuenteovejuna* (1612–14), *La dama boba* (1613), and *El castigo sin venganza* (1631) show up most frequently on syllabi and marquees alike, lauded for their timeless themes that allow modern audiences and readers to continue to identify with the material and characters. *Fuenteovejuna*, for example, portrays a town's revolt against a despotic leader, a theme that can be transposed to just about any setting – as Repertorio Español attempted to do in their 2013 production set in a modern office, with an overbearing boss taking the place of the cruel *comendador*. Lope's other plays, especially those that are pre-*Arte nuevo* and considered "early Lope," are often cast aside, particularly when they lack a clear connection to the modern world. That is not to say that these plays are without merit, and in the right hands can be brought back to life in a way that allows for theatrical identification with a modern public, but it takes a formidable effort to do so. This chapter will discuss one such "early" Lope play, *El príncipe ynocente*[1] and the efforts of the Mexican acting troupe EFE TRES Teatro (henceforth ETT) to connect a noble love triangle to the injustices of the modern world.

El príncipe inocente (1590) was relegated to obscurity for over four hundred years; it was considered lost until the first half of the twentieth century, and was virtually unknown until the acting troupe ETT from Mexico City brought it back to the stage – or quite possibly staged it for the first time[2] – in 2014. The play does not appear to lend itself to any modern retelling, although it does contain elements that are repeated throughout the history of literature, from the Bible to fairytales: a long-lost prince, raised by peasants, comes into his inheritance through a series of mishaps and petty crimes. However, by placing the story into their own invented, modernized frame, ETT is able to turn a relatively benign *comedia de capa y espada* into a social commentary on the gap between rich and poor, a disparity that still exists today.[3]

ETT's performance goes beyond a simple staging of the original text. With their addition of the frame story, with its own characters and internal world, it must be considered a modernized rewrite of Lope de Vega's *El príncipe inocente*. The frame story not only begins and ends the play but interweaves itself seamlessly into the original. Adaptations, much like translations, are tied uniquely to the time and space in which they are created from the original text, which is itself tied to its own "chronotope" or time-space. Mikhail Bakhtin borrows the word "chronotope" from Einstein's theory of relativity as a metaphor for the "inseparability of space and time" in literature (84) and, as such, literary works, whatever the genre, are tied to the time and space in which they are created. Adaptation, however, gives us a new creation, one that is repetitive, but not necessarily directly replicative (Hutcheon 7). Repetition allows us to maintain contact and familiarity with the original, and yet even a repetition never directly replicates the original, and thus the adaptation becomes a new creation in a new chronotope. Adaptations are often more fleeting than originals, and yet open up a space in which a text that might seem out of reach for the audience is made new and relevant, albeit such relevance is tied to a very limited moment. Paradoxically the originals survive, waiting for new audiences to discover them. Lope de Vega's vast oeuvre contains a number of *comedias* that survive and thrive on today's stage, while others have been relegated to a secondary or even tertiary status, remaining unpublished, under-read, and/or rarely performed. The chosen few tend to be performed over and over, often in traditional dress and setting, thus avoiding what Linda Hutcheon calls the "predictable lamentations from the ... fans" (42) which arise when the audience has expectations, based on previous experience, of how these famous works should be adapted, and thus force directors to make a difficult choice between (financial) success and artistic expression. When directors push too far, particularly with a popular source text, they risk losing the audience. For example, Repertorio Español's 2013 adaptation of *Fuente Ovejuna* was panned in a *New York Times* theatre review. Although *Fuente Ovejuna*'s plot can be boiled down, in the most general terms, as that of underdogs finally taking revenge upon their oppressor, the specifics of the play – a wedding, rape by the *comendador*/boss character, and his eventual death – are unfit for the office setting: "Presumably this [the setting] is intended to make the story more relatable, but it usually just leads to incoherence: there are bad bosses, and then there are bosses who invoke droit du seigneur" (Rampell C3). In spite of the potential problems that can arise within modern adaptations, strict fidelity to the original chronotope can also create audience detachment; the societal touchstones of early modern theatre can often clash with modern expectations of social norms. Skilful adaptations of both well-known and more obscure works can induce theatrical identification of modern audience members, allowing them to see themselves and the issues pertinent to them in an accessible and intriguing manner, but they have to be done with purpose and coherence.

Choosing a play that is lesser-known does take some of the pressure off the adapter to fulfil audience expectations and opens up a wider range of creative possibilities. ETT's choice of a long-ignored Lope play, rather than one of the canonical pieces, gives them the opportunity to "romper con todas las reglas ortodoxas definidas tácitamente y montar a Lope de Vega de la manera más teatral posible partiendo del juego de niños: transitando, ambos actores, por todos los personajes planteados, sin reverencia, sin sobriedad, lúdico ... que no se vea aburrido ([break with all the tacitly defined, orthodox rules and produce Lope de Vega in the most theatrical way possible, drawing from children's games: both actors playing all of the proposed characters, without any reverence or sobriety, playfully ... so that it is never boring]"[4] (Flores, Memije, and Villa). They are able to accomplish this by the addition of a frame story, in which the two actors, dressed in stereotypically striped prison garb, decide to tell each other a story to pass the time. Often plays that are transposed onto a different time and place can leave the audience feeling disjointed. ETT's adaptation, *El príncipe ynocente*, is mediated through a framework created by the trio that shows two prisoners who act out the story in order to pass the time, using only their imagination and a few items one might find in a jail cell as props. Although the frame story's time period is left ambiguous, the diction, actions, and materials used by the prisoner-actors give the feel of a more modern age. The frame creates a transtemporality in which the actors and audience are able to connect a sixteenth-century courtly play to a twenty-first-century prison, made all the more convincing by the prisoners' breaks in the action to discuss motivation and technique as they try to perfect the performance. This approach allows for ETT to implement their theatrical philosophy, as outlined in Villa Proal's prologue to this volume, which allows the audience more freedom to relate to and interpret the performance. Likewise, ETT's reliance on early modern approaches to the stage – such as the *ñaque* style and *desengaño* theory, both of which will be discussed in detail later on – create a bridge between the two epochs and link the prisoner's story to that of the source text. It becomes clear in the asides and breaks from the original text that the prisoners are rehearsing and repeating something that they have done before, and will do again, even if their only audience member will ever be the lone guard to their cell. The use of the prisoner characters in the frame story opens up possibilities of audience connection, while giving a purpose to a story that otherwise would seem incongruous with the intentions of ETT to bring classical theatre to modern audiences. In an interview panel at the 2017 Association for Hispanic Classical Theater conference, Fernando Villa Proal, one of the co-founders of ETT, explained the justification of this imposed framestory:

> Hacer la puesta en escena con solamente dos personas era una de las premisas que planteamos para la escenificación, sin importar el resultado, esa tendría que ser una condición inamovible. El ñaque estaba dado por sentado. La historia de los presos la encontramos al necesitar un marco que encuadrase la puesta en escena. Todo sucedió cuando un vestuarista nos cuestionó sobre nuestro "marco estético." No tuvimos una respuesta. Así que tras mucho diálogo y lluvia de ideas sobre cómo enmarcar nuestra propuesta llegamos a la conclusión de que la temporalidad sería importante ... y el universo que una prisión nos brinda resultaba un terreno donde cimentar con toda lógica la historia de un pícaro y burlador que resulta exonerado por ser príncipe. (Villa Proal)

> Creating a performance with only two people was one of the premises we had imposed for the staging; whatever the results, that was an immovable condition. *Ñaque* was a given. We figured out the prisoner story when we realized that we needed a structure in which to frame the staging. It all came together when a costumer asked us what our "esthetic style" was. We had no response. Thus, after a lot of dialogue and brain-storming about how to frame our proposal, we came to the conclusion that the time period was less important, and the universe that a prison would provide, would result in a field on which we could base the story of a scoundrel and a trickster who could be exonerated simply for being a prince.

The ETT rewrite begins, and ends, with two prisoners, sitting in cramped cages. They sing a song lamenting the downfall of the justice system and their lack of voice, given their status as poor labourers and petty thieves. To pass the time, they tell each other the story of *El príncipe ynocente*. Like any theatrical production, the original text is truncated and adapted to fit their needs. ETT's production, unlike most theatrical productions, allows the frame story they've created to bleed over into the original text, with the prisoners stopping to consult on how to fix a scene that isn't working, or to complain about each other's idiosyncrasies, as Villa Proal attests: "plantea una posibilidad metateatral para jugar y para poder aclarar cosas que por el lenguaje y el contexto del texto teatral pudieran resultar ajenas al público [it lays out a metatheatrical possibility to play with and be able to clarify things that, because of the language and theatrical context, could seem foreign to the audience)." These insertions of the prisoner-characters into the original text are what allows for the audience's theatrical identification and twists an otherwise banal love story into a comment on modern social ills.[5]

At first glance it seems unsurprising that the original play had sat on the shelf for so long. With too many characters and a rather banal and overdone storyline of a lost prince who only realizes who he is when he is thrust back into the world of courtly intrigue, the play is overly complex and difficult to follow. Centred around the two daughters of the Duke of Cleves, both of whom fall in love with the same prince, Alejandro, while one is also courted – unbeknownst to her – by two other men. Alejandro is an exiled prince who finds himself at the mercy of the Duke, who in turn offers to help him regain his throne, and all in the midst of a love triangle between the Duke's two daughters. When Rosimunda, the first daughter, rejects the prince so that he will favour her younger sister, Hipolita, he resigns himself to the less interesting sister and scorns the first. Finding herself scorned, Rosimunda immediately falls in love with him. In a twist on the usual love triangle, Lope adds another two suitors for the daughters: the Duke's secretary, an awkward man who knows his status will never bring him up to the standards of Rosimunda and yet cannot help but love her, and Torcato, a mute peasant who miraculously finds his voice – and the true nature of his birth – when confronted with the nobility of Rosimunda and Hipolita. With Alejandro focusing his attention on Hipolita, Rosimunda's affections are then vied for by her father's secretary and Torcato. Torcato turns out to be far more cunning than his simple upbringing would suggest, and is able to manipulate both the secretary and Rosimunda into believing he is working on behalf of Alejandro, and that Alejandro will give Rosimunda his hand in marriage, in exchange for one night's bliss. She consents, and under the cover of darkness Torcato steals into her room. As the play unfolds, all of the characters – including Rosimunda – learn the truth of her dishonour, and, eventually, Torcato's status as a lost – "innocent" – prince.[6] The two pairs – Alejandro and Hipolita, and Rosimunda and Torcato – are married, with the blessing of the Duke and the King of Sweden.

The plot is further convoluted by the breaking of Lope's own rules on the unity of time and action (*Arte nuevo* 181–7). The play's main action takes place in the palace of the Duke, but there are also scenes in the forest, in which Torcato is introduced during a hunting expedition that the Duke and his daughters undertake as they await the much-anticipated arrival of Alejandro. During this sojourn into the countryside, Torcato and his rustic counterparts are shown playing crude word games, and the Duke and his daughters are implausibly forced to spend the night in their home. Showing his first signs of hidden nobility, Torcato is suddenly able to speak in aristocratic tones, and saves the sisters from the attack of a lion. Charmed by his simple but noble nature, he is invited back to the Duke's palace. There are also scenes that take place outside the Duke's palace, in the garden, and on the battlefield, creating a complex and difficult set.

Adding to the complexity are at least nineteen characters,[7] two love triangles, and four rulers vying for power. ETT, however, does not seem to struggle with these issues at all. In fact, they choose techniques that help minimize the complexity, such as using the *ñaque* style of baroque theatre, in which only two actors are on stage, playing all of the different parts. In order to explain this stylistic choice, however, ETT adds a metatheatrical, transtemporal framework and two additional characters. The use of *ñaque* allows them to successfully follow through on almost all of their pre-production objectives:

> Explorar las posibilidades de comunicación con el público y experimentar con la teatralidad de las convenciones ... Concretar en una [sic] resultado artístico el proceso creativo que va de la dirección a la ejecución ... Romper el prejuicio del público en general con el teatro del siglo de oro: es aburrido, no se entiende, no es vigente, es tedioso, lento ... Que la gente se divierta y la pase bien más allá de generar una reflexión profunda. (Flores, Memije, and Villa)

> To explore the possibilities of communication with the audience and experiment with the theatricality of conventions ... To create an artistic result that incorporates the creative process from direction to performance. To break preconceived notions of the theatre of the Golden Age: that it's boring, not understandable, that it isn't relevant, it's tedious, slow ... For the audience to have fun and enjoy themselves, more than generating profound reflection.

I say almost all of their objectives because I disagree with their final statement. Although it is undeniable that they provide an entertaining

A Social Justice Framing of the *Comedia* 125

Photo 7.1: Fernando Villa Proal and Fernando Memije play Rosimunda (with cards) and Torcato (with scarf) respectively. The cards indicate that one of the prisoners is playing a leading lady and the scarf flipped over the shoulder indicates a leading man. Photo credit: Barbara Riquelme.

and relaxing atmosphere for the audience, the frame story also undoubtedly adds meaning and generates plenty of opportunity for the spectators to reflect on the justice system and their own situation in society.

The two characters added by ETT are prisoners and as such they are bound by the walls of their cell, not just in terms of space but also by way of props. All of the costumes, set pieces, and props are restrained by what you might find in a jail: playing cards, a guitar, a chain, and two cages make up the majority of the onstage objects, with the chain delineating the boundary of the cell, confining the prisoner-actors while on stage (see photo 7.1). Time in jail slows almost to a halt, and so in order to "matar el tiempo [kill time]" (Memije and Villa, *El príncipe ynocente*) they tell each other the story of an "innocent" prince. The framing of the story inside a modern prison, however, sheds light on the underlying implications of the plot: that the prince might have been naive about his noble status but is far from innocent, which in turn allows for a dialogical relationship between the chronotopes that can then comment on the continuing class injustices in the twenty-first century. According to Bakhtin, chronotopes can coexist and interact, but without the possibility of the dialogue entering the world represented within the literary work (252). ETT's addition of a frame-story set in a different, yet unspecified, time, however, allows for the external characters to comment on the original chronotope, creating an internal dialogue that informs the audience perception. This dialogue is mediated throughout by the prisoner characters, whose use of acting techniques and the postmodern recognition of the audience's presence (albeit an audience of one), opens the door to their new interpretation to take on its own life, both separate from and in concert with the original story.

By opening up a space for these two chronotopes – modern prison and early modern royal court – to coexist, ETT not only gives new meaning to the original play, but also invokes the baroque concept of *desengaño* (disillusionment) for the audience. *Desengaño* in Spanish baroque literature came out of the realization on the part of artists and writers that the world they had been sold by religious and political leaders was not as it seemed, and that truth was being hidden from them behind a veil of outward appearances (Egginton, "Baroque as a Problem of Thought" 144). What is behind the curtain is always just out of reach, but through baroque art we can catch glimpses of the truth when the artist peels back the layers of propaganda and lies; scepticism and satire are used to draw the audience's attention to the hypocrisy inherent in the system. Although Lope is not known for taking part in the *desengaño* movement, the participants in the ETT production embody *desengaño* in their performance of *El príncipe ynocente* by breaking the fourth wall repeatedly, stopping to ask each other how to perform a certain scene, summing up particularly complex scenes in prose, acknowledging audience engagement, or humming familiar tunes to themselves as they perform the function of stagehand during scene changes. They draw the audience into their fiction and present it as truth: the fiction is the internal play; reality belongs to the realm of the prisoners. The culmination of this technique occurs when the Duke is being attended by his Secretary: after a difficult hunt the Duke falls ill and, to drive this point home, begins sneezing uncontrollably throughout the Secretary's speech. After several "salud" (bless you) and "gracias" (thank you) exchanges have been made, the prisoner playing the Secretary stops the scene and questions the other prisoner's motives in constantly interrupting him. The prisoner playing the Duke claims that he is only trying to play up the verisimilitude of the scene, to which the prisoner-as-secretary replies, "¡Qué no te enfermes del realismo! [Don't make yourself sick with realism!]" (Memije and Villa, *El príncipe ynocente*). The effect of this scene – aside from the audience's amusement – is twofold: one, they are reminded that the play-within-the-play – that is to say, Lope's original play – is not grounded in their reality, and therefore cannot be taken literally; and two, the prisoners are confirmed as that which is actually real. Still, the intense focus of the prisoner-as-secretary demands that the game being played by the two prisoners be taken seriously. Reality is a sickness, and if the prisoners take it too seriously, they will be more harmed by focusing on their depressing surroundings of the jail cell. They need the escapism inherent in their re-enactment of the play to keep themselves healthy and sane. The prisoners have already experienced *desengaño* in their unjust treatment; they need *engaño* to persevere in the face of such a harsh reality.

The setting of the frame in a modern-day prison cell pushes the concept of *desengaño* even further, allowing the frame characters to expose the contradictory nature of the early modern conception of honour. That they are prisoners only enhances the effect, as it is as if the prisoners are breaking the chains of their own captivity by entertaining themselves – and yet the final song demonstrates just how aware they are of the lies told to them by society. Although the original play itself ends in the traditional all's-well-that-ends-well denouement of a wedding announcement (a double wedding in this case), the prisoner's lament of social injustice shines a spotlight on the crimes of the so-called innocent prince, who has, in fact, raped the Duke's oldest daughter and heir. They know that the reality of their own imprisonment is unjust and yet they have only fiction with which to console themselves.

The use of the *ñaque* style – previously considered suitable only for shorter plays or individual scenes (Rojas Villandrando, Libro I) – as a way to introduce the transtemporal frame story, along with the sloweddown time of imprisonment gives them the space to attack what Bakhtin calls "historical inversion"[8] and prove that the past was, in fact, no better than the present. The prisoners have not only "killed time" in both the metaphorical and literal sense, breaking down the walls between past and present in order to prove that the thesis presented in their opening song is as relevant to today's audience as it was in early modern society

> Que no importa lo que hagas
> si tú tienes sangre real,
> amigos o algún puesto muy formal,
> siempre habrá algún juez dispuesto
> que por unos pesos o un favor
> te pueda él exonerar. (Memije and Villa)

> It doesn't matter what you do if you have royal blood, friends, or some high-ranking job, there will always be a ready judge that for a few pesos or a favour can exonerate you.

The original play is thus relegated to the background and the frame story or adaptation takes centre stage. The asides and interruptions of the prisoners are portals through which even the novice viewer can infiltrate early modern *desengaño* and see the contradictory nature of reality. Their use of transtemporality as a time machine between sixteenth and twenty-first centuries breaks open the periodization that so often hinders modern audiences. ETT uses the connections made between old and new chronotopes to open up a portal for the audience to gain new insight and understanding of both the historical space/time and their own. They give agency to the audience to use their own imagination to take the stark reality of an unjust prison system and turn it into a palatial love affair. In the end, however, their playful, time-passing game has been just that. By ending back in the prison cell, the audience members are not only denied the catharsis often supplied by the traditional wedding denouement, but are left contemplating contemporary social issues and their own precarious space within society.

For ETT's production of *El príncipe ynocente*, the expansion of time has a corresponding contracting effect on space. This is a delicate balancing act in which physical space becomes limited while time becomes transversable. A chain placed on the stage delineates the jail cell walls, within which the entire action of the play will take place. The actors begin the performance inside cages too small for them to stand up or stretch out fully. Likewise, the economy of space also requires an economy of costume changes and props – the jail cell setting requires that props and costumes be limited to that which a prisoner might have access:

> valiéndonos de la convención teatral se re-significan todos los objetos, entonces, un juego de cartas sirve para conformar los abanicos que representan a las damas, un recogedor de basura se transforma en el bastón del Viejo del pueblo y en una espada, una tuerca representa el anillo del príncipe, e incluso la misma celda se modifica para convertirse en los diferentes espacios de la obra. (Villa Proal; see Photo 7.1)

> Taking advantage of the theatrical conventions, all of the objects take on a new significance; thus a hand of cards serves as the fans that represent the ladies, a trash picker transforms into the cane of an old villager and a sword, a nut [of the construction variety] stands in for the prince's ring, and even the cellblock can be modified to demarcate different spaces on the stage.

To facilitate the *ñaque* style, many of the minor characters are played in turns; only the two protagonist pairs are played by set actors. That is to say, one of the actors always plays male protagonist number one, while the other plays his female love interest, and vice-versa for the second set. For example, in Photo 7.1, Villa plays Rosimunda to Memije's Torcato, and always does so, just as Memije always takes the part of Hipólita opposite Villa's Alejandro. To avoid confusion, the actors rely on subtle changes to their stripped jumpsuits, props, and gestures/posture to convey their current character status. The prison frame, as confining as it might appear, opens up the space for the actors to travel back to the sixteenth century and provide a show for their one-man audience (a never-seen security guard). This performance-without-an-audience, however, only underlines more sharply their condemnation of a society that punishes poverty and turns a blind eye to the suffering of their fellow human beings. It is the moral equivalent of the tree-falling-in-the-forest – if we do not see it, then it cannot truly affect us.

One must wonder, then, why the prisoners continue their rehearsals and repetitions, attempting to perfect various scenes and make the characters appear more relatable. If no one – save the one guard outside their cell – will likely ever see it, why bother? The prisoner-actors give us one reason – to kill time – but there is another, even more existential reason: to prove their worth, even if not their innocence. Although the audience is never told the exact crime or sentence of the prisoners, there are clues given in the songs they sing:

> Aquí mi compadre, por robar para los suyos
> pues no alcanza la doble jornada laboral,
> y tú por andar de revoltoso
> promoviendo tus ideas locas
> de igualdad y libertad.   (Memije and Villa)

> My buddy here, who stole for his own, since a double shift does not suffice, and you for running around in revolt promoting your crazy ideas of equality and liberty.

Thus, their crimes appear to be, on the one hand, petty theft, presumably to feed his family he cannot support in spite of working two jobs, and, on the other, promoting justice for all. Crimes, they go on to qualify, that are far less grave than the crimes the upper class gets away with, as those with money and friends in high places will find a way to get around the justice system (Memije and Villa). In Lope's denouement, Torcato's new-found status as a prince allows him to escape capital punishment for his rape of Rosimunda, while Alejandro is forgiven for having kidnapped Torcato as a baby, in spite of showing little remorse.

Throughout the original play, there are two separate discussions of justice. The first is ETT's critique of a corrupt justice system that rewards the rich simply for their social status corresponds directly to Alejandro's attempt to circumvent the King of Sweden's orders. When he arrives at the Duke's castle, the King of Sweden sends an envoy to explain Alejandro's transgressions but the Duke questions the King's right to wage war on him simply for giving the prince refuge:

> LEONISO: No te puedes quejar del Rey, gran Duque,
>   que en efecto, si guerra te promete,
>   en razón y justicia va fundada.
> DUQUE: ¿Qué justicia y razón vuestro Rey tiene
>   para que tome contra mí las armas?
> ERICINO: Amparar en tu tierra a su enemigo,
>   y no sólo en tu estado y de secreto,
>   sino públicamente y en tu casa.
> DUQUE: Más razón y justicia es ampararle
>   que no el hacerle, como dices, guerra,
>   pues él injustamente le ha quitado
>   su estado y reino. (2.1488–99)

LEONISO: Great Duke, you cannot complain about the King, whose promise of war is founded in reason and justice.
DUKE: What reason and justice can your King have to take up arms against me?
ERICINO: Protecting his enemy in your lands, and not only in your estate and in secret, but publicly and in your home.
DUKE: It is more reasonable and just to protect him, and not to make war, as you say, against him, as he has unjustly taken from him his estate and kingdom.

The Duke is convinced of Alejandro's innocence and will not falter in his conviction, even as Leoniso and Ericino, the King's ambassadors, explain to the Duke that Alejandro is a son of the King's brother, but not the legitimate heir, who disappeared mysteriously as a child. The King suspects that Alejandro had something to do with the disappearance and has either kidnapped or killed the true prince. Nevertheless, the Duke is unmoved, sure in his belief that the King of Sweden is the one who is trying to unjustly usurp power from his nephew, Alejandro. Ericino accuses the Duke of being more interested in his own gains – that one of his daughters might marry the prince and become queen of Dacia – than the truth. The meeting is thus cut short, with both sides promising war.

The other discussion of justice comes towards the end of the play when Rosimunda realizes that her sister has received a promise of marriage in the form of a letter from Alejandro, the man whose ring she received in return for a night of pleasure, which she also believed to be a promise of marriage:

¡Oh villano Alejandro! Aquesto pasa:
– cubierta estoy de un temeroso hielo –
dite entrada en mi alma y en mi casa,
bien a costa del Duque y de mi honra,
y el nuevo amor de Hipólita te abrasa.
Dé voces a los cielos mi deshonra;
pida justicia del crüel tirano
que dos hermanas, sin amor, deshonra.   (3.2282–9)

Oh Alejandro, you villain! This is what happened – I'm shrouded in icy fear – I gave you entry into my soul and into my house, at great cost to the Duke and my honour, and now love for Hipolita burns in you. May my dishonour call out to the heavens; may it beg justice from the cruel tyrant that dishonours two sisters without love.

For the modern audience the justice that Rosimunda receives – that is, the revelation that it is Torcato who tricked his way into her room and, as a newly discovered crown prince, can marry her and take his rightful place on the throne – would ring hollow; this is why ETT quickly glosses over the original denouement, returning the prisoners to their cramped cages and concluding inside the frame story.

Nevertheless, the Duke's unwavering defence of Alejandro's innocence speaks directly to the critique presented by ETT's staging; that is, as long as one has friends in high places, the law will not be applied so directly or as punishingly as it would to someone of lower status. Even when, at the end of the play, when the King of Sweden finally appears and Alejandro admits his guilt and Torcato is revealed to be the true successor to the crown, the Duke feels that it would be unjust to leave Alejandro with nothing:

> DUQUE: Todo se sabe, y resta solamente
> que de las bodas [se decida] el día.
> Y pues ha de heredar forzosamente
> Torcato, a Dacia y Frisia, y ha quedado
> Alejandro tan pobre injustamente,
> a Hipólita le doy con mi ducado. (3.2507–12)

> DUKE: Everything is now known, and it only remains for the weddings to determine the day. And since Torcato must inherit Dacia and Frisia, and Alejandro is left so unjustly poor, I give him Hipolita, along with my duchy.

Alejandro not only escapes punishment, but is also rewarded, albeit not with the title he originally presumed to take.

The original play does not punish the transgressions of any of its characters, from Alejandro's attempt to expropriate Torcato's inheritance, to Torcato's rape of Rosimunda, both of which are crimes that a modern audience would likely find difficult to condone. Rather than linger on the incongruities of the play with modern life, ETT creates the prison frame to draw parallels of the (in)justice system across time and generate theatrical identification between the audience and the prisoner-actor characters. To facilitate the audience-character connection, they use a familiar tune: the melody of the "Oo-de-lally" song, as originally sung by Alan-a-Dale (or "The Rooster") in Disney's 1973 cartoon version of *Robin Hood*. In its pre-production notes, ETT uses a number of references from popular culture to flesh out how the company itself would conceive of the characterization and presentation of all of the characters onstage, so that, even with sixteen different roles,[9] the audience would remain constantly aware of which of the two prisoners is playing which character at different moments throughout the play. The use of the songs from *Robin Hood* opens up a space of familiarity for the audience members, whose acquaintance with the Robin Hood plot will help them recognize that this performance is not really about the original play's interior love triangles, but rather a metaphor for the imprisonment of the two frame characters.

Although the *ñaque* style might create some confusion with such a large cast of characters, ETT is able to keep the audience informed through the use of simple props as well as the identifiable caricatures they create for each of the interior characters; since the two male and female leads would only ever be played by one of the two actors (one male and one female lead per actor), the more minor characters, like the Duke and Secretary, need strong characteristics to differentiate them visually and audibly on stage as the actors switch off on playing them as necessary. The Duke's portrayal, for example, was built on the following ideas: "Delicado, padre de Rosimunda e Ypólita, negociador, interesado, histeriquito, líder por posición, no por vocación, militar, crédulo [delicate, father of Rosimunda and Hipolita, negotiator, self-interested, slightly hysterical, leader based on position, not vocation, military man, gullible]" (Flores, Memije, and Villa). Included in the production notes are pictures of fictional characters that might fit the description; Foghorn Leghorn, Mr Magoo, and the King of Hearts from the Disney version of *Alice in Wonderland* characterize the Duke, for example. Certainly, the influence of the last two can be seen in the actors' physical performances, as they get into a low, crouched position, indicating a shorter stature, and force themselves to painfully shuffle around the stage, with a flipped-up collar and high-pitched voice. These characteristics continue to populate the space even when the prisoners embody multiple characters at a time; holding a fan of playing cards at arm's length indicates that their current character is engaging with one of the female leads, while staring down towards the ground where the Duke formerly stood in his crouched stature allows the audience to continue to see him there in their mind's eye. Blocking is thus crucial in this *ñaque* version of the play, as the actors must interact with the phantoms of the other characters, as if they themselves were still embodying the now-empty spaces.

Although the play itself was hitherto unknown to modern audiences, the use of the familiar in the current chronotope allows the frame story to open up a new avenue of interpretation for the play's denouement. As Hutcheon explains, "adaptation is a form of intertextuality: we experience adaptations (*as adaptations*) as palimpsests through our memory of other works that resonate through repetition with variation" (8, emphasis in the original); thus through the use of more modern tropes

ETT is able to create a palimpsest for a previously unknown play, which in turn makes it almost already familiar for its audience. This familiarity is what allows ETT to turn the play's internal motivation on its head. By associating the internal characters with external ones, the associations that the audience makes are not with sixteenth-century values but rather with more modern ones. The return over and over throughout the play to the tune from Disney's *Robin Hood* links the play to the prison, and the prisoners to the ideals of a ne'er-do-well thief with a heart of gold, a conceit that primes the audience to accept that the characters of the external frame read this story as an example of the injustices of the class system. Torcato, as prince, is instantaneously forgiven all his wrongdoings as a rustic peasant, in spite of committing what would now be considered rape; the two prisoners, however, as petty, lower-class criminals, will likely spend the rest of their days in jail. Using the *Robin Hood* tune they lament not only their particular situation but the two-tiered system that privileges the wealthy.

Adaptations, by their very nature, allow for a new audience to identify with the staged material, a process which can impose new meaning or interpretation onto the source material. Issues pertaining to what we now call social justice were not uncommon in theatrical works of Spain's Golden Age, but often they seem inaccessible to the modern audience member. The Spanish Code of Honour, which required that women remain virginal and men protect them from the evils of the world, might seem antiquated now, but a deeper look can find much more relatable characters, such as *Fuenteovejuna*'s Laurencia, who fight for women's honour and right to choose what to do with their own bodies and lives. Without the framing adaptation of ETT, Lope's *El príncipe inocente* would appear ludicrous to the modern audience. Who would believe that the rustic, adoptive son of a shepherd would get away with raping the daughter of a Duke because he is really a long-lost prince? Leaving credibility aside, how many modern audience members would expect to enjoy such a plot point? By shifting the focus away from the original denouement and back into the jail cell of the modern prisoners, the ETT production highlights the injustice inherent therein, and is able to demonstrate that the political and judicial systems are still rife with similar problems, in that the lowest of us suffer the greatest consequences, while those with money and power are able to get away with much greater crimes.

The adaptive framing imposed by ETT has the potential to open up a whole new set of plays outside of the traditional canon, plays that can become relevant even to the most sceptical audience members[10] and impose new interpretive meaning onto plays that were once relegated to the dustbin. For Lope de Vega and his contemporary audiences, there would have been little – if any – concern over the potential injustice in Torcato's return to power, even if the rape and ensuing marriage with Rosimunda seem jarring to the modern spectator. Rather, for Lope's time, the double marriage end to the play would be the most logical and even expected denouement. Instead of grappling with the improbability of such a conclusion, ETT moves away from the original story and back to its own frame, singing about happy endings: "Aquí sin libertad yo quisiera ser rey ... Pero en su lugar prefiero más justicia al final [Here, without freedom, I might have wanted to be King ... But instead I would much rather have justice in the end]" (Memije and Villa). Although the prisoners dream of being able to order people around and make – and even break – the fates of their subjects, they quickly realize that justice for all is the only way to be truly free. Villa Proal's prologue in this volume underscores just how vitally important this idea of true justice – even if we do not see it in our own lifetime – is to the end goal of ETT's conscientious theatre. The addition of the frame story creates a palimpsest for the modern audience out of a play that was previously irrelevant and almost incoherent in its complexity. The use of early modern techniques and theory – *ñaque* and *desengaño* respectively – allows ETT to comment on the presence of absence in today's social order: the never-seen prison guard stands in for the power structure that ignores the plight of those who are lesser-than, such as the prisoner-actors whose petty crimes are disproportionately punished. In spite of their claim to be interested only in "el puro placer de montarlo [the pure pleasure of performance]" (Flores, Memije, and Villa), as the light dims on the prisoners back inside their cramped boxes, the audience does not leave with the cathartic, traditional marriage ending in their minds, but rather with the questions raised by ETT regarding the societal divide between rich and poor, and the justice system that fails all but the most affluent. Although adaptations are often considered, as mentioned above, to be constrained to one particular chronotope, I would argue that ETT has found the perfect balance between modernization and ambiguity – never mentioning the exact place or time in which the prison frame is set – which allows their version of the play to endure and succeed across a variety of spaces and times.

NOTES

1 The only surviving copy (and, presumably, the original manuscript) was titled thusly, with *inocente* spelled with a "y." EFE TRES Teatro's production maintained the original spelling of "ynocente." For the sake of clarity,

I will from here on use "ynocente" when discussing the production and "inocente" when discussing the text itself, in keeping with the spelling that Tania de Miguel Magro and I have employed in our edition of the text.

2 As Tania de Miguel Magro and I note in our introduction to the critical edition of this play, there is no recorded staging of this play during Lope's lifetime and the original manuscript was lost, leaving only a handwritten copy from 1762, which in turn remained unknown until it was rediscovered in 1945.
3 The Organisation for Economic Co-operation and Development (OECD) notes that, although Mexico is the eleventh largest economy in the world, income inequality, corruption, and crime in that country continue to prevent real progress across the board (14).
4 All translations are mine unless otherwise noted.
5 For more on ETT's approaches to theatre and social commentary, see the interview with cofounders Fernando Villa Proal and Allan Flores in the third section of this book.
6 It must be noted that Torcato's "innocence" as a prince has only to do with his lack of knowledge regarding his high station in life. His actions prior to this revelation are anything but innocent in nature.
7 The exact number would really depend on staging and interpretation. There is a "paje" or page listed in each of the acts, with the page of the first act given a name. The other two acts just state that "un paje" speaks. Thus, all three pages could be the same, first one named in Act I, or there could be three different pages, meaning that the total number of characters would then reach twenty-one.
8 "The essence of this inversion is found in the fact that mythological and artistic thinking locates such categories as purpose, ideal, justice, perfection, the harmonious condition of man and society and the link in the *past*" (Bakhtin 147).
9 The original text has a staggering eighteen characters – if the "dos cazadores" and "dos pícaros" are counted as four individual characters – but ETT cuts two characters, Ericino and Leoniso, the ambassadors of King Dinacreo of Sweden. One might argue that there are really only fourteen characters in the ETT version, as the "dos pinches" – which stand in for the "dos pícaros" here – are not really true characters, as they are portrayed simply by the *cocinero* wearing oven mitts as puppets. Although the ambassadors do not appear on stage in the adaptation, ETT puts their accusatory lines (cited above) into a letter from the King which the Duke reads out loud, much to the same effect.
10 Of whom I was previously one, as I mention in my review of the performance at the Chamizal Siglo de Oro Festival in 2016.

8 Systemic Oppression in Morfeo Teatro's Adaptation and Production of *El coloquio de los perros*

GLENDA Y. NIETO-CUEBAS

La sabiduría en el pobre está asombrada;
que la necesidad y miseria son las sombras
y nubes que la escurecen

Wisdom in a poor man is always overshadowed; for necessity and poverty are the shadows and clouds which blot it out[1]

Miguel de Cervantes, *El coloquio de los perros*

In the last pages of *El coloquio de los perros*, Miguel de Cervantes tells us that human needs and misery obscure the wisdom of the poor (358). This phrase adequately describes the theatrical atmosphere and the dramatic performance of Morfeo Teatro's adaptation of Cervantes' novel. This production premiered in 2011 and was adapted and directed by Francisco Negro.[2] In it the dogs Berganza and Cipión are transformed into men with dog-like lives. Berganza is transformed into an impoverished nobleman and Cipión is a beggar who suffers any number of misfortunes. This chapter looks at how Morfeo's humanized dogs capture the voice of the oppressed and the socially marginalized. I propose that the desolation of the environment and the scraggly physical aspect of Cipión, as well as the deteriorated appearance of Berganza, represent the misery experienced by many human beings who are victims of systemic oppression; as a result of this oppression these individuals become alienated, powerless, and voiceless. These characterizations expose the prejudice many suffer as they are ostracized and disenfranchised in different social contexts. Cipión and Berganza help us reflect on the injustices that existed in Cervantes' society, in which powerful institutions exploited groups of people based on their social class. At the same time, Morfeo transfers this notion to the present in the Western world, where minorities fall victim to bigotry, violence, and oppression. In both cases, the conditions reveal asymmetrical power structures that privilege some individuals over others on the basis of class, gender, religion, sexual orientation, and other forms of social identity.

Marginalization and classism are examples of systemic oppression insofar as they prevent members of particular groups from meeting basic needs and from fully participating in society, privileging one group over the other (Scholz, *Political* 210). In "The Challenge of Systemic Oppression," Sally J. Scholz explains that

> in systemic oppression at least one group benefits or is privileged in some way due to the oppression of another group ... This condition is important for two interconnected reasons. First, since the nature of the oppression is systemic, or rooted in the structure of society, rather that there being a specific oppressor group, no social group is held morally blameworthy for the oppression of another social group. This in turn legitimatizes the privileged status of the group or individual benefitting from the oppression of another social group (or individual members of oppressed social groups). That is, because systemic oppression arises out of attempts to formulate the just state, the oppression of some may be taken to be justified on the basis that it is for the common good or simply that nothing alternatively can be done without reformulating the state entirely. Or, again due to the attempt to theorize a just state, the oppression or exclusion may not be recognized, especially by those who benefit from it. Second, there is no incentive on the part of the privileged group to change the social conditions that result in the systemic oppression of some. Doing so would change or even remove their privileged status. (170)

In modern times, the principle of equality has become better understood and defended than in the past,[3] but discussions of inequality and what oppression entails have been presented in various ways throughout the centuries. Inequality has been a frequent topic in works of literature. Early modern Spanish texts reveal Miguel de Cervantes as one of the leading literary figures who, through his writing, exposed disparities rooted in the structure of his society. As has been well noted, Cervantes understood first-hand the extreme difficulty of successfully climbing the social ladder and the struggles of less privileged individuals who lived in a society hegemonized by the noble class.

Within Cervantes' *Novelas ejemplares*, *El coloquio de los perros* gives us a good example of how stratified seventeenth-century Spanish society was. Berganza explains to Cipión how some members of groups are marginalized mostly owing to their socio-economic status and how much scarcity and corruption there is in the world. The dogs' dialogue makes this short novel well suited for the stage because it offers abundant theatrical possibilities in aesthetic and ideological terms. Most important, Cervantes' text exposes social injustices and poses a call to action. Probably because of its engagement with social issues, this text has been adapted numerous times for the stage over the last fifteen years. On most occasions, the productions have highlighted social concerns such as racism, inequality, injustice, unfair taxation, oppression, and corruption. These adaptations include *Solo y Cía* (Dir. Pepe Ortega, 2005), *Teatro de la Abadía* (Dir. Fefa Noia, 2010), *Morfeo Teatro* (Dir. Francisco Negro, 2011), *[In]constantes Teatro* (Dir. Emilio del Valle, 2012), *Els Joglar* (Dir. Ramón Fontserè, 2013), *Laboratorio Escénico de la Universidad del Valle, Colombia* (Dir. Ma Zhenghong and Alejandro González Puche, 2013), and *La Carnicerí* (Dir. Gastón Borges, 2016). In this chapter, I analyse Francisco Negro's production of *El coloquio de los perros* because it portrays systemic oppression in early modern Spain as well as in modern times. It does this by showing Cipión and Berganza living a dehumanized existence in a society that neglects the poor and privileges the rich. I will first provide an introduction to Morfeo's work and then briefly discuss their production of *La escuela de los vicios*. This discussion will illustrate the kinds of repercussions Morfeo faced because of their commitment to social justice. I will follow this with a more in-depth analysis of their adaptation and production of *El coloquio de los perros*.

Morfeo Teatro's work calls out injustice and prejudice. Their theatrical adaptations of Spanish classical narratives focus on contemporary social issues and are deployed as means to denounce social injustice and corruption. Morfeo is based in Burgos, Spain, and it is well known for rescuing classical texts, as well as contemporary ones, from obscurity. Some of the works they present were not necessarily written for the stage. Francisco Negro and Mayte Bona co-own Morfeo Teatro. They focus on transforming their work into stagecraft with which the audience can engage through the often rhythmic dialogues and the visually stimulating stage and costume designs they create. In the last fifteen years they have adapted and produced seven performances based on Spanish classical texts: *El buscón*, by Francisco de Quevedo (2005); *De burladores y burlados*, based on interludes by various authors (2007); *La Lozana Andaluza*, by Francisco Delicado (2008); *El coloquio de los perros*, by Miguel de Cervantes (2011); *La escuela de los vicios*, by Quevedo (2014); *Fiesta barroca*, an anthology of theatre, poetry, and music of the Spanish

Golden Age (2015); and *El retablo de las maravillas*, by Cervantes (2016). Most of these performances have been well received by audiences in and outside Spain. However, Morfeo's work has been threatened by censorship in the last four years. *El coloquio*, for example, is a production that, in Negro's words, "siempre enternece y conmueve [al público] [always touches and moves the audience]," while other productions have provoked anger and outrage due to its highly critical content ("Re: Entrevista").

Their productions show a deep reflection on the authors' work and its connection with today's society. They reveal an insightful, often ethically charged, view of social and political issues that affected Spanish society four hundred years ago and that continue to be relevant today. In a country that is still politically divided and generally leans towards conservativism, Morfeo's work has not always been well received by audiences and by cultural agencies and politicians, many of whom are not interested in supporting their work[4] or would rather they put on less politically charged productions. In Negro's words:

> Tener opinión y ofrecerla – y el teatro cuando es teatro, y ofrece verdad y no sólo entretenimiento fútil – es una plataforma que ofrece opinión para que los demás la pongan en entredicho o aplaudan – acarrea tanto premios como castigos. Estamos muy valorados, a veces entusiastamente, como compañía con unos compromisos éticos, con un "proyecto" intelectual; pero también sufrimos la censura de muchos gestores o políticos en cargos culturales que no les interesa nuestro trabajo, y no nos contratan escudándose en que el teatro deber servir a la diversión más que a la reflexión, que el público lo que quiere es "pasarlo bien." Como si pensar o emocionarse, o poner a prueba nuestro sentido crítico con ironía e inteligencia, fuera "pasarlo mal." También hay una parte del público que se siente incómodo con nuestras obras, no lo vamos a negar, que comparten la visión de que es mejor no opinar de ciertas cosas. El conservadurismo siempre ha sido enemigo de los ideales. ("Re: Entrevista")

> Having an opinion and offering it – and theatre, when it is [proper] theatre and offers truth and not only futile entertainment – is the stage that offers an opinion for others to question or applaud. This brings as much merit as it does punishment. We are valued, sometimes enthusiastically, as a theatre company with ethical commitments, with an intellectual project; but we also suffer censorship from many agents or government officials working for cultural entities that are not interested in our work and do not hire us, under the pretext that theatre performances should entertain rather than promp reflection, or that what the public wants is to have a

good time. As if thinking or getting excited or testing our critical sense with irony or intelligence means "having a bad time." There is also part of the audience that feels uncomfortable with our plays; we are not going to deny it. They share the notion that it is better not to have an opinion about certain things. Conservativism has always been the enemy of ideals.[5]

Although Morfeo's adaptation of *El coloquio de los perros* has not been generally perceived as a controversial piece, at least one of its other productions has. Its production of *La escuela de los vicios*, based on satire and political discourse, was seen as a politically charged piece. In this adaptation, the devil tries to trick two foolish men through the "escuela de los vicios" (school of vices). The academic credentials that could be acquired through this school are a bachelor in lying, a licensure in deceiving, a doctorate in stealing, and a full professorship in corruption. The two fools commit to their lessons, acquiring excellent results, and at the end are named Minister and Magistrate, but both titles are stained with corruption. This production, as Negro describes it, "refleja la realidad de la maquinación política [reflects the reality of the political apparatus]" ("Re: Entrevista"). For the adapter and director, it was important to represent Quevedo's words and point of view explicitly. Negro did not want to hide anything, especially when Quevedo described Spain's current political situation so well. As Negro points out: "[a] Quevedo le metieron en la cárcel por estos escritos, no queremos ocultar nada de lo que dijo, para que el espectador vea en qué manos estamos [Quevedo was sent to jail for his writings, we don't want to hide what he said so that the spectator sees who is in charge today]" ("Re: Entrevista").

The opening of *La escuela de los vicios* (Burgos, 1 February 2014) coincided with a mass uprising in Spain, "the Gamonal protests," that took place in Burgos a few weeks before the opening of this play, on 10 January, 2014.[6] These protests were intended to expose years of graft and corruption by local politicians who put financial gain above the real needs of the people of these cities ("Battle").[7] After a week of protests, the residents of the Gamonal were able to stop the government's plan to spend millions of dollars towards the construction of a boulevard. Interestingly, during the opening of *La escuela de los vicios*, the enthusiasm of some of the victorious residents of the Gamonal and their supporters reached the Teatro Principal de Burgos. At the end of the performance, many in the audience stood up yelling excitedly "Sí, se puede [Yes, we can]." This led many conservatives to see Morfeo Teatro as a radical liberal troupe and to label them as "rojos [reds]," indicating that they were leftists or communists.[8] The intention of the company, as has been mentioned before, was to pay homage to Quevedo's genius and to expose the relevance of his work in modern times. They did not have a political agenda. Still, the company took a stance against ultraconservative views, which is clearly expressed in the description of the play as published in the company's website:

> Advertencia: Este espectáculo, como buena farsa, es políticamente incorrecto, tiene una alta dosis de inquina, es hiriente, cáustico y por ende provoca risa inteligente (mérito en su mayor parte del autor), por lo que puede desaconsejarse su ingesta a públicos con mentalidad ultraconservadora, o que vayan al teatro sólo a pasar un buen rato y no pensar. (Morfeo Teatro Web)
>
> Warning: This performance, like a good farce, is politically incorrect. It is full of disdain. It is offensive, hurtful, and caustic. Therefore it causes intelligent laughter (owing primarily to its author, Quevedo). In light of this, it might not be appropriate for audiences with an ultraconservative mentality or for those who only go to the theatre to have a good time and to avoid thought.

Owing to the perceived provocative nature of this production and its direct criticism of political corruption, it was censored by government and cultural officials. The censorship took the form of sudden requests that the company cancel planned performances of *La escuela* and schedule other productions from their repertoire instead. Local theatres cut their contracts by 40 to 50 per cent. This, as expected, significantly affected the company economically, and by extension, the economic security of its cast. Despite the conservative backlash against the production, it was extremely well received by the critics, some of whom applauded its risky approach and its sharp criticism of corruption (I.L.H.).[9]

Even though Morfeo's *El coloquio de los perros* has not been perceived as being as politically charged as *La escuela*, it addresses issues that are relevant today, such as poverty and privilege, and in a subtle way, condemns them. Since its premiere in 2011, this production has been presented more than thirty times in and outside Spain and it has been well received by audiences and reviewers. Most of the reviews praise the high calibre of the actors, costumes, and stage design. Some point to how the company was faithful to the style of classical theatre, in its effective elocution and the design of the costumes (Frías A16). *El correo de Burgos* pointed out how "la amargura, el desencantamiento y la desilusión [bitterness, disappointment, and heartbreak]" are observed in this play without forgoing "el humor, la ironía y la sorna malintencionada, propias del Siglo de Oro [the humour, the irony, and the ill-intentioned sarcasm that is typical of the Golden Age]" (Vill, "Descarnado"). Additionally, in a review published in the *Bulletin of the Comediantes*, Gladys Robalino notes that Francisco Negro reinstates the central space Cervantes gives to ostracized characters: "Negro recupera la centralidad que da la obra de Cervantes a las voces marginales, es decir la voz de quienes no tienen voz ... La voz de estos seres marginados, 'desechos del universo,' ocupa en la adaptación de Negro todo el espacio teatral [Negro reinstates the centrality that Cervantes gives to marginal characters, the voice of those who do not have a voice ... The voice of those marginalized beings, 'waste of the universe,' occupy the central space in Negro's adaptation]" (175).

Mofeo's adaptation of *El coloquio de los perros* follows the original narrative structure and incorporates many of the passages where Berganza recounts his experiences with many of his masters. However, it is recounted as a continuation of the original text and takes place thirty years after the dogs had their night-long conversation at the Hospital de la Resurrección in Valladolid. The spectacle transports us to a dark and foggy street from the beginning of the seventeenth century, where an apparently blind beggar – interpreted by Mayte Bona – drags a shattered cart and takes centre stage, begging for Christian charity in a melodic and exaggerated way:

> CIPIÓN: ¡Por las animas de Purgatorio sean pronto perdonadas! Una caridad cristiana ... Ay, Cipión, mala noche cargas ... ¡Por santa Catalina de Siena que no callaba ni al matalla! Una caridad cristiana ... Nadie por la calle pasa ... ¡Y estas tripas que me rugen ... ¡Cristianos, mala noche les dé Dios, sino me aguijan una dádiva! Una caridad cristiana. (Negro, "El coloquio" 2)

> CIPIÓN: May the souls in Purgatory find forgiveness! Show me Christian charity ... Oh, Cipión, suffering this foul night ... By Saint Catherine of Siena, who was never silent, not even as she was martyred! Show me Christian charity... How my gullet growls ... Christians, may God cast this foul night upon thee if you cannot spare alms! Show me Christian charity.

Although this can be considered a comedic scene, Cipión's calling out for charity is not intended as a joke. It voices the anguish of the needy, of an outcast who has become silent and invisible in his isolation. Cipión's pleading chant is unheard by those who have a moral responsibility to help the poor. They are nowhere to be seen, but they are not the ones who have been erased, unlike individuals like Cipión, who have been discarded by society. His invisibility stresses how society lacks moral values and fails to assist the needy.

Cipión is eventually heard and approached by Berganza, an individual as powerless and disadvantaged as he. The newcomer seems to recognize Cipión as his old friend, but the latter does not recall ever meeting Berganza and threatens him with all kinds of abuse. His attitude changes once Berganza promises to share some provisions. The characterizations of the dogs-made-men that we see in Morfeo's adaptation draw upon a past when little heed, especially by those in positions of power and privilege, was paid to understanding and addressing the disparities, subjugation, and segregation suffered by those who came from low economic or different religious backgrounds.[10]

The alienation in this context is seen onstage through the set design, the characters' costumes, and the stage props. The scenery situates the characters in what looks like a remote part of the woods, excluded from society. At the beginning of the performance, we see a sombre backdrop, inspired by the dark, cloudy, and tempestuous sky of El Greco's *View of Toledo* (1600). The set, designed by Regue Fernández Mateos, recreates the secluded scenery in the outskirts of the city as portrayed in El Greco's painting. In *View of Toledo*, the chaotic and wavy clouds that encompass a topographically altered Toledo seem to point at a tumultuous and dark world that exists beyond the walled city. In fact, to describe the atmosphere and the characters we see onstage, we can use the same words Azorín used to describe El Greco's work in his *Diario de un enfermo*: "personajes ... penosos, en negruzcos tintes, azulados violentos, violentos rojos ... dan la sensación angustiosa de la vida febril, tumultuosa, atormentada, trágica [sad characters, in dark shades, violent blues, and reds ... They give off a sensation of anguish, of a feverish, tumultuous, tormented, and tragic life]" (75). A turbulent and isolated atmosphere is also used in Morfeo's production to visually frame the plot and the social exclusion in which the characters live; it is segregated and marginalized from mainstream society. Negro explains that in this production:

> Retomamos pues una iconografía de la época de Cervantes, que está en el inconsciente colectivo del espectador para ubicarle con facilidad en el tiempo de la acción. La desolación del paisaje es reflejo de la de los personajes, la dureza del entorno es la que ha rodeado sus vidas. ("Re: Entrevista")

> We took the iconography from Cervantes' period, which resides in the collective unconsciousness of the spectator in order to easily situate them within the era of the narrative. The desolated scenery reflects the

characters' landscape, the harshness of their surroundings has encircled their lives as well.

In this sense, this visual context and the gloomy open scenery reflect the characters' condition and help the audience understand the social climate that surrounds them. It opens up to the viewer a shadowy and solitary world in which two raggedy individuals discuss their misfortunes without the possibility of ever escaping the literal and figurative darkness of their situation.

The characters' lack of material possessions, shown by a minimalist use of stage props, a dead tree trunk and an old wooden cart carried by Cipión, emphasizes their social circumstances and exposes their shared social identity and disadvantaged situation.[11] There is no doubt for the spectators that they have in front of them two unfortunate individuals surrounded by an unjust world that does not welcome them. According to Negro:

> Para, como reza el subtítulo de la obra, "Pues hay perros que como nobles personas proceden, y personas que como perros se comportan": mostrar esa humanidad y la contradicción de intentar ser "buenos" en un ambiente hostil a la virtud. Esa humanidad se magnifica al ser dos personajes desposeídos de cualquier tipo de fortuna material. Además, necesitábamos que los perros se "vistiesen" de personas para favorecer la comprensión del espectador, para que la anécdota de dos perros hablando no distrajese el discurso cervantino, para que la fabula, que se defiende por si sola y brillantemente en la novela, no se viera opacada por la interpretación en escena de unos actores simulando ser perros, no teniendo estos la misma carga emocional que dos personas. (Entrevista)

> As the subtitle of the work goes, "there are dogs that behave like nobles and people that behave like dogs." [This is intended] to show that humanity and the contradiction of trying to be "good" in an environment that is hostile to virtue. That humanity is magnified by two characters who are dispossessed of any type of material fortune. We also needed the dogs to be "dressed" like people to facilitate the understanding of the audience, so that the image of the talking dogs did not distract from the Cervantine discourse, and so that the fable, that defends itself brilliantly in the novel, was not obscured by actors interpreting dogs onstage, which would not have had the same emotional charge of two people.

The world that surrounds them seems tainted, disturbed, and untamed, like the characters' physical appearance. Cipión opens the play wearing

Photo 8.1: Cipión and Berganza facing the public as they speak. The first one wears extremely filthy clothes and the other resembles a crestfallen version of a nobleman. Photo courtesy of Francisco Negro (Morfeo Teatro). Photographer: Fran Álvarez

extremely filthy and ragged clothes. His hair is unkempt and dirty, and his posture is that of a tired and despondent man. Berganza, on the other hand, looks like a crestfallen and rumpled version of a nobleman. Both appear down on their luck and everything that surrounds them points to their misery and loneliness.

Through the staging of this piece, a paradoxical relationship between the visual and the oral takes place. Cipión's interventions will make the audience laugh and momentarily dissipate the reality in which the characters live. This character's discursive mediation is fundamental to the comedic character of the play. At the beginning, the beggar enlivens the play with his sprightly movements, dances, popular sayings, and witty comments. Despite his condition, Cipión never loses his sense of humour and charisma, and exhibits a penetrating point of view that perceives the evils that affect society. His scepticism and pragmatism contrast with Berganza's idealism. However, this will change as the plot develops:

> BERGANZA: En el sentido figurado. Que de lo que has dicho vengo a suponer que lo que hasta aquí he pasado es sueño y apariencia; y que en verdad no somos hermanos sino hombres con vida de perros, yo de loco y vos de cuerdo... y la Fortuna, la Fortuna es sólo una moneda al aire que juega con nuestras ilusiones, y en lo que cae, la vida se ha pasado. (Negro, "El coloquio" 26)

> BERGANZA: In a figurative sense. From what you have said I have come to assume that what happened here was only a dream, an illusion; we are not real siblings, only men with doglike lives. I am crazy and you are sane ... and Fortune, Fortune is only a coin cast into the air that plays with our aspirations, and by the time it lands, life has already passed.

Throughout the play, Cipión denies remembering being a dog and accepts his life as it is. In contrast, Berganza starts to lose his initial optimism, and eventually exteriorizes the angst caused by the social exclusion he is facing. At the end of the play Berganza reveals his disappointment, showing a more pessimistic and realistic view of life.

During most of the production, Berganza and Cipión take centre stage. However, they are momentarily interrupted and upstaged by the apparition of the old Cañizares (played by Felipe Santiago), a witchlike character that emerges from within Berganza's narration. Like in Cervantes' original text, although the reader can clearly visualize the old hag – thanks to the detailed description given in the narrative – she is a subject of the past and not of the present. Onstage, Cañizares is represented as a phantomlike figure – inspired by Francisco Goya's *Black Paintings* and the character of Macbeth in Akira Kurosawa's film *Throne of Blood*[12] – that emerges from the darkness, illuminated by a dark red light. She talks and moves like a spectre while narrating the supposedly true story of the dogs' births. According to Cañizares' account Berganza and Cipión, born as humans, were soon converted into dogs by an envious sorceress called Camacha. While the apparition of this character would seem to connect the human-dogs to others, because they are no longer alone onstage, it only emphasizes how lonely and socially excluded these individuals are. Berganza remains in the left corner and Cipión at the right of the stage, frozen and mute, while the overwhelmingly powerful figure and voice of the old witch take over, erasing them from the scene. Therefore, when this powerful figure emerges onstage,

Photo 8.2: Berganza and Cipión on opposite sides of the stage while Cañizares tells her story. Photo courtesy of Francisco Negro (Morfeo Teatro). Photographer: Fran Álvarez

both human-dogs become invisible. Even though this invisibility is mainly sensed by the spectator at that moment, it is clear that individuals like Cipión and Berganza have always suffered within a society that privileged the affluent classes and subjugated less fortunate ones.

As Martin Halliwell has noted about Cervantes' *El coloquio de los perros*, Francisco Negro's adaptation also "typif[ies] the picaresque" narrative (1002). The picaresque is an exemplary genre for understanding "social justice." It deliberately exposes the injustices of a society constructed by and for the upper classes. *Lazarillo de Tormes* is the best-known example of the genre. According to Antonio Pérez-Romero the novel

> is a merciless critique of the whole official worldview and of the apparent glitter and glory of the Spanish empire; this system had thrust vast sectors of the Spanish population into misery and alienation. According to the protagonist, anyone who manipulated and dehumanizes others inevitably

becomes corrupt and alienated. Corruption and dehumanization, then, could allow the nonprivileged to survive in the cruel world created by the owners of society, but would ultimately ensure their alienation and lack of fulfillment. An important subversion in *Lazarillo* is the exaltation of the ideas and aspirations of the poor, which appear in stark contrast to those of the upper classes. Despite the "jungle" environment imposed upon everyone, this novel gives us glimpses of the solidarity of the poor in the face of adversity and oppression. (233)

Like the titular character of *Lazarillo*, Cipión and Berganza are forced to survive in a world that is far from being fair and benign; it is a brutal environment built by a society that favours only a privileged few. Dishonesty – as we see when Cipión pretends to be blind in order to get charity – and learning to cope with life's adversities help them survive. This is presented as a social critique of a powerful system that drove its less advantaged population into poverty[13] and, by extension, as a critique of our own society. Berganza, like a *pícaro*, is portrayed as an individual who is unsuccessful in climbing the social ladder.[14] He shows signs of being rejected by the system and ostracized. This is suggested visually by his clothing, which seems to have once been of good quality but is unkempt and dirty. As Negro notes of his characters' appearances: "Sus caras, sus vestimentas, están ajadas, como sacados de un cuadro de Velázquez, con esa mirada triste y limpia que tienen los que han pasado por el mundo siendo desgraciados, pero honestos [Their faces, their attire, are aged, as if they had been taken from a Velázquez painting. With the desolated and empty look of those who have gone through the world living a miserable life, but who are honest]" ("Re: Entrevista"). Indeed, Berganza carries the sadness Negro describes, but I would like to add that he also conveys an air of elegance seen in many Velázquez models. Berganza's attire, also inspired by Francisco Domingo Marqués' painting *Un lance en el siglo XVII* (1866), consists of a velvet hat with narrow brim, grey and burgundy pants, a white undershirt, a front-tied grey jerkin with sleeves puffed to the wrist, and a green cape. In contrast to the filthy long, hooded cassock – inspired by the one in Francisco de Zurbarán's painting *Saint Francis of Assisi in His Tomb* (1630–4) – Cipión wears a jerkin and trousers. Berganza's outfit stands out as that of a man of high rank. However, it is wrinkled, dirty, and wrecked. It shows signs of a sophisticated past and hints at what Cruz calls the "appearance of wealth," which a person of his status might have tried to acquire, but was unable to, owing to his exclusion and marginalization from the dominant class (86).

On the other hand, another well-known topos of the picaresque novel revealed in this adaptation is the characters' hunger; like two authentic *pícaros*, Berganza and Cipión are both impoverished and starving. Hunger serves as a contradictory topos; it is tragic and comic at the same time. "Hambre" – hunger – is a word that appears in the piece often, ten times, to be exact. Each time, it is used emphatically to denote the characters' deprivation past and present, and how it has had an affect on them. For instance, at the beginning of the play, Berganza tells Cipión that he had forgotten that he was a dog because hunger made him forgetful and shadowed his judgment: "Atended, que habéis perdido el juicio con tanta letanía y malandanza, y el hambre os volvió olvidadizo y nubló vuestro discernimiento [Pay attention. You have lost your mind with so much litany and misfortune, and hunger has made you forgetful and shadowed your understanding]" (Negro, "El coloquio" 4).

In this production, Berganza's account stresses his hardships and mentions how he experienced hunger to the point that, deceived by his master's evil servant, he ate a cat, thinking it was a rabbit:

> Una noche vino y tiró junto a mí un animal desollado: "Toma perrito bueno, come perrito bello, cómete este conejo y hagamos paces y trato." ... y comime el conejo entero dejando solo su pelleja. A la mañana siguiente, la negra dijo al amo que habíame encontrado arañando la puerta de la despensa, y al reprenderme, en un ataque de rabia, había matado al gato. Vi entonces la mi cena: ¡lo que de noche era conejo, de mañana gato era! ¡Maldita la trampa del hambre que te hace comer a ciegas! (Negro, "El coloquio" 13)

> She came one night and threw a dead animal next to me: "Here, good doggy. Eat, cute doggy, eat this rabbit and let's make amends" ... and I ate the whole rabbit, leaving only the skin. The next morning, the woman told our master that she found me scratching at the door of the pantry and that, as she reprehended me in a fit of anger, she killed the cat. I then realized what I had had for dinner. What had seemed like a rabbit at night was shown to be a cat by morning! Hunger is a damnable trap that makes you eat blindly!

Towards the end, hunger and sorrow become synonyms, and by overstating this distress, the play highlights a predominant topic in the picaresque novel:

> CIPIÓN: Que qué me pasa dice ... Ay, qué pena.
> BERGANZA: Querreis decir hambre. (Negro, "El coloquio" 21)

CIPIÓN: What ails me, he asks ... Oh, such sadness.
BERGANZA: You must mean hunger.

All of the situations where hunger is mentioned share an element of humour. In fact, they support the comic character of the piece. However, they also lend a gloomy undertone. As this last line reiterates, the grief that Cipión is referring to is caused by famine. Cipión only agrees to listen to Berganza's story in hope that he will get dinner in exchange. However, what he envisioned as a big feast is no more than a rotten grape, a cheese rind, spoiled wine, and bread:

> BERGANZA: Pues aquí viene. *(Abre un zurrón y saca una gran hogaza.)* Pan, hogaza más grande y crujiente no la hubiera visto un rey.
> CIPIÓN: *(Coge la hogaza contento y tras probar su dureza con su tranco se desalienta.)* Grande es, mas crujiente, ¡no hay quien le meta un diente, dura cual roca está!
> CIPIÓN: ... *(Deja el pan.)* Venga la fruta. Jugosa y fresca como del jardín del Edén salida. *(Saca Berganza un gran hatillo que desenvuelve... Sigue quitando trapos dejando el hatillo muy pequeño.)*
> BERGANZA: *(La muestra.)* ¡Una uva! Gigante y hermosa estaba cuando aquí la guardé ... mas parece haberse vuelto pasa ...
> CIPIÓN: ... ¡Una pistola! ¡Un arcabuz! ¡Que tengo de matalle! ¡Pues no me prometió cena y he cenado una pasa! (Negro, "El coloquio" 20–1)

> BERGANZA: Here it comes. *(He opens a bag and takes out a large loaf of bread.)* Bread, a loaf so large and crusty no king has ever seen.
> CIPIÓN: *(He takes the loaf with joy and is disappointed when he realizes how hard it is.)* It is large and crusty, but none can bite into it. It is as hard as a rock. ...
> CIPIÓN: ... *(He drops the bread.)* Bring me the fruit. Juicy and fresh as if it came from the garden of Eden. *(Berganza brings out a big bundle that he unfolds... Berganza keeps unfolding it, making the bundle smaller.)*
> BERGANZA: *(He shows it to him.)* A grape! It was beautiful and gigantic when I took it ... but now it seems it turned into a raisin. ...
> CIPIÓN: ... Give me a pistol! An arquebus! I have to kill him! Didn't he promise dinner? I have only eaten a raisin!

Although this scene is probably the funniest one of the play, owing to the dialogue exchange that ends up crushing Cipión's expectations, it also ends up showing the reality of the disfranchised "other," as mentioned above. Having both characters observe how the food is unwrapped and then discover it is no more than decayed fruit, cheese, wine, and bread constitutes a realistic depiction of their society. Cipión explicitly calls the meal the "dinner of the poor":

> CIPIÓN: Esta es la cena del pobre que todo el mundo ya sabe, sueña comer manjares y con mal vino se rehace ... Cuente vusted el final de la historia que no es culpa suya el desastre; tanta es el hambre que atraso que no hay ya quien la repare. Al menos dadme el real, que podré desayunar mañana ya que hoy ceno tan mal. (Negro, "El coloquio" 21)

> CIPIÓN: This is the dinner of the poor. As everyone knows, they dream of enjoying a big feast and need to settle for spoiled wine ... Keep telling me your story. This disaster is not your fault; my hunger is so strong that no one can take it away. Since I will not have dinner tonight, at least give me that coin so I can have breakfast tomorrow.

A feast for two individuals like them seems unattainable and exposes the harsh reality of their hunger and desolation. Even though in this play Cipión might resemble the "fraudulent beggars"[15] that, according to Cruz, roamed early modern Spain, in this characterization the disenfranchised are not demonized (21). Cipión is instead humanized and wins the empathy of the spectator with his charisma. The inequalities they suffer transcend the performance; they take the audience from moments of hysterical laughter to moments of reflection upon the bitter truths exposed in this scene.

The gloomy environment, however, contrasts with the intense comic exchange between the humanized dogs. It reveals a world that does not leave space for idealism and characters that are unable to change or elude their circumstances, even though they laugh and make the audience laugh. For Negro, this laughter

> es un acto de generosidad para con la vida, un acto espontáneo que muestra nuestra perplejidad en este inmenso universo y el gozo de estar vivo. La risa es empática. Cipión y Berganza pueden ser unos pobres miserables, pero ríen abiertamente, frivolizando sus penalidades. La empatía, en nuestra opinión, es uno de los pilares que sustentan esta delicada novela ejemplar cervantina. Los marginados siempre remueven nuestros corazones, nos vemos en su lugar, con sus pesares, y nos sentimos mal por su desgracia, confraternizamos, ese [es] el bello fondo de nuestra naturaleza. ("Re: Entrevista")

> is an act of generosity for our life, a spontaneous act that shows our perplexity in this immense universe and the joy of being alive. Laughter is

empathic. Cipión and Berganza might be poor, miserable individuals, but they laugh openly, making light of their hardship. Empathy, in our opinion, is one of the pillars that sustain this delicate Cervantine exemplary novel. The marginalized always move our hearts; we are able to see ourselves in their place, enduring their hardships, and we too feel bad for their misfortune. We can relate and that is the beautiful foundation of our nature.

Although these characters do not lose their sense of humour and make us laugh, they are unable to climb the social ladder. As Francisco Negro affirmed at a talk presented on 23 September 2016 at Ohio Wesleyan University, Berganza is a masked agent through which Cervantes can speak. Berganza's dog-like life resembles the author's life and his conversation with Cipión can be considered a dialectic on the art of writing. In an allegorical sense, according to Negro, the author enhances the story through satire and the strong irony of Berganza's reflections. However, Cervantes' work shows a radical realism in which there is little space for poetry and which shows a pessimistic view of existence and of morality. Cervantes ridicules humanity, not only by portraying the dogs as a more intelligent species but also by representing human nature as inferior (Negro, "Cervantes").

Although Berganza's clothing might signal his ability to hold on to some sort of privilege, he is unable to move up through a social and political system that benefits only the upper class. By turning these characters into humans with dog-like lives, this adaptation shows us voiceless individuals transported from the margins to the centre, a place society denied to them. The characterization of the dogs recaptures the voice of the oppressed and the forgotten. It exposes the prejudice many suffer. Their oppression does not allow them to be heard. Cipión begs on the streets for money but he is only heard by the other characters who are in a similar situation. They are not heard beyond the space they occupy personally; although we as the audience have their undivided attention, we are unable to cross the fourth wall in order to save them.

However, as suggested by Cervantes' text, our duty as an attentive audience is not to save the characters, but to build a social conscience and pave the way to critical thinking and social change. This starts happening when we recognize that what we see onstage is not far from what is happening in our society. The message, although pertaining to Cervantes' time, can be applied to the present day and the inequalities that still exist, making the story relevant for modern audiences. Cervantes paves the way for us in his social and political commentary, in pointing out social disparities. Poverty and hunger still exist. Many minorities are exploited and rendered invisible. The disadvantaged work in unsafe conditions and earn low wages. Cervantes' *coloquio* can be used as a discursive tool to promote social justice because it seeks to give voice to the voiceless and issues a call to action. It reminds us that social inequality transcends the stage and is part of our reality. It forces us to contend with issues of disparity, alienation, corruption, oppression, and dehumanization. Negro's adaptation is a unique call to arms, demonstrating that solidarity might be the key to addressing these inequalities.

Finally, in Francisco Negro's adaptation, oppression is manifested as economic and social inequality. The characters' dialogue explores their subjugation and their dehumanization, which persists. This dehumanization is perpetuated by the failure to provide for basic human needs, such as food and shelter. The types of systemic oppression that Cervantes experienced first-hand surface in these characters, who were not able to escape their realities. They do not show frustration or hostility as a result of their disadvantages. Deep down, they recognize the perpetuation of the institutionalized class system, but they are still portrayed as optimistic and their solidarity with one another leads the spectator to reflect on their hardships and to sympathize with them. In the end, it is understood that by transforming Cervantes' dogs into humans, a deeper message, already embedded in the seventeenth-century text, is exteriorized: that is, the need to share and to communicate is a primary existential need. Conferring the ability to speak to Berganza and Cipión gives them the ability to exist as human beings. Francisco Negro's adaptation thus reflects on the nature of humanity and while bringing the marginalized into a central space, not only onstage but also in our consciousness.

NOTES

1 Translation by Byc A. Jones.
2 I would like to thank Francisco Negro and Mayte Bona, owners of Morfeo Teatro, for their time and generosity in providing me with their scripts, videos, and an interview. I would also like to thank Felipe Santiago, actor in Morfeo Teatro, for kindly responding to questions about their production *La escuela de los vicios*. Their knowledge and experience have been extremely valuable for this chapter.
3 As explained by Ann E. Cudd in her book *Analyzing Oppression*, it was not until the beginning of the liberal movement and of the idea that "human beings are roughly morally equal" that oppression became an important topic in political philosophy (5).

4 In Spain, the municipalities administer public theatres. Therefore, public theatre contracts are managed by the government cultural agencies whose decisions could, at times, be politically motivated.
5 All English translations are mine unless otherwise noted.
6 The Gamonal is a province of Burgos; its population is mostly working class. As documented in numerous news articles, the conflict arose when the city council decided to spend 8 million euros on the construction of a boulevard. The residents of the Gamonal argued that the project was unnecessary and too expensive; it would also eliminate two-lane roads and reduce free parking space in the city. They pointed out that the province had other pressing needs, such as building housing for low-income people. There were many conflicts between police and protestors, and the city went through nights of repeated rioting. The protests spread to other Spanish cities, such as Madrid and Barcelona. The national uprising was known as the "efecto Gamonal [the Gamonal effect]." See the online article: "Gamonal: Ocho días que hicieron de Burgos el epicentro de la protesta ciudadana" (20 Minutos). This story was also featured in numerous national and international newspapers. I consulted the following online articles: "The Battle for Burgos" (Workers Solidarity Movement), "Spain Austerity: Spending Protest Grips City of Burgos" (BBC), "Burgos activists hunker down against construction project" (El País), and "Support for Burgos Rebels Spread to Other Spanish Cities" (El País). Complete bibliographical references are listed in the works cited.
7 This issue is well elaborated in an article entitled "The Battle for Burgos," published by the Workers Solidarity Movement. It explains that "Burgos may be, at first sight, an unlikely flashpoint for a Spanish-state wide uprising, but the long-standing problems underlying the local conflict have resonances with similar problems all over the country. The story behind the proposed development in Gamonal reveals a decades long problem of local shenanigans between corrupt developers and bought and paid for local politicians, that have ridden roughshod over the needs of urban residents and workers to the financial benefit of a tight inner circle and at the expense of local social services and laying waste to urban public space." Also, see the following online article: "Spain Austerity: Spending Protest Grips City of Burgos."
8 Felipe Santiago shared this information with me during a conversation in October of 2017.
9 See the review, "Morfeo convierte en teatro los discursos políticos de Quevedo," by I.L.H. and published in *El diario de Burgos*.
10 The figure of a man forced to live a dog's life is a well-known trope. One of the best-known twentieth-century literary examples can be found in Osvaldo Dragún's play *Historia del hombre que se convirtió en perro* (The Story of the Man Who Turned into a Dog), staged for the first time

in 1957. Dragún's work denounces injustices perpetuated by a repressive political system. The main character in this play is forced to work as a watchdog, the only line of work available to him. He ends up internalizing his role to the point of loosing his voice and ability to fully act and walk like a human. Like Morfeo's Berganza and Cipión, this man is a victim of systemic oppression; his story portrays issues of inequality, subjugation, and dehumanization still present in our societies.

11 Oppression, as Scholz describes it, is a "group phenomenon. It is as a member of a group that an individual becomes subject to oppression. The individuals within the oppressed group share some social identity that both identifies them as a group and serves in some way as justification for their unequal position in society" (*Political* 210).

12 In a talk given at Ohio Wesleyan University in September 2016, Francisco Negro explained that his characters' attire and characterization were, for the most part, inspired by Spanish painters. In this case, Cañizares was inspired by Goya and a character in a 1957 Japanese film (Negro, "Cervantes' *El coloquio*").

13 For a complete discussion on poverty and the picaresque, see Anne J. Cruz' *Discourses of Poverty: Social Reform and the Picaresque Novel in Early Modern Spain.*

14 Anne Cruz reminds us that "As Maravall makes clear, pícaros had little opportunity to enrich themselves or climb up the social ladder ... In their need to advance, he tells us, the pícaros could only resort to the appearance of wealth and the usurpation of a social status that guaranteed them the same leisurely lifestyle enjoyed by the indolent ... Although wealth had become the key to well-being across most social spheres, it also created a bind for those commoners and lower nobles who attempted to better their position through their acquired riches ... The climbers who, like the pícaros ... enjoyed a precarious success that lasted only until they were found out and rebuffed by the same social forces to which they aspired" (86).

15 When discussing relief for the poor and the status of the poor in early modern Spain, Cruz explains the differences, as perceived in this period, between the "true or legitimate poor" versus the "fraudulent beggars who were not physically incapacitated to work but would injure themselves to fake an incapacity (21).

9 *El Trato de Argel* and the Immigrant Crisis

MINA GARCÍA JORDÁN

During the celebrations of the fourth centenary of Cervantes' death the city of Madrid filled its streets with banners with quotes from the author that could speak to and connect with people in their everyday lives, waiting for the bus or walking the dog. One of those quotes, taken from *El Trato de Argel*, seems especially relevant in the face of the current immigration crisis: "la insufrible vida que padezco, de hambre, desnudez, cansancio y frío, determino morir antes huyendo, que vivir una vida tan mezquina [and the unbearable life I endure, with hunger, bareness, fatigue, and cold, I would rather die escaping than live such a miserable life]" (Cervantes III, 50–3).[1] These words echo the desperate situation of many immigrants today, who, in search of a better life, leave their places of origin and venture across their borders.

This is the premise of *Tratos*, a 2016 performance of the Cervantes' play by the Centro Dramático Nacional in which this connection was explored. Instead of the African jail where Cervantes was kept captive for five years, we are transported to a centre for undocumented immigrants in Spain, where the poor treatment of the newly arrived is brought to centre stage and immigration policies are questioned with every word. All of a sudden, a play from the sixteenth century becomes contemporary again, its claim for social justice more relevant than ever.[2]

In this chapter I will explore the way in which both versions make us think about individual responsibility towards social justice, especially in encounters with other cultures. Although the scenarios depicted in the plays reflect the nearly five-hundred-year distance between the two versions, I will argue that both of them, while making us confront the moral dilemmas that arise in the presence of the Other, advocate for political activism and raise awareness about other people's suffering.

In September 1575, Cervantes set sail on the galley *Sol* from Naples to Barcelona, with letters of commendation to the king from the Duke of Sessa. On the morning of 26 September, as the *Sol* approached the Catalan coast, it was attacked by Ottoman pirates and taken to Algiers, which had become the centre of corsair activity in the Mediterranean. Algiers was one of the most prosperous cities of the Ottoman Empire, largely owing to the revenues acquired by piracy; at times the city held as many as 25,000 captives (Fernandez 9). Cervantes was held in captivity between 1575 and 1580. After a long imprisonment in Algiers, and four unsuccessful escape attempts, he was ransomed by the Trinitarian friars and returned to his family in Madrid.

Cervantes wrote *El Trato de Argel*, also known as *Los Tratos de Argel*, around 1581–3, only a few years after his release from captivity. It is a testimony of his traumatic experience after years of being deprived of freedom and facing an uncertain future in a prison in North Africa. Ernesto Caballero, director of the 2016 adaptation, argued that this idea of confinement led him to explore the connections between the two plays and thus, when asked to make Cervantes' theatre relevant for today's spectators he answered, "Pensé en esta obra porque contaba la dura experiencia del cautiverio de los cristianos secuestrados por piratas berberiscos. También en las personas que, de la misma manera, son objeto de reclusión en nuestros días [I thought of this play because it told the harsh experience of the captivity of Christians kidnapped by Barbary pirates. Also of the people who, likewise, are confined nowadays]" (qtd. in López Rejas). This is the common point of departure of these two plays, presented centuries apart, that flow along similar lines but that also make the audience confront the unique challenges of their own times, challenges that are considerably different, as are the circumstances in which they came to light, as well as the political circumstances they reflect.

The similarities start in the name of the main characters: as in Cervantes' play, Aurelio, Silvia, and Saavedra, together with Ysuf, Zahara, and Fatima, complete the cast of the 2016 version. Another thirty-some characters join them in Cervantes' play, but despite the difference in number, both of the plays manage to create an intimate portrait of captivity in which the reality shared by many is told by one person at a time, without distractions, making each case unique and unbearable in its own right, increasingly amplified by the echo of many others.

This sense of oppression created by the accumulation of individual tragedies, told one after the other, is also conveyed by the sparse scenery used in both plays as a reflection of the emptiness that filled the lives of those who knew they had no control over their own future. The modern version uses a very empty stage where the metallic shine of the surfaces and the constant banging of metal on metal filled the space.

It only consisted of a catwalk with a landing on each side that housed opposing worlds, sometimes men vs. women, sometimes captors vs. captives, and always stressing a clear opposition between groups that were able to share the stage but never cross to the other side. In the words of Ernesto Caballero, this scenery was designed "para crear una brusca, violenta segmentación entre dos grupos humanos con el objetivo final de apelar a la necesidad de ponerse en el lugar del otro [to create a sharp, violent division between two human groups in order to ultimately appeal to the need to put oneself in the place of others]" (Agencia EFE). To this catwalk, Caballero adds a chair and a table, both metallic like the rest of the elements and like the prison bars that can be seen on both sides of the stage. All these objects make the stage look functional, cold, noisy, and above all, very impersonal, a place where nobody wants to stay and where these people find themselves because of adverse circumstances, which they hope will change very soon.

In Cervantes' case, the scenery is non-existent, that is, there are no references in the text to anything that was used onstage, making the words and the actions of the characters work that much harder to create a scenery that was just not there. I have to assume that it was not Cervantes' intention to reproduce the physicality of the bathhouses where he and his fellowmen from the galley *Sol* had been living since no attempt was made to describe their environment in the play.

Friedman refers to the *baños* as large corrals, sometimes with different floors where multiple captives would live.In them a hospital, a pharmacy, a chapel,[3] and other facilities could be found, creating a community where prisoners would not remain behind bars at all times, but rather were free to move about (60).[4] They would remain there until ransom was paid for their freedom, either by their families, if they were able to take care of the payment, or by either one of two religious orders, the Trinitarians or the Mercedarians, who had made it their mission to rescue as many Spanish captives as possible, using mainly donations for that purpose.

Cervantes designed a play that can be described as a collection of vignettes of the suffering of multiple captives, unrelated to one another, but that all together tell the complex story of the experience of the Christian slaves in Algiers. Among those captured at sea are two Spanish young lovers (Aurelio and Silvia), an Italian family (parents with several children), a Spanish soldier called Saavedra, and various slaves. In the first act, Aurelio laments his condition while his owner, Zahara, tries in vain to seduce him. Fatima, a servant, tries to intercede in the name of Zahara but is also unsuccessful. Other captives appear such as Saavedra, who addresses Philip II and urges him to liberate the

Spanish captives that remain in Algiers, chasing the pirates away with the armada that was being prepared. We also meet Leonardo, who has become the lover of his Moorish mistress, and Sebastián, who tells the news of a Morisco justly executed in Sargel, and that of a Valencian priest who had fallen victim of infidel brutality.

In the second act Ysuf, a Spanish renegade (a Christian who converted to Islam) and Aurelio's master, confesses his love for Silvia, a newly arrived slave who is also Aurelio's bride. From there we are transported to a slave market where a family with young children is torn apart, treated like animals, and sold to different bidders. The mother implores her children to remain strong in the Christian faith, as she fears she will never see them again. Ysuf insists on courting Silvia in vain. When Zahara is introduced to her new slave, Silvia, she finds out that she knows Aurelio. In desperation Zahara asks Silvia to help her seduce him, not knowing that they are a couple. Fatima, the servant, conjures up a demon to help Zahara in her pursuit. Unable to manipulate a stalwart Christian, the demon summons Necesidad and Ocasión (Need and Occasion) to steer Aurelio into Zahara's arms.

The two final acts show Aurelio's internal struggle when confronted with these two allegorical figures; the escape attempts of two slaves; the reunion of the two brothers sold in the market, now enemies after the conversion of one; and the final liberation of the young lovers by the king of Algiers, Hasan Pasha. In the final scene, a group of slaves prays to the Virgin Mary and thanks her for the arrival of a ship bringing ransom money from the friars to rescue multiple captives. The ending, however, is bittersweet because while many find freedom, many more are left behind, hopeless and forgotten.

This series of vignettes, loosely related to each other, paints a picture of some of the aspects of being a Christian captive in Algiers, a wound inflicted on the mind of the playwright himself, who lived in captivity, an experience that haunted him throughout his life and work (Garcés 3). These episodes are pieces of a complex mosaic that Cervantes used to convey the many facets of the tragedy he witnessed, turning the drama into a collective testimony, the sum of all that happened to him and around him. As Garcés explains: "As a fragmented text ... *El Trato* reflects both the breakdown of understanding and the literal reenactment of traumatic events. Entering into a dialogue between the individual and the collective, these fragmented scenes and discourses render a collective testimony of captivity in Algiers" (12). Therefore, although not every person suffered all the injustices described, the group presented in the play did, as a collective entity, as the representatives of the many anonymous captives that the audience never encountered (Stackhouse 14).

This is the same idea that moves the fragmentary structure of the 2016 version, presented as a series of scenes developed on the same space but with very obvious changes between them. These transitions normally involve changes in the placement of furniture done by the actors onstage who, by moving furniture while in complete silence, emphasize the sharp break with the preceding scene. In doing so, both plays make apparent the discontinuity and the fragmentary features of their experience in captivity, a place where one is not able to decide one's own future, where all control over one's own destiny is lost, and where even concepts of time and space are challenged. Captivity then becomes, be it in the Early Modern bathhouses in Algiers or in the current Spanish CIE (Centro de Internamiento de Extranjeros [Immigration Detention Centre]) a no-place with no time, a political and legal limbo, an unregulated parenthesis where arbitrariness and abuse become law.

> YUSUF: Así es. Tú te preguntas por qué estás aquí, cómo has llegado hasta este lugar, mejor dicho, a este no-lugar. A nadie le gusta estar aquí, a mí tampoco me ha quedado más remedio que aceptar este destino, también tengo que sacar a los míos adelante. (52)

> YUSUF: That's right. You wonder why you are here, how did you get here to this place, or rather, to this no-place. Nobody likes to be here, I don't have any other choice either. I have a family to feed.

In this place with no time and no space, we see in the characters in both plays a pervasive lack of individuality. Not only do the main characters share names, they have lost their identities. This point is made very clear in Caballero's play where the interns are identified by numbers and not by their names:

> ZAHARA: ¿Cómo te llamas?
> AURELIO: Aquí soy el 631 ...
> AURELIO: ¿Cómo se llama?
> ZAHARA: Zahara.
> AURELIO: 631.
> ZAHARA: Encantada (17, 20)

> ZAHARA: What is your name?
> AURELIO: Here I am 631...
> AURELIO: What is your name?
> ZAHARA: Zahara.
> AURELIO: 631.
> ZAHARA: Nice to meet you.

As we can see, Aurelio is not Aurelio; He is number 631. And Silvia is not Silvia. She is number 335, while Saavedra becomes number 202 in a world made of a long list of numbers that take over the humanity of the people left behind, that erase their identities and hide their lives, eliminating any connections with their past and their uniqueness (Campos).[5] But as Saavedra quickly points out, it is the personal responsibility of the intern, Aurelio in this case, not to lose himself in the system, to preserve his own identity and sense of self in spite of the number he was given, and to not let the bureaucracy get the best of him. "Si te tratan como un delincuente te conviertan en un delincuente [If they treat you like a criminal, they make you into a criminal]" (32), or in the words of the great Bob Marley, quoted in the 2016 play, "Nadie más que uno mismo puede liberar su mente de la esclavitud [None but ourselves can free our minds from slavery]" (32).

This obsession with being liberated from captivity drives both versions of the play, and the actions of all the characters, in the pursuit of freedom, are pushed to their limits. In the case of Cervantes' Aurelio, his quandary lies in the difficult decision he is confronted with: to choose between his loyalty to Silvia and his Catholic faith. This internal struggle is personified on stage by two allegorical figures, Necesidad and Ocasión (Need and Occasion), who display Aurelio's thought processes for others to see. They are visible only to the audience but they make his struggle take physical shape onstage. Aurelio nearly surrenders to Zahara's seduction and Ocasión appears when Ysuf is not at home. Aurelio is presented with a very difficult decision because he does not know how long his captivity will be and he can see an immediate chance to improve his living conditions.

Both Need and Occasion witness Aurelio's self-questioning of the possible consequences of his transgression against his faith and Silvia. They are witness to the degenerating effects of prolonged captivity and the need to remain vigilant against constant temptation. In the end, Aurelio chooses his faith and his bride, that is, his religion and his people, over his personal gain:

> AURELIO: ¡Cristiano soy, y [he] de vivir cristiano;
> y, aunque a términos tristes conducido,
> dádivas o promesa, astucia o arte,
> no harán que un punto de mi Dios me apar[te]! (III, 288–91)

> AURELIO: I am a Christian and I have to live like one; and even if I end up badly, gifts and promises, cleverness and tricks, are not going to push me away from God.

This inner dialogue is a symptom of the fragmentation that has taken place inside the character, struggling to make the right choice and above all, a choice that he can live with for the rest of his life.[6] But this fragmentation also allows for the possibility of choosing differently, a route that Cervantes explored in the character of Leonardo, who is in reality Aurelio's alter ego, the one who chose differently. In his case, he chose to be seduced by his mistress, thus improving his living conditions but compromising his loyalty to his country and his religion in the process.

This practice of using quasi-doubles, or characters that are paired but that differ in one crucial aspect, as we just saw in Aurelio-Leonardo, could be interpreted as Cervantes' way of presenting the lack of individuality that captives endured in Algiers. If in the 2016 version of the play the characters are assigned numbers, Cervantes designs pairs, emphasizing the fact that somebody else also finds himself in the same situation at all times, and therefore none of them is unique. Other pairs that can be found in the play are the two brothers sold in the market (one converts to Islam and the other remains Christian), the two captives that attempt to escape (with very different outcomes), and the other captive who asks for the king's mercy at the end. He is not as lucky as Aurelio and Silvia in obtaining the king's mercy. But maybe the easiest set of doubles to spot is Aurelio and Saavedra. Whereas Aurelio represents the figure of the captive confined to a private home, Saavedra, his double, belongs to the street in both versions; both characters inverted and complementary, often mirroring each other as on a distorted glass (Garcés 153).

But Cervantes' play goes even further in suggesting that living in captivity is actually not a way of living but of dying, a destiny worse than death itself. Since Christianity denounces suicide, this sense of hopelessness justifies all the irrational decisions to escape detailed in the play. Most of these attempts are futile, but they keep proliferating in the plot. For those living in captivity, these impossible attempts appear much more attractive than dying in captivity because at least, they allow for the agency of the captive; there is a chance to intervene in one's own destiny. In contrast, staying put, not doing anything, waiting for death seem like suffering impossible to bear, like being buried alive.
In this grim scenario, the survivor is the one who remains alive after his body and/or psyche has been forever altered by the introduction of death (Garcés 152).

This is where Aurelio and Leonardo finally differ, in the fact that they choose to go in opposite directions when faced with the same challenge, emphasizing the idea that it is not the circumstances that drive their decisions, since they were both placed in identical scenarios. It is the personal convictions and values that each holds dear that make them lean one way or another and determine their future with every choice, a message very much in line with the Catholic belief in free will. In any case, both men are lucky enough to have choices in the first place, and to be able to exercise their freedom when choosing so that, even in extreme situations, they both are given agency, a precious commodity while in captivity.

While they are trying to make captivity as bearable as possible, the captives in Algiers wait for an outside intervention, the only way to break the cycle and reintegrate them back into mainstream society. Therefore, although none of the characters in either play are criminals (neither the captives in Algiers nor the immigrants in the modern version) they find themselves trapped in the situations they are in, hoping for the intervention of others, or for a stroke of luck and, although both prospects are unlikely, the main characters in both plays manage to abandon their imprisonment in the end, a small victory that feels entirely unsatisfactory.

In an attempt to make sense of his own traumatic experience and to give the internal chaos some narrative structure, Cervantes turned to existing literary genres and conventions such as testimony. It is important to remember that both plays are based on direct testimonies, that is, either first-hand experience with tragedy, as in Cervantes' case, or on the direct testimony of immigrants who lived in detention centres, as in Caballero's case. They are as close as we can get to unfiltered accounts of what they witnessed or suffered in the first person and thus give voice to a situation that the audience knows about but that is largely removed from their everyday worries. Cervantes' traumatic experience is clearly more mentally unprocessed since it was written in the years right after the playwright's release; it feels raw, both in form and in content. In this play, the very first that he wrote, the act of writing and holding on to literary conventions provided him with a much-needed security blanket through which to express his personal fears and repressed feelings.

Cervantes turned to the conventions of martyrology narratives, here found in the play in the torture and death on the Valencian priest. To complete the picture, Cervantes adds the traditional elements of this genre, that is, the cruelty of the torturer, the resistance of the condemned in the face of pain, and, above all, the exultation of the Christian faith, a leitmotif that will dominate *El Trato de Argel* (Fernández 17). The resort to conventional genres allows Cervantes to channel his pain and the horror of his memories (an early modern form of post-traumatic stress disorder, or PTSD) into a frame of spiritual literature that offers religious comfort. As Fernández puts it, "*Los Tratos de Argel* es la cura de urgencia de memorias acuciantes que resulta en un mosaico que comparte con el discurso redentorista de la época, la vocación testimonial y muchas estrategias textuales, pero lo sobrepasa ampliamente [*Los Tratos de Argel* is the emergency cure to the pressing memories that result in a mosaic that shares with the redeeming discourse of the period the testimonial commitment and many more textual strategies, but that surpasses it widely]" (22).

Writing therefore becomes a safe place of expression where Cervantes could rely on genres such as testimony, martyrology, and hagiography to give him the structure he needed to process his experiences, much-needed therapy after surviving a harrowing ordeal. Examples of the religious elements he leaned on can be found in the scene of the tamed lion, based on the prophet Daniel's encounter; in the frequent references to bread and wine as spiritual nourishment; and the allusions to Oran as the promised land (Fernández 18).

All these elements served him well as a means to an end, that is, as ways of achieving his final objective. Time had come to release all those repressed feelings and to make the audience aware of the injustices that were being committed in the name of progress, to denounce the situation that has become the background of their lives and, more important, to intervene and call for change. In this encounter between witness and listener (the spectator), the theatre offers the perfect platform to give a voice to the anonymous captives of both worlds, to learn about their situations and fight for their rights. Therefore, the play, as least in Cervantes' case, serves a dual purpose: as therapy for the afflicted and as public denouncement of the situation of the captives, both of them pillars of testimonial literature. In any case, the staging of both dramas has made possible an encounter between the survivor and the listener, so that individual and collective testimony could take place and reach a large audience (Ohanna 120).

The call for political action takes slightly different directions in the two plays, and I will refer to their differences later in this chapter. Let me first address basic commonalities of the plays. Both express the need to assume personal responsibility for our actions, even in desperate situations, in the interests of human dignity and moral integrity. Both plays also teach the audience to treat others with respect and to put yourself in other people's shoes before judging their behaviour, inviting us to look kindly at the weaknesses of others, lessons that are relevant in any context.

But each play gets to these final lessons through very different paths. The first aspect in which they differ is the context in which they are set. Whereas Cervantes' play follows the difficulties of a group mainly composed of Spaniards wanting to leave Algiers, living in a foreign land and longing for home, the situation is diametrically opposite in

Caballero's play. In it, we get to know a small group of Africans (one from Cameroon, another from Guinea, and a third who only identifies himself as coming from a Third World country) who desperately want to stay in Spain and who understand living in Europe as a sign of progress. In this migration from Africa to Europe in the 2016 play we see Aurelio and Silvia, who overstay their visas and fail to have their paperwork renewed by the time they are arrested, and Saavedra, who jumps the fence in Melilla to cross into Spanish territory. To these scenarios we could add the thousands of people who attempt to cross through the Strait of Gibraltar every year, hoping to reach the beaches in southern Spain. All of these migrants have something very basic in common: their desire to find a future in Spain, and to not be sent back to their places of origin, where the political and financial situations are precariousAnd then there is the shame associated with the ones who left and were returned, the ones who failed to make it in Spain:

> AURELIO: Mi padre me decía que los emigrantes somos los cazadores modernos, que deben regresar con cosas buenas para su gente. ¿Qué cosas buenas para mi familia o para mi pueblo voy a conseguir aquí encerrado? No nos podemos quedar de brazos cruzados, algo hay que hacer. (36)

> AURELIO: My father used to tell me that the emigrants are the modern hunters, bringing back good things for their people. What good things can I get for my family or my people while I'm locked up in here? We can't sit back and do nothing. We need to do something.

Both plays, therefore, reflect a desperate situation, whether that of captives in Algiers or of immigrants trying to reach Europe. We see desperate measures like jumping the fence in Melilla, or attempting to escape from the bathhouses, mere glimpses of the grim reality behind these actions. For the protagonists, dying during an escape attempt is preferable to dying in prison and, likewise, risking deportation or even their own lives when trying to enter Spain seems like a better option than staying in their countries of origin or being sent back. In both cases, Spain is depicted as the Promised Land.

This is the background of Caballero's play, the struggle of Aurelio and Silvia to stay in Spain, where they have arrived hoping to earn a decent living. Aurelio, a professor of literature specializing in Cervantes, and Silvia, a former student of Aurelio's with a bachelor's degree in Spanish literature, try to renew their paperwork through the official channels. Owing to a number of random circumstances (the clerk assigned to their case is on maternity leave, no internet access on the day of their appointment, and so on) that delayed the process, they are arrested as undocumented immigrants and sent to the Immigration Detention Centre, where they are put in separate quarters for men and women. That is where Aurelio meets the streetwise Saavedra, who has been in those centres before as well as in prison, and who teaches the quixotic professor some valuable life lessons. We thus witness the same Cervantine characters struggling to survive in today's world, from captives of war to captives of the bureaucratic system, just as heartless and as arbitrary as the one Cervantes had to confront.

In the detention centre the story line is tripartite since the male and female detainees cannot interact with each other. To these two segments we have to add the interactions between the detention officers: Yusuf and Fatima, corresponding to the original characters. But if Yusuf was the master and Fatima was the servant in his house, in the 2016 version he is the director of the centre and she is his successor, who takes over his position after his retirement. The tension between those two characters is undeniable: a tired director reluctant to make changes vs. a new officer caught between her defence of the interns' human rights and the need to follow the rules and maintain her newly acquired position. In an ironic twist the woman who used sorcery and conjured up demons in the original play is now cast as the new director of a centre for undocumented immigrants, a context where she will also try to work her magic and strike the right balance between the opposing forces she encounters in her new job.

> FÁTIMA: Soy la primera que considera este modelo como un mal menor necesario, lo único que estoy planteando es que hagamos un esfuerzo por respetar los derechos humanos en la medida que se pueda. (42)

> FÁTIMA: I'm the first one who considers this model a lesser evil; the only thing I'm suggesting is that we make an effort to respect human rights as much as possible.

This is the intention she has when she takes the job. Soon she realizes that Aurelio is being beaten at night (with the unspoken suspicion that the beatings where orchestrated by Ysuf, the director of the centre, to teach him a lesson in humility), that Ysuf is also interested in Silvia, and that Zahara, the doctor for all the refugees in the centre, is willing to bend the rules to achieve social justice, which is nowhere to be found. She is the only one who takes a personal interest in the internees, who makes an effort to learn their names, who worries about their injuries, and who tries to help them with the few resources she has: acetaminophen and falsified reports. This loophole in the system was first opened by Ysuf to gain more time with Silvia and hopefully to have something she needed to thank him for.[7] By alleging that she had been the victim of sexual abuse, her case could be delayed and her chances of staying in Spain could increase exponentially. Zahara then adds to this allegation Aurelio's beating as a reason for both of them to be hospitalized and therefore not deported. This is when Zahara's well-intentioned plan meets with Fatima's opposition; she is not willing to lie openly, not even in the name of social justice.

In the final scene of the play, Cervantes himself appears on stage (bearing a very close resemblance to the retired director), wondering how the play ends. It is then that we learn that Fatima "forgot" to send the couple's deportation papers by the deadline; once they maxed out the days they could be in the centre, Silvia and Aurelio are released. As in the original, this liberation, which is the happy ending that the audience has been waiting for, feels somewhat bittersweet. Although the couple manages to find jobs in France, teaching Cervantes, they carry with them the guilt of those who made it out, leaving behind numerous inmates and a broken system, a bureaucratic jungle that keeps reproducing the same patterns of social injustice that they endured. Like Cervantes, they are filled with survivors' guilt.

One of the points where the two plays differ the most is the matter of agency, more precisely, who has agency and who does not, or rather, whose actions are the focus of attention: those of the captors or those of the captives. Regarding this point, the 2016 version revolves around the activities of the detention officers, their choices in how to treat the inmates, how they relate to each other, and how they relate to a culture other than their own, leaving the captives with little room for action. Under these circumstances, the only thing that Aurelio can do is complain about the social injustices that he has to live with, and the only response he gets in return is periodic beatings and the director's desire to rush his case to get rid of him as soon as possible. But he is not confronted with a dilemma he has to solve, a decision he has to make. In the modern Aurelio's case, the only choice is to be strong and survive his ordeal.

Cervantes' play instead focuses on the dilemma that the prisoners face. As opposed to the modern play where the agency is with the captors, and the captives appear only as the victims of their decisions, with no agency at all, Cervantes chooses to present in detail the struggles of those imprisoned. In order to do so he presents a game of double identities, alluded to above, that shows the effects of the different options that are available to the captives, that is, that allow room for choices to be made, and reinforce the presence of free will even in the most desperate situations.

This change in agency also presents the audience with a different reality to judge. In the 2016 play we, the audience, find ourselves questioning the injustices of the immigration policy in Spain and the way it is implemented, resulting in numerous forms of social injustice, but we never question the captives or their actions, since the agency does not lie with them. It is, therefore, the responsibility of the detention officers to provide humane treatment and to preserve the dignity of the inmates; it is their moral responsibility towards those in their care.

Very different, though, is the job of the audience in Cervantes' play where the agency lies with the captives. As a matter of fact, it is emphasized throughout the play that it is the individual responsibility of the captives to maintain their faith and their moral commitment towards their country, their people, and their religion, regardless of the difficult situations they have to endure. The double character motif, that is, the fragmentation of one person into two parallel characters, shows the audience examples of those who followed suit versus those who deviated from the high expectations inflicted upon the Christian captives in Algiers, who would be judged by the audience and in years to come.

Also unable to escape the scrutiny of history is Philip II of Spain (Filipo in the play), whom Saavedra addresses directly, asking for immediate military intervention:

> SAAVEDRA: Su gente es mucha, mas su fuerça es poca,
> desnuda, mal armada, que no tiene
> en su defensa fuerte muro o roca.
> Cada uno mira si tu armada viene,
> para dar a los pies el cargo y cura
> de conseruar la vida que sostiene.
> De la esquiua prision amarga y dura,
> adonde mueren quinçe mill christianos,
> tienes la llaue de su zerradura. (I, 429–37)

> SAAVEDRA: Their people are many, but their strength little, naked, badly armed, they don't have in their defence a strong wall or rock. Everyone keeps an eye on your armada and relies on their feet to save their own lives. You have the key of the lock where fifteen thousand Christian die in a hard, bitter, and distant prison.

This military help will never arrive. In fact, Aurelio and Silvia are liberated by the King of Algiers and not by their own, which speaks volumes about the situation of neglect that the captives in Algiers were enduring. But military intervention is only one aspect of the demands made by the play, the other being directed to the audience in their ability to contribute to the liberation of the captives in Algiers with donations:

> AURELIO: O, si de oy mas, en caridad deshechos
> se viesen los christianos corazones,
> y fuesen en el dar no tan estrechos,
> para sacar de grillos y prisiones
> al christiano catiuo, espeçialmente
> a los niños de flacas intençiones!
> Es esta sancta obra ansi exçelente,
> que en ella sola estan todas las obras
> que a cuerpo y alma tocan juntamente. (III, 361-9)

> AURELIO: O, if only more Christian hearts were overwhelmed by charity and were generous when giving to free from prison and shackles the Christian captives, especially the young ones, lacking in strong intentions! This holy act is excellent since it contains within all the deeds that join body and soul.

Cervantes, therefore, is not using his writing only to raise awareness about the slave trade that was taking place in the Mediterranean. He also had the interests of those who stayed behind in the forefront of his political agenda and was a strong advocate for the captives that were still in Algiers. In protesting the political situation that allowed this trade to take place his play had a role in achieving social justice for the captives.

But in both cases, regardless of whether they are the captives, in the one play, or the captors, in the other, the agency is always with the Spaniards/Christians. We go from Spaniards/Christians imprisoned in Africa to Africans imprisoned in Spain, from captives who desperately want to leave, to others who would do anything to stay, and yet, in spite of these reverse situations, the agency always remains with the Spaniards. What, then, is the role of the other culture? How is it regarded in the plays? What is the function of the other culture in these plays?

In this regard the answers could not be more diametrically opposed, reflecting the five-hundred-year distance between the two texts, the different political climate, and the advance of globalization.

In Cervantes' case we have to remember that the play was conceived to reflect two antagonistic worlds: Muslim Algiers and Spanish Christianity, with no common ground in between. Everything in Algiers appears evil and distorted in comparison to the reality the captives had left at home; love is contaminated by convenience, families are torn apart, couples are separated, and moral values are not respected. Human beings are sold in the market and a sorceress conjures up the devil at whim. Everything points to an immoral, evil land, where holding on to the Christian faith would be very difficult for the captured. Nevertheless, converting to Islam is presented as the worst possible outcome for the captives and there was even an epithet created for such people: "renegade," a word used to describe those who abandoned their faith in the pursuit of worldly gain. Those who have chosen this path are disdained by their relatives:

> FRANCISCO: ¡Abraçame, dulçe hermano!
> JUAN: ¿Hermano? ¿De quándo aca?
>   ¡Apartese el perro alla;
>   no me toque con la mano! (III, 328–31)

> FRANCISCO: Hug me, dear brother!
> JUAN: Brother? Since when? Go away, dog; don't touch my hand!

Conversion to Islam is therefore met with rejection and scorn; it is regarded as taking the easy way out, almost as committing spiritual suicide. In this light, then, we should not expect respect or appreciation for the Muslim religion or culture, or an effort to understand them, but rather a desire to be as far away as possible from a menace that endangered the future of Christianity.

In this context, the Muslim Other in Cervantes' play is presented to make explicit the danger that loomed over the Christian captives and to force a moral dilemma in the psyche of the captives with one goal in mind: to reinforce the redeeming values of Christianity (closely linked to Spanishness in the play) as the only force that guarantees salvation, as the only hope in such dire circumstances. This final message is crystallized in the final scene when some of the captives are about to be liberated and thank the Virgin Mary. The prayer shows the devotion to the most exalted and idealized woman in Christianity, but also emphasizes the final shift from the Other to the M(other) as the captives leave the land of the infidels (Garcés 162). Moreover, it also marks the end of the metaphoric absence of the mother (country) to which the captives are about to return.

The sociopolitical situation that is reflected in the 2016 version is very different. Unfortunately all kinds of barriers still exist between the two cultures, not only the physical one in Melilla that Saavedra jumped to get into Spain, but also the mental ones, which are harder to jump. Interestingly enough, skin colour is never mentioned as a barrier in Caballero's play, but being poor is presented as an insurmountable stigma:

> SAAVEDRA: ¿Y qué fue de mí?
> AURELIO: Te volvieron a encerrar. Si te sirve de consuelo, desde la cárcelconcibió la idea de escribir El Quijote.
> FÁTIMA: Saavedra, tu condena no está en tu apellido ni en el color de tu piel, sino en venir de la miseria ...
> SILVIA: Así es, pues el delito mayor del hombre es haber nacido ...
> TODOS: ... Pobre.
> CERVANTES: Dos linajes solo hay en el mundo, que son el tener y el no tener. (100–1)

> SAAVEDRA: ¿And what happened to me?
> AURELIO: You were locked up again. If it is any consolation, he thought of the idea for Don Quixote in jail.
> FÁTIMA: Saavedra, your sentence is not in your last name or in the colour of your skin, but in coming from poverty.
> SILVIA: So the biggest crime is to have been born ...
> ALL: ... Poor.
> CERVANTES: There are only two breeds in the world: the haves, and the have nots.[8]

Both plays then, in spite of the five hundred years that exist between them, recognize the privilege of the rich and the pain suffered by the poor, no matter their place of origin.

In the 2016 play, the call for action is, in my opinion, even more difficult since it does not depend on the action of one king. Saavedra argues that "El rey Filipo de ahora dice que un rey llega hasta donde llega [Today's King Philip says that a king can only do so much]" (101). What Caballero's play asks for is individuals to exercise their collective responsibility to social justice. He urges us to get out of our comfort zone and try to understand the plight of the immigrants, to put ourselves in their shoes and imagine their struggle, to respect their differences, and to treat them with the humanity they deserve. Caballero thus advocates for building international, interfaith, and intercultural relations with others, across socio-economic and racial lines. His play is therefore not only a reflection on past struggles but also a contemporary call for cultural openness, acceptance, and an invitation to treat others like we would like to be treated. In an era when politicians advocate travel bans from Muslim-majority countries and the building of border walls, our commitment to cross-cultural understanding and social justice is needed more than ever.

NOTES

1 All translations are mine.
2 For the sake of clarity, I will use *Tratos* when discussing the 2016 production and *El trato de Argel* when discussing Cervantes' play.
3 In general, the Christian faith was very much respected in the *baños*, and so were the clerics that were imprisoned. They were allowed to celebrate mass, Holy Week, and holy days. In fact the "the captives that were expected to command a good rescue price were not allowed to convert ... because they would lose the rescue price" (Friedman 89), since they would become free upon conversion.
4 From a figurative point of view, Cervantes associates the dungeon of Algiers with Dante's *Inferno*, where horrible torments were inflicted upon captive Christians. In that sense, *El Trato* draws a picture of the captivity in Algiers as a place close to the sufferings only expected in hell, a city represented in the play as an actual dungeon (Garcés 10–12).
5 Childers argues that "Spaniards ought to be more tolerant of newcomers because so many emigrated in search of work during the difficult years of the Franco regime" (168); he attributes this treatment to fear. "The belief is widespread that Spain has become more dangerous as a consequence of the new immigration, and the events on 11 March 2014 have only added to that perception. Thus the xenophobia Spaniards consciously disavow resurfaces in a growing feeling of insecurity, out of all proportion to any real increase in crime" (167).
6 This split of Aurelio's personality can also be seen in the opening scene of the play when he laments his situation and, dressed in rags, we feel pity for his misfortune, only to find out later that the actual reason for his grumbling is that his heart is imprisoned by Silvia's love (I, 29–32).
7 It is implied that Silvia had to surrender to Ysuf's request, as can be seen in the following exchange:

> SILVIA: La Ocasión y la Necesidad ... Cervantes también tuvo que ceder a los requerimientos de su carcelero, Dali Mali, para sobrevivir en Argel ...
> AURELIO: ¿Qué quieres decir con "también"?
> SILVIA: Eso mismo: también.
> AURELIO: Dejémoslo así.
> SILVIA: Sí, dejémoslo así.
> AURELIO: Fuimos fuertes, ¿verdad?
> SILVIA: Sí, fuimos fuertes. (95)
>
>> SILVIA: Need and Occasion ... Cervantes also had to give in to the requests of his warden, ali Mali, to survive in Algiers.

AURELIO: What do you mean "also"?
SILVIA: That: "also".
AURELIO: Just leave it.
SILVIA: Yes, we better leave it.
AURELIO: We were strong, weren't we?
SILVIA: Yes, we were strong.

8 This is a direct reference to *Don Quixote*, Part II, chapter 20.

10 Chirinos and Chanfalla Go to America: Social Justice in Adaptations of *El retablo de las maravillas*

CHARLES PATTERSON

Despite his best efforts, Cervantes never travelled to Spain's colonies in the New World. His play *El retablo de las maravillas* (The Stage of Wonders) makes no mention of the Americas, and its conflict is firmly rooted in Old World concerns about blood purity. The play's satirical critique of this early modern institution, however, has proven to be an irresistibly fertile model for twentieth-century adapters who have deployed Cervantes' interlude to address social justice issues in a New World context. I will analyse how the critique of unjust institutions evolves from Cervantes' version through two adaptations of it: Manuel Altolaguirre's *Las maravillas* (1958), which is set in colonial Mexico and the United States of the 1950s, and José Sanchis Sinisterra's *El retablo de Eldorado* (1985), which explores the theme of the Conquest.

According to David Miller, social justice "concerns the distribution of benefits and burdens throughout a society, as it results from the major social institutions" (22). Social justice theorists provide specific criteria for evaluating the justice or injustice of a social institution, which can be organized into five categories. The first is the guarantee of basic liberties. According to John Rawls, in a just institution "each person is to have an equal right to the most extensive basic liberty compatible with a similar liberty for others" (60). These guarantees include political liberties, such as freedom of expression, as well as personal liberties, such as freedom from arbitrary arrest. Basic liberties may not be abrogated for any reason, even to meet the second criterion (Rawls 61). The second is the distribution of benefits and offices. For Rawls, "social and economic inequalities are to be arranged so that they are both (a) reasonably expected to be to everyone's advantage, and (b) attached to positions and offices open to all" (60). The third is respect for just-making differences. In the arrangement of inequalities, a just institution must "respect some though not all differences," according to William K. Frankena (13). He writes that while "differences in capacities and needs" must be respected, "differences in blood or color ... are not just-making" (13–14). The fourth is the need for consistent and well-publicized rules. Participation in a just institution involves an understanding of its rules and trust that they will be applied consistently (Rawls 56). According to Rawls, there must be "a common basis for determining mutual expectations," which requires that everyone involved be familiar with the institution's rules (56). Finally, rules must lead to positive outcomes. For Rawls, an institution's rules not only need to be universally understood, but they also "should be set up so that men are led by their predominant interests to act in ways which further socially desirable ends" (57).

While there is no controversy in claiming that early modern Spain's blood purity laws were an unjust institution, or that Cervantes' *El retablo de las maravillas* is a critique of their injustice, the concepts that I have outlined up to this point provide a useful framework for specifying these claims. The institution of blood purity deprived New Christians of basic liberties and excluded them from offices of power on the sole basis of their ancestry, breaking the first three criteria of a just institution: guarantee of basic liberties, distribution of benefits and offices, and respect for just-making differences. The institution that enforced the blood purity statutes, the Inquisition, also failed to meet the requirements of justice. Its rules were neither consistently applied nor well-publicized, and they led to socially undesirable behaviour, such as the universal need for dissimulation, violating the fourth and fifth criteria of evaluating a just institution.

In *El retablo de las maravillas*, Cervantes critiques these injustices by having the tricksters Chirinos, Chanfalla, and Rabelín take advantage of them in order to swindle the town leaders with their fake puppet show. As Chanfalla tells them, "ninguno puede ver las cosas que en él se muestran, que tenga alguna raza de confeso, o no sea habido y procreado de sus padres de legítimo matrimonio [no one can see the things that are shown in it who has any New Christian ancestry, or who was not had and procreated by his parents in legitimate matrimony]" (162).[1] Chanfalla distributes the show's benefits based on ancestral privilege rather than capacity or needs, and therefore mirrors and parodies the broader institution of blood purity. The town leaders demonstrate that they are accustomed to such an unjust system by readily embracing this requirement and proclaiming their own fulfilment of it, as Juan Castrado declares, "Juan Castrado me llamo, hijo de Antón Castrado y de Juana Macha; y no digo más, en abono y seguro que podré ponerme cara a cara y a pie quedo delante del referido retablo [Juan Castrate I call myself, son of Antón Castrate and Juana Macha, and that is all I have to say in guarantee and pledge that I will be able to stand face-to-face and firm-footed before the aforementioned puppet show]" (166). For Castrado, his ancestry guarantees his share of the benefits.

Chirinos and Chanfalla's parody of blood purity further reveals it as an unjust institution in terms of its rules. As I explained above, for Rawls a just institution must have rules that apply consistently, but the *retablo* does not. For example, the last figure that appears is "la llamada Herodías [the so-called Herodias]" (177). The woman described is actually Salome, Herodia's daughter, but the two are conflated because, according to Cory Reed, in the biblical narrative Herodias is the actual enemy of John the Baptist, while Salome is merely doing her bidding ("Dirty Dancing" 9). As Salome dances, Benito Repollo asks, "pero, si ésta es jodía, ¿cómo vee estas maravillas? [but, if she is Jewish, how does she see these marvels?]," to which Chanfalla responds, "Todas las reglas tienen excepción, señor Alcalde [All rules have exceptions, Mr Mayor]" (178). The fact that some are exempt from the *retablo*'s requirements demonstrates that the rules are not consistently enforced. Similarly, the nobility in early modern Spain were usually exempted from the disadvantages of being New Christians (Castillo and Egginton 449).

Another characteristic of a just institution is that its rules "should be set up so that men are led by their predominant interests to act in ways which further socially desirable ends" (Rawls 57). The rules of the *retablo* do not comply with this criterion. For example, the Gobernador succumbs to dishonesty when he fails to see the figures in Chirinos and Chanfalla's show: "Basta, que todos ven lo que yo no veo; pero al fin habré de decir que lo veo, por la negra honrilla [Enough! Everyone sees what I do not see; but in the end I will have to say that I see it, because of my damn reputation]" (173). At the end, the *retablo*'s rules lead not only to dishonesty, but also to violence. The town leaders are so determined to prove their privileged status that they turn against the Furrier (Quartermaster) when he enters and fails to see the figures in the *retablo*. Responding to their accusation of "Dellos es, dellos el señor Furrier, dellos es [He's one of them, he's one of them, the Quartermaster is one of them]," the Furrier attacks them: "acuchíllase con todos [he swings his blade at all of them]" (181–2).

As these observations demonstrate, the criteria for a just institution provide a useful approach to explaining the injustices that Cervantes addresses in *El retablo de las maravillas*. Even though blood purity is fairly specific to early modern Spain, Cervantes' general method for critiquing it has proven useful for twentieth-century writers, who have adapted his work to address other injustices. One of these was Manuel Altolaguirre (1905–59), a poet of the Generation of 27 who, in his later career in cinema, wrote a script for a film adaptation of *El retablo de las maravillas* titled *Las maravillas* (1958).

Altolaguirre manifested an enthusiasm for Cervantes and other classical writers throughout his career. Like other members of the Generation of 27, he viewed Golden Age works as being tied to the present and future of Spain, and began adapting them as Republican propaganda pieces during the Spanish Civil War. He penned, for example, a now-lost play on the Germanías rebellion that included elements of Cervantes' *La Numancia* (Crispin 91; Torres Nebrija 351). During his postwar exile in Mexico, the classics provided Altolaguirre with a sense of connection to Spain, and he emphasized their continuity into the present. In his essay "En el campo de la poesía primitiva" he wrote, "En nuestro idioma no existe mejor fuente de inspiración que la de la poesía primitiva, tan clásica, tan romántica, tan moderna, a pesar de los años [In our language there does not exist a better source of inspiration than the primitive poetry, so classic, so romantic, so modern in spite of the years]" (275). Altolaguirre also viewed the classics as a link to the future. In "Nuestro teatro," he wrote, "Tenemos un gran teatro que conservar y un gran teatro por hacer [We have a great theatre to preserve and a great theatre left to make]" (211).

Given his sense of continuity with the Golden Age, it is unsurprising that a large part of Altolaguirre's film career was devoted to adapting works from that period. The first film he directed was a version of Tirso de Molina's *El condenado por desconfiado* in 1947 (Wheeler 76), and his last film, an adaptation of Fray Luis de León's *Cantar de los Cantares,* was featured at the San Sebastián Film Festival to rave reviews just before his death (Aranda 296). According to James Valender, editor of his complete works, Altolaguirre's personal papers include two lists of literary works that he planned to adapt to cinema, including several from the Golden Age (Altolaguirre 341–2). One project brought to partial fruition was his 1958 adaptation of Cervantes' *El retablo de las maravillas*. Titling it *Las maravillas*, Altolaguirre wrote an incomplete script for a theatrical performance, and a complete screenplay for a film version, which he never managed to produce (Valender 342–3). The screenplay contains three acts. The first is titled "El retablo de las maravillas," the second, "El telar de las maravillas" (The Loom of Wonders), and the third, "El filtro de las maravillas" (The Filter of Wonders). In each act, Altolaguirre adapts Cervantes' model in order to critique more contemporary injustices.

The first act is a fairly minimal adaptation of Cervantes' version. For the most part, there are only minor changes, such as adjustments to the language in order to make it more accessible for a twentieth-century audience and a reduction in the number of characters. There are two modifications, however, that are consequential in terms of adapting the work to the social justice concerns of the 1950s. First, the directions indicate that the *retablo* the tricksters carry is a movie screen (427). This reveals that, in spite of this act's sixteenth-century setting, the viewers are encouraged to think about its relevance to their own time.

This melding of past and present, characteristic of Altolaguirre's attitude towards the classics, explains the second major modification. Whereas in Cervantes' version those of illegitimate birth or *confeso* origin are excluded from seeing the figures, in Altolaguirre's, Chanfalla says the following: "que ninguno puede ver las cosas que en él se muestran que tenga alguna sangre judía, porque aquellos que desciendan de padres israelitas pueden despedirse de ver las cosas jamás vistas ni oídas de mi Retablo [no one can see the things shown in it that have any Jewish blood, because those who descend from Israelite parents can say goodbye to seeing the never seen nor heard things in my puppet show]" (429). Gone is the exclusion of illegitimate children, and Jews are explicitly mentioned instead of New Christians. On this first point, Gregorio Torres Nebrija posits, "Hay que suponer que, desde el nuevo ámbito en el que Altolaguirre pensaba ofrecer su adaptación, el tema de la ilegitimidad ... no tendría la fuerza de choque social que en 1615 [One must suppose that, in the new setting in which Altolaguirre planned to offer his adaptation, the theme of illegitimacy ... would not have the same power of social shock as in 1615]" (364). While it may be that illegitimacy would be somewhat less controversial in 1958 than in 1615, it was still more shocking and comprehensible to a twentieth-century audience than the complexities of early modern blood purity. My own view is that Altolaguirre eliminated the legitimacy requirement in order to focus on the issue of race. He further emphasizes this issue by changing "confeso" to "judío," converting it from a reference to early modern blood purity to a reference to more recent antisemitism, such as that experienced in Nazi Germany. It is an invitation to connect the sixteenth-century institution of blood purity to the twentieth-century institution of antisemitism and other forms of racism.

The second act, "El telar de las maravillas," is primarily an adaptation of Hans Christian Andersen's "The Emperor's New Clothes" set in eighteenth-century Mexico, but includes many elements from Cervantes' *El retablo de las maravillas*. For example, the tricksters are once again Chirinos, Chanfalla, and Rabelín, and many phrases echo ones from Cervantes' work. The con artists' victims this time are a vain and corrupt Viceroy and an adulterous Vicereine, for whom they promise to weave a cloth visible only to those who do not harbour any disloyalty to the king of Spain (442). The cloth is, of course, non-existent, but only an insurgent against the crown is willing to tell the truth about it.

In "El telar de las maravillas" the institution that Altolaguirre critiques is that of government corruption, particularly as it results in the unjust distribution of offices and benefits. One of the first indications of this critique is when the tricksters arrive and find the Viceroy out hunting while dressed in a "traje suntuoso [lavish suit]" (440). Chirinos remarks, "Imposible que con esos impedimentos pueda cobrar una sola pieza [It's impossible for him to make a single kill with those impediments]," to which Chanfalla replies, "No las cobra, sino las paga. Son sus cortesanos quienes derriban las perdices y conejos, aunque confiesen que es el Virrey quien acertó en el blanco [He doesn't make kills, he pays for them. It's his courtiers who knock down the partridges and rabbits, although they confess that it was the Viceroy who hit the mark]" (441). This example of the Viceroy receiving an unjust share of benefits (credit for shooting animals) without merit (hunting skills) is emblematic of his position as Viceroy, which he also does not deserve. For example, his vanity prevents him from governing effectively: "Tanto se viste que en lugar de reunir cada mañana su consejo de oidores, reúne cada mañana y cada tarde su junta de sastres [He dresses so ostentatiously that instead of meeting each morning with his council of ministers, he meets each morning and afternoon with his council of tailors]" (440). He is also corrupt, as seen when he decides to pay for the magic cloth using the king's gold:

> MINISTRO: Al fin y al cabo, el Rey de España no va a ser menos rico porque reciba una barra de oro más o menos.
> VIRREY: Ni se enterará.
> MINISTRO: Claro que no. Nuestra lealtad tiene sus limitaciones. (445)

> MINISTER: In the end, the king of Spain is not going to be less wealthy because he receives one bar of gold more or less.
> VICEROY: He will never even know.
> MINISTER: Of course not. Our loyalty has its limitations.

The reason he has his position in spite of his vanity and corruption has nothing to do with deserts or needs, but simply because his wife slept with the king, as implied in her declaration: "Mi conducta fue siempre de la más apasionada sumisión [My conduct was always most passionately submissive]" (444).

While Act I touches on the issue of race as an unjust form of differentiation, and Act II on the unjust distribution of offices and benefits within a corrupt colonial system, Act III, titled "El filtro de las maravillas," takes place in the United States of the 1950s, and takes on the institutions of consumerism, racism, and McCarthyism. This time, the perennial tricksters, Chirinos, Chanfalla, and Rabelín, arrive in a dry county selling a magic filter that they claim can turn water to whiskey. Excluded from being able to taste that whiskey are "aquellos que están afiliados a organizaciones de las llamadas progresistas [those who are affiliated with so-called progressive organizations]" (452). When they present this new product to the Governor and the Sheriff, the former invites them to bring it to the wedding party of the latter's daughter, where they both hope to use it to identify political enemies. After a number of individuals claim to be able to taste the whiskey, an African-American dentist and a priest both tell the truth about the beverage: it is only water.

Although this act is not a direct adaptation of either Cervantes' *El retablo de las maravillas* or of Andersen's "The Emperor's New Clothes," it nevertheless mirrors closely Cervantes' critique of an unjust institution. In this case, that institution is McCarthyism instead of blood purity, as indicated in Chanfalla's introduction to the authorities: "Yo, señores, soy Montiel, el representante que anuncia y vende el Filtro de las Maravillas. He sabido de la existencia de una comisión investigadora del Senado y vengo a prestarles mis servicios [I, good sirs, am Montiel, the representative who announces and sells the Filter of Wonders. I have heard of the existence of a Senate investigative committee and have come to offer them my services]" (452). As explained above, for Rawls a just institution's rules must be universally understood, consistently applied, and lead to socially desirable behaviour. In the following examples, the screenplay demonstrates that McCarthyism fails these requirements.

In the first example, based on the dialogue between Teresa and Juana in Cervantes' version, Teresa informs Martita, the bride, of the requirements for tasting the filter's whiskey:

TERESA: sólo pueden beberlo aquellas personas que no sean lo que tú eres.
MARTITA: ¿Y qué es lo que soy?
TERESA: ¡Quién sabe! (455)

TERESA: the only ones who can drink it are those who are not what you are.
MARTITA: And what is it that I am?
TERESA: Who knows!

The filter, therefore, is representative of McCarthyism: it is not universally understood what constitutes a crime. It also, like Cervantes' *retablo*, encourages dishonesty, a socially undesirable behaviour, as when Teresa communicates to Martita the Sheriff's wishes: "que, cuando tragues el agua, digas que es un whisky riquísimo. No quiere que quedes mal ante todo el mundo [that, when you swallow the water, you will say that it is a most delicious whiskey. He does not want you to look bad in front of everyone]," to which Martita replies, "Descuida. Si no es más que eso, estoy dispuesta a fingirme borracha [Don't worry. If that's all there is to it, I'm willing to pretend to be drunk]" (456).

This dialogue also reveals that, for Altolaguirre, in this context "progressivism" is simply a derogatory epithet applied to social justice in order to demonize it. In answer to Martita's question "¿Y qué es lo que soy? [And what is it that I am?]," Teresa replies, "Lo cierto es que has invitado al señor Persting. Y el doctor Persting es un negro. Y sólo una persona progresista, dice tu padre, puede invitar a un negro a sus fiestas [The fact is you have invited Mr Persting. And Dr Persting is a black man. And only a progressive person, according to your father, can invite a black man to his parties]" (455). Martita then points out the injustice of differentiation based on race: "El doctor Persting es mi dentista y es mi amigo, sea negro o sea rojo ... Gracias a él tengo esta sonrisa y gracias a esta sonrisa voy a casarme. Hasta que me arregló el doctor Persting mi dentadura, no encontré novio. Cómo no lo iba a invitar [Dr Persting is my dentist and he is my friend, regardless of whether he's black or red ... Thanks to him I have this smile and thanks to this smile I am going to get married. Until Dr Persting fixed my teeth, I couldn't find a boyfriend. How could I not invite him?]" (456). In response to an unjust, race-based distribution of benefits (in this case, a wedding invitation), she emphasizes a distribution based on deserts: Persting had earned his invitation by fixing her teeth.

In another example, when the Governor learns that the requirement for tasting the whiskey is not having progressive ideas, he also does not know if he qualifies: "¿Qué clase de ideas son esas? Debo confesarle que en mis compañas políticas, antes de las elecciones, me han llamado muchas veces progresista, pero de eso a que yo lo sea ... ¿Cree que gustaré de ese whisky? [What kind of ideas are those? I must confess that during my political campaigns, before the elections, they called me many times a progressive, but as to whether I really am one ... Do you think I will taste that whiskey?]" (454). Once again, this dialogue points to the injustice of an institution whose rules are not universally known. To answer his question, Chirinos shows him a drawing depicting rich people eating at an expensive restaurant, while the poor watch from outside. When she asks him to identify the good and the bad people in the picture, the Governor replies: "A ver. A ver. La cosa no es muy complicada. Los buenos son los que están dentro, disfrutando del producto de los beneficios obtenidos con el honrado trabajo. Y los malos son los de afuera, los vagos, los maleantes, los envidiosos [Let's see. Let's see. This is not very complicated. The good guys are the ones who are inside, enjoying the product of the benefits obtained through honest work. And the bad guys are the ones outside, the lazy, thuggish, jealous ones]" (455). This answer satisfies the requirement, so Chirinos replies, "No tenga usted la menor duda de que beberá del buen whisky [Don't doubt in the slightest that you will drink the good whiskey]" (455). While in Cervantes' version the Governor must pretend to see figures that do not exist, here the Governor forces a just interpretation of an unjust situation. He assumes that the beggars outside of the restaurant deserve their poverty in some way, and so to exclude them from the distribution of benefits is just. The ironic manner in which Altolaguirre depicts this attitude prompts the viewer to consider the myriad other factors besides lack of merit that could explain their situation, such as unjust institutions, like racism and the class system, which have prevented them from benefiting from capitalism in an equitable manner.

The act continues with a series of characters who pass similar ideological tests, until first Dr Persting, and then a priest, declare the beverage to be water. Through the priest's condemnation of those going along with the filter scam, Altolaguirre sums up his criticism of American society for having abandoned the principles of social justice. After referring to "las tradiciones liberales de este gran país [the liberal traditions of this great country]," he declares: "Muy peligrosas son esas borracheras, amigos, porque no son causadas por ningún espíritu, ni siquiera por el espíritu del vino, sino que son el efecto y la consecuencia de una mentira engendradora del miedo y de las peores *injusticias* [Those intoxications are very dangerous, my friends, because they are not caused by any spirit, not even by the spirit of wine, but are the effect and consequence of a lie that engenders fear and the worst *injustices*]" (463, italics mine).

Another twentieth-century playwright who has adapted *El retablo de las maravillas* to address social justice issues is the Valencian playwright and director José Sanchis Sinisterra (1940–present). His version of *El retablo de las maravillas*, titled *El retablo de Eldorado* (1985), does not take place in a modern setting like Altolaguirre's, but rather in sixteenth-century Spain. It is, however, like *Las maravillas*, a critique of an unjust institution set against an American backdrop – in this case, the Conquest.

Sanchis is one of the most prolific and celebrated Spanish theatre professionals alive today. He has been active since the 1960s as a playwright, director, and theorist, and is best known for his play ¡*Ay, Carmela!*, the film version of which won thirteen Goya awards, including best picture, in 1990. Although conceived of and performed as a stand-alone work, *El retablo de Eldorado* forms part of Sanchis' *Trilogía Americana* (American Trilogy), which also includes *Lope de Aguirre, traidor* (Lope de Aguirre, Traitor, 1992) and *Naufragios de Álvar Núñez* (The Shipwreck of Álvar Núñez, 1992). This trilogy is a reflection of two of Sanchis' main intellectual and artistic interests: Latin America – particularly the history of the Conquest – and Hispanic Golden Age theatre.

Manuel Aznar Soler estimates that Sanchis is the most performed Spanish playwright in Latin America (393). By all appearances, the affinity is mutual. The playwright describes three reasons for his connection with Latin America: 1) his uncle was part of the Republican exodus to Mexico after the Civil War; 2) he views the various leftist political movements in Cuba, Chile, and Nicaragua as "modelos de transformación política [models of political transformation]," and 3) he has a long-standing fascination with the chronicles of the Conquest, which he says reveal to him "ese choque traumático de culturas, esa terrible y miope relación con lo otro [that traumatic clash of cultures, that terrible and myopic relationship with the Other]" (Serrano 18). It is not just the clash of cultures that fascinates Sanchis, however, but also the cultural hybridity that it produced. According to Aznar Soler, the Americas represent for the playwright "la conciencia de la diversidad [the awareness of diversity]" (395).[2]

In addition to his avid reading of the chronicles of the Conquest, Sanchis also has a fascination with Golden Age literature in general, and particularly theatre. In one of his essays, titled "La condición marginal del teatro en el Siglo de Oro" (The Marginal Condition of Theatre in the Golden Age), he questions the notion that the *comedia* served the interests of the powerful, arguing that it was instead "una poderosa máquina de transgresión que socava todo el poderoso edificio de la sociedad monárquico-feudal-eclesiástica que aspira a detener los flujos de la historia y de la libido durante nuestro brillante Siglo de Oro [a powerful machine of transgression that undermines the powerful edifice of the monarchical-feudal-ecclesiastical society that aspires to stop the flows of history and libido during our brilliant Golden Age]" (87). This admiration for the classics does not lead Sanchis to consider them sacrosanct, however. In "Sobre la revisión crítica de los clásicos" he advocates for

> una revisión de nuestros clásicos a partir de un criterio dialéctico. El teatro por el teatro, como el arte por el arte, no tiene nada que hacer en un mundo de exigencias inmediatas y urgentes, y, muy especialmente, nuestra sociedad necesita una seria revisión de todas sus creaciones ideológicas desde la perspectiva enriquecedora de una sociología objetiva. (64)

a revision of our classics starting from a dialectic criterion. Theatre for the sake of theatre, like art for the sake of art, has no role to play in a world of immediate and urgent demands, and, most especially, our society needs a serious revision of all its ideological creations from the enriching perspective of an objective sociology.

One classical work that Sanchis has revised is, of course, *El retablo de las maravillas*. His version, *El retablo de Eldorado*, is based primarily on Cervantes' version, but also incorporates, in an intertextual tour de force, abundant materials from other early modern Spanish and colonial works, many of which he credits in the play's acknowledgments (253). This interweaving of early modern texts into his own writing is emblematic of Sanchis' effort to universalize the issues of social justice in the work – for him, they are not dependent on time or place. While his version focuses on the period of the Conquest, it also invites the audience to connect its themes to the present.[3] For example, the opening stage directions establish that the play takes place in the sixteenth century, but, as in Altolaguirre's version, this setting is ambiguous:

> Lugar: Del texto se deduce que la acción podría transcurrir en una lonja abandonada, a las afueras de un pueblo tal vez andaluz ... Pero también podría emerger de las tinieblas de un escenario.
> Tiempo: Algunos de los personajes creen existir en los últimos años del siglo XVI ... Pero también hay quienes sospechan – como el público – que el único tiempo real es el *ahora* de la representación. (252; italics in original)

> Place: From the text it is deduced that the action could occur in an abandoned market, in the outskirts of a possibly Andalusian town ... But it could also emerge from the darkness of a stage.
> Time: Some of the characters believe that they exist in the last years of the sixteenth century ... But there are also some who suspect – like the public – that the only real time is the *now* of the performance.

This ambiguity of time and place encourages the audience to think about the main character's conflict between official discourse and lived experience as applicable to a broader context than the period of the Conquest alone.

El retablo de Eldorado, subtitled *Tragientremés en dos partes*,[4] takes place sometime after the action of *El retablo de las maravillas*, and features, like *Las maravillas*, the continuing antics of the tricksters Chirinos and Chanfalla, but not Rabelín. They have entered into a partnership with a veteran conquistador named Rodrigo de Contreras and an Aztec woman called Sombra in order to raise funds for an expedition to find the mythical city of Eldorado. Their plan is to make money by putting on a play depicting Rodrigo's exploits in the New World. Finding themselves in a town where most of the inhabitants are attending an *auto-de-fé,* and therefore will not be there to watch their play, Chirinos and Chanfalla hire a group of ruffians to pose as town leaders in order to trick the visually impaired Rodrigo into rehearsing. Although this play-within-a-play is meant to depict the glorious aspects of the Conquest, Rodrigo continuously interjects reminders of its brutalities and injustices, and reveals that his objective in seeking Eldorado is to bring healing and redemption to the New World. When he realizes the futility of this quixotic quest, he commits suicide.

El retablo de Eldorado depicts, primarily in the figure of Rodrigo, both the official discourse regarding the Conquest and the subversion of that discourse. On the one hand, Rodrigo has from a young age been steeped in an official discourse that justifies the Conquest as necessary for the good of the Native peoples of the Americas. For example, in the play-within-the-play depicting the life of Rodrigo, a thief (played by Chanfalla) approaches the young Rodrigo (played by Chirinos) and encourages him to go to the New World, saying, "Que como aquellos naturales no conocen al verdadero Dios y Señor, están en grandísimos pecados de idolatría y perpetua conversación con el diablo [Since those Natives do not know the true God and Lord, they are in the most grievous sins of idolatry and perpetual conversation with the Devil]" (314). From this official perspective, it is permissible to suspend the basic liberties of the indigenous people because of their religion. This is, of course, a violation of the first criterion for just institutions, which asserts there is never any justification for suspending basic liberties, as well of as the third criterion, which requires respect for religious difference. Rodrigo appears to embrace this official discourse promoting an unjust, anti-indigenous view. For example, he and the tricksters also include in their play-within-the-play Fray Tomás Ortiz's sermon justifying the enslavement of the indigenous peoples (324).

Rodrigo generally seems unaware of the injustices inherent in the official discourse, even as his own words ironically subvert it. For example, after a mention in the play-within-the-play of the Native sex slaves that the conquistadors took advantage of, Rodrigo interrupts to say,

> Sólo a los capitanes. (*Chanfalla le mira, sorprendido.*) Las indias, digo, que sólo a los capitanes se daban, y a algunos caballeros. Que nosotros, los meros soldados, por muy contentos nos teníamos si podíamos haber

alguna niña o vieja o, cuando no, mujer ya muy parida. (*Se va indignando.*) Y ello a las prisas, con los calzones puestos, y aun con las armaduras, a las veces al trote de una marcha o en el respiro de una escaramuza. (336)

Only to the captains. (*Chanfalla looks at him, surprised.*) The Indian women, I mean, were only given to the captains, and to a few nobles. But we, the grunt soldiers, considered ourselves very fortunate if we could have some girl or old woman or, otherwise, a woman who had given birth multiple times. (*He grows indignant.*) And even that was in a rush, with our underwear, and even our armour, still on, and sometimes on the march or during a break between skirmishes.

The irony consists in the fact that Rodrigo views himself as a victim of the violation of the second criterion – that the unequal distribution of benefits (in this case, indigenous women) is only justifiable if it benefits everyone – while completely ignoring his own far more egregious violation of the first criterion: the indigenous women involved have lost the basic liberty of control over their own bodies.

As another example of Rodrigo's failure to perceive an unjust situation, in a conversation between himself and Chanfalla before the start of the play-within-the-play, Rodrigo describes the acceptance of homosexuals among the Amerindians. The dialogue continues:

CHANFALLA: (*Indignado.*) ¡Malditos sodomitas! ¡Debieran matarlos a todos y ensartarlos por las agallas, como sardinas en lercha!
RODRIGO: En cierto lugar echamos a los perros hasta cincuenta de estos putos que encontramos, y luego los quemamos, informados primero de su abominable y sucio pecado. Y cuando se supo por la comarca esta victoria y justicia, nos traían muchos hombres de sodomía para que los matásemos y tenernos así contentos.
CHANFALLA: Ahí se echa de ver los grandes beneficios que trae consigo cristianizar a esos bellacos. (295)

CHANFALLA: (*Indignantly*) Damn sodomites! They ought to kill them all and string them up by the gills, like sardines on a stringer!
RODRIGO: In a certain place we threw to the dogs about fifty of these fags that we found, and then we burned them, having been informed first of their abominable and dirty sin. And when this victory and justice became known throughout the region, they brought us many men of sodomy for us to kill, thus keeping us happy.
CHANFALLA: So we see the great benefits that come from Christianizing those scoundrels.

The irony of Chanfalla's words is clear to Sanchis' twentieth-century audience: the Conquest has brought no benefit whatsoever to these fifty victims, and has introduced a socially unjust element to a culture previously tolerant of sexual minorities.

In spite of his embrace of the official discourse, however, Rodrigo's lived experience has led him to also espouse attitudes that undermine that discourse. For example, the dialogue cited above about the slaughter of homosexuals continues:

> RODRIGO: No todo son beneficios ...
> CHANFALLA: ¿Qué dice vuestra merced?
> RODRIGO: No, nada. Sino que, algunas veces, por la demasiada devoción con que se los quiere cristianar, quedan las almas algo dañadas (295)

> RODRIGO: It's not all benefits ...
> CHANFALLA: What's that you say?
> RODRIGO: No, nothing. Just that, sometimes, because of the excessive devotion with which we try to Christianize them, the souls end up somewhat damaged.

In almost the same breath in which Rodrigo seems to deny the humanity of the Native peoples, he also recognizes that humanity. This contradictory attitude is reflected in his surname ("de Contreras"). According to Sprinceana: "The particle 'de Contreras' in his last name, intended to indicate his place of origin, refers to a person who speaks contrary to his acts or vice versa. This inconsistency is present from the first moment he appears on stage to the last moment of his life, when he commits suicide against the will of his shadow (Sombra)" (61). In Rodrigo's own words: "Has de saber, Chirinos, que no hay verdad sin dos caras y dos bocas, amargas las unas, dulces las otras [You should know, Chirinos, that there is no truth without two faces and two mouths, one bitter, the other sweet]" (276–7). He is able to see the injustices of the Conquest, usually ignored by the official discourse, because he has witnessed them personally: "Yo he visto con mis ojos multitudes de hombres perdidos y estragados, muy peores que fieras sin entrañas, cometer mil traiciones y maldades en aquel vastísimo y Nuevo Mundo de las Indias [I have seen with my own eyes multitudes of lost and ruined men, much worse than heartless beasts, commit a thousand treasons and evil deeds in that vast and New World of the Indies]" (275).

Another aspect of his lived experience is his relationship with Sombra, the Aztec woman who has accompanied him to Spain. He is particularly defensive of her humanity. For example, when Chanfalla is unable to pronounce her real name, Ahuaquiticlan Cuicatototl, he sarcastically asks, "¿Qué importa su nombre? [What does her name matter?]," to which Rodrigo responds, "Importa tanto como el tuyo [It matters as much as yours] (296). He reinforces the idea that, at least in her case, race is not a just-making difference when he responds to Chanfalla's question as to whether Sombra is his concubine by angrily replying, "¿Y por qué no mi esposa sacramentada? ¿Acaso por ser india no puede ser tan buena cristiana como tú y como Chirinos? [And why not my lawful wedded wife? Just because she is an Indian, can she not be as good a Christian as you or Chirinos?]" (297).

This tendency to defend Sombra's humanity, and his awareness of the injustices resulting from the Conquest, are Rodrigo's motivation for finding Eldorado. He sees this mythical treasure city as the solution to the inequalities in the New World, as communicated in a song about it included in the play-within-a-play: "allí solo hay señores, / nadie es criado [there are only masters there, / no one is a servant]" (307). At one point, he reveals the scars on Sombra's back and says to his imaginary audience, "De tantas violencias que en aquellas gentes y tierras se han hecho y se hacen, vuestras mercedes serán, yo mediante y esta mi gran jornada, los nuevos redentores [Of the much violence that has been and is being done upon those peoples and lands, you will be, through me and my great expedition, the new redeemers]" (345). Later, when asked what he will do with the riches of Eldorado, he confirms this purpose: "¿Qué he de hacer, sino enmendar este Nuevo Mundo de la desolación que el Viejo le ha causado? [What else will I do, but rectify in the New World the desolation that the Old has caused it?]" (352).

The play-within-the-play ends when Chanfalla and Chirinos flee from the Inquisition officials. Rodrigo, after realizing his play has not accomplished its objective and that his quixotic quest to find Eldorado will be impossible, decides to commit suicide. His death signals the futility of hoping for a deus ex machina solution to the injustices inflicted upon the peoples of the New World, which he expresses to Sombra by exclaiming, "¡Tus dioses y los míos nos han abandonado! [Your gods and mine have abandoned us!]" (357).

The analysis of these three works reveals an evolution in the way the authors approach unjust institutions and the fictions that uphold them. Cervantes' *El retablo de las maravillas* parodies blood purity's unjust rules in the nonsensical requirements set forth by Chirinos and Chanfalla for viewing a puppet show. The three acts of Altolaguirre's *Las maravillas*, by transposing Chirinos and Chanfalla to different times and places in the Americas, demonstrate the universality of injustice and its supporting fictions. In each act, by choosing to see something non-existent, Chirinos and Chanfalla's victims call attention to a similar tendency to see injustice as justice. Sanchis not only builds upon Altolaguirre's efforts to universalize the theme by centring his version on the Conquest but also dramatizes the internal tension produced when discourse comes in conflict with lived experience. Rodrigo simultaneously embodies Cervantes' villagers, who choose to believe in fictions that justify unjust institutions, and the Furrier, whose personal observations compel him to bear witness to a different reality. Just as in Cervantes' play the tension between the villagers and the Furrier ends in violence, in Sanchis' work it ends in suicide, revealing the inherent incompatibility of these two versions of justice.

NOTES

1 All translations are my own.
2 Sanchis' interest in Latin America coincides with Spain's opening to that region. In 1977, the same year that the playwright began work on *El retablo de Eldorado*, Spain's transitional government, with support from across the political spectrum, re-established relations with Mexico (Tusell 256).
3 Sanchis describes this intention, saying, "Un espectáculo, una obra, no es una emisión unilateral de signos ... sino un proceso interactivo ... en el que el texto propone unas estructuras indeterminas de significado y el lector rellena esas estructuras indeterminadas [A performance, a play, is not a unilateral emission of signs ... but rather an interactive process ... in which the text proposes some indeterminate structures of meaning and the reader fills those indeterminate structures] ("Por una dramaturgia" 67).
4 "Tragientremés" is a neologism that combines "tragedia" (tragedy) with "entremés" (interlude).

11 Social Networks, Social Justice, and the People's Right to the Golden Age Canon: The SGAE or the *Comedia* Villain of the Digital Age?

ELENA GARCÍA MARTÍN

Fuente Obejuna[1] and Zalamea are two of a handful of rural localities that have developed amateur theatre festivals entirely undertaken by the residents and dedicated to the presentation of classical dramas set on location. After more than twenty years of celebrations in some cases, these initiatives recently found themselves at the centre of a virulent financial controversy, generated by the SGAE (General Society of Spanish Authors), concerning the people's rights to the canon. According to authorities in these localities, the SGAE had claimed astronomical copyright fees (30 and 24 thousand euros respectively) for works of classical authors in the public domain. The SGAE claimed that the fees were in fact extracted for the work of the modern adapters who had been involved in making the texts more accessible to contemporary audiences unfamiliar with early modern Spanish language and performance codes.

While the SGAE, which controls copyrights laws in Spain, attempted to tax the meagre earnings which help to make possible these rural festivals run by volunteers and unpaid actors, the local communities joined in protest against what they perceived as oppressive forms of authority that mirrored those of the historic plays they re-enacted. In an attempt to unravel some of the issues involved, I briefly review contemporary copyright and intellectual property laws and examine the power of media and social networks to question ethics and organize against unfair practices. The investigation aims to unveil the extent to which the socio-economic present of these communities remains interwoven with their historic and literary past. But, more specifically, I emphasize the particular significance for rural communities of the dynamics that link cultural and economic capital.

Local municipal initiatives of rural development have had much success establishing touring theatre projects among small, otherwise non-touristy, communities. The main project to this day, called "Teatro pueblo a pueblo [theatre, one village at a time]," attempts to increase tourism, lend cultural visibility to the festivals, and strengthen resistance against the copyright tax. The impact of these rural communities on the national conversation on the classical canon hinges on a twofold process that shapes local identities through the construction of place in site-specific theatre. The process encompasses a shift in the structure and distribution of cultural and economic capital, and the influence of social networks and the media on the social fabric and structures of knowledge within these communities.

It is hard to overestimate the importance of the classical dramatic canon for communities such as Zalamea and Fuente Obejuna, where site-specific plays have had the power to turn place into a source of cultural, economic, and symbolic capital. These are communities whose cultural recognition and self-perception have been altered through their presence and participation onstage and their subsequent involvement in the historical dialectics of the Golden Age.

Despite the national and global popularity of dramas such as Calderon's *El alcalde de Zalamea* and Lope de Vega's *Fuenteovejuna*, it was not until the SGAE controversy caught the eye of the media that these remote and isolated towns, which often up till then existed in the popular imaginary as mere literary creations, gained visibility and recognition. Thus, for the localities involved, these Golden Age festivals represent a process of resistance against spatial erasure and a positive creation of place. The history plays have become, for the residents of Zalamea and Fuente Obejuna, essential to the construction of a geographically centred politics of identity that inserts rural participants into national historical narratives reconstituting place as a form of symbolic capital.[2] Given the importance of the dramatic canon as a form of institutional cultural capital, objectified by national education and legitimized by entities such as the Real academia de la lengua and the Teatro clásico nacional, its symbolic value to the towns, now placed at the centre of this tradition, comes as no surprise.[3]

As performers of the theatrical tradition, the residents of Zalamea and Fuente Obejuna become endowed with embodied cultural capital, understood as "long-lasting dispositions of the mind and body" (Bourdieu 242). The significance of these theatrical productions derives, in part, from their cultural inclusivity:[4] both annual productions, Zalamea's and Fuente Obejuna's, are undertaken entirely by the residents. Over six hundred actors from all age groups, including many shepherds, farmers, and construction workers, participate in each locality annually. It is estimated that more than 20 per cent of the residents of these small towns have been onstage, and that more than half the population of each town has participated over the years on- or offstage (Agencia EFE, "Zalamea"). These texts have been appropriated by the residents as cultural capital that has been incorporated into their everyday lives, and are thus invested with economic as well as symbolic value.

In Fuente Obejuna, thanks to popular initiatives, an association has been created for the preservation of the cultural patrimony of the town, the reading of Lope's drama has now replaced recitals of *El Quijote* in the annual "day of the book," and *Fuenteovejuna* has been newly established as required reading in local high schools (Martín Fernández). Even children playing around town are known to recite the classical text they consider part of the local patrimony. An actor from Fuente Obejuna recognized that "la gente no viene hasta aquí para ver a profesionales, para eso van a Madrid. Vienen por el sentimiento; nadie puede sentir esta obra como nosotros la sentimos nada más que con leerla en un libro [people do not come here to see us act professionally, they can go to Madrid for that. They come for the feeling; nobody can feel this play the way we do just from reading it in a book]" (qtd. in Delgado Llano). The director of *El alcalde* also points out that their performances differ from those of professional productions:

> Todo un espectáculo, una acertada fórmula que convierte una obra clásica e inmortal en un plato para todos los gustos, no solo para minorías selectas. Todo un pueblo sobre el escenario convertido en improvisados actores dando vida a un momento de su historia ... Todo un pueblo, donde niños, jóvenes, adultos y ancianos, recitan como algo usual, todos y cada uno de los versos de *El alcalde de Zalamea*. Todo un pueblo, que cada verano ocupa sus horas de ocio en convertirse en Pedro Crespo, Chispa, Isabel, Rebolledo, don Lope, Juan, don Mendo, Nuño, etc. en aprender esgrima, verso, dicción, o a subir y bajar de un caballo con destreza y naturalidad. (Albuisech, *El alcalde*)

> It is a great spectacle, a successful formula that turns a classic and immortal play into everybody's cup of tea, not just a production for select minorities. A whole village onstage, turned into improvised actors who bring to life a moment of their history ... It is about a whole town where children, adolescents, adults, and elders routinely recite verses from *El alcalde*; a whole town that each summer takes its leisure time to become Pedro Crespo, Chispa, Isabel, etc., to learn fencing, recitation, diction, or to mount and dismount a horse with grace and skill.

The 2003 performance playbill includes claims of the residents' mastery of the text and of the continuity and reinforcement of practices (textual and performative) that have become part of the local tradition.

Following Bourdieu's distinction among forms of capital, the statement can also be read as a claim that, through the time investment and habitus that transform "the external wealth into an integral part of the person," the residents can be said to have become endowed with embodied cultural capital (Bourdieu 43). Bourdieu draws further distinctions:

> It should not be forgotten that [cultural capital] exists as symbolically and materially active, effective capital only insofar as it is appropriated by agents and implemented and invested as a weapon and a stake in the struggles which go on in the fields of cultural production (the artistic field, the scientific field, etc.) and, beyond them, in the field of the social classes – struggles in which the agents wield strengths and obtain profits proportionate to their mastery of this objectified capital, and therefore to the extent of their embodied capital. (245)

The struggles and tensions related to the Golden Age theatrical patrimony have been key in the national conversation about cultural heritage and production. Spanish contemporary culture seems intent on revisiting its colonial past, defining literary heritage, and introducing a retrospective cultural calendar in the popular imaginary. We only need to look at a few examples of recent government-funded celebrations: the last 1992 World Expo, the 2005 and 2015 four hundredth anniversaries of both parts of *El Quijote*, the four hundredth anniversary of the publication of Lope de Vega's *El arte nuevo de hacer comedias en este tiempo*, and the establishment of theatre festivals, tourist routes, and municipal festivities commemorating key figures of the Aurean tradition. Though this phenomenon is far from new, given the pervasive presence of Golden Age drama in schools, theatres, and the press of Republican and early Francoist Spain, this legacy has only recently acquired the quality of an energetic and profitable industry. While these plays have been inscribed with a number of divergent ideological and aesthetic goals, particularly in the first part of the twentieth century,[5] it is no less important that the plays today not only remain culturally contested but continue to be appropriated to articulate and dispute unresolved tensions involving local autonomy and collective rights. Moreover, these plays, which feature the rape of rural maidens by powerful military authority figures and result in peasant revolts, have served to document political violence and, on occasion, have functioned as justification for popular rebellion. While these early modern *comedias* continue to be an important component of the national literary canon and of the repertoire in major venues and theatre circuits, their contribution to rural cultural heritages is particularly significant.[6]

As seen above, Spanish early modern plays set in specific rural communities, such as Fuente Obejuna and Zalamea, have had an undeniable cultural impact on the lives of the local communities that have adopted them, and their contribution to economic development has been considerable. The precarious economies of these rural towns have resulted in dwindling populations, a trend directly related to the displacement of the rural economies by service economies and by high unemployment.[7] However, thanks to modest ticket prices, 12 euros and 8 euros respectively in 2016, performances in each locality have consistently sold out since the 1990s. Fuente Obejuna's municipal page boasts a total of more than 10,000 visitors each year the festival has been held since 1992. In 2014 the mayor of Zalamea, Francisco Paredes, estimated that since 1994 productions of plays by Calderón had brought to the municipality more than 170,000 spectators (Agencia EFE, "Zalamea"). Yet, owing to the magnitude of the productions, which require annual budgets of over 150,000 euros,[8] the main profit does not come from the box office, as ticket sales do not suffice to cover basic costs. In fact, the municipality of Fuente Obejuna has occasionally been forced to cancel the annual festivals owing to prohibitive costs. Since 1992 municipal authorities have been able to fund them on only eight occasions.[9] The mayor of Fuente Obejuna, Isabel Cabezas, attempts to schedule a theatre cycle every three years in order to make it economically feasible.[10] Nonetheless, she recognizes that the productions bring to the town forms of economic development that are not easily quantifiable: "'una vez que se pone todo en movimiento pasan por Fuente Obejuna miles de personas, tanto de España como del extranjero,' afirma la alcaldesa. 'Los alojamientos rurales, el hotel municipal y las casas de alquiler cuelgan el cartel de completos y los empresarios tienen la oportunidad de obtener importantes beneficios,' señala Cabezas [once everything is in place thousands, Spanish as well as foreigners, come through Fuente Obejuna. Rural lodgings, hotels, and rental properties alike switch on the 'no vacancy' signs, and commerce profits greatly]" (Cantador 7). Though the mayors of both towns recognize that the productions themselves result in budget deficits, they acknowledge that the annual theatre productions undeniably contribute to strengthening the local economies. In the case of Zalamea, the mayor, Francisco Paredes, speaking at the 2014 conference Olmedo Clásico, said that not only is the Golden Age festival a cultural resource, it has generated about forty regular jobs and has contributed to the travel industry by adding three hundred hotel rooms to its infrastructure, a clear testimony to the increase in tourism (Agencia EFE, "Zalamea").

The effects of site-specific productions of Golden Age theatre have been significant in terms of reappropriation of tradition, the consolidation of place, and the subsequent gains in embodied and symbolic capitals; their impact on economic growth through the promotion of heritage industries and cultural tourism has also been significant. Particularly in this case, economic capital hinges upon the recognition, valorization, and transmission of cultural capital. In other words, the SGAE controversy has brought attention to the invisibility and cultural marginalization of these regional festivals and the interdependence of cultural and economic capital in rural communties. For these reasons, it is vital to look beyond economic factors and examine the role of new modes of cultural diffusion in the digital age.

The media, social networks, and what Manuel Castells terms "space of flows"[11] have played key roles in the public controversy and have generated new spaces of resistance. In what follows, I re-examine key dramatic works of Golden Age Spain within the context of the digital age and review them as tactics of popular resistance against unfair copyright taxation by the rural communities who claim the texts as their rightful cultural inheritance. Up until 2009, these rural performances were almost exclusively addressed to local or provincial audiences. Yet, the attention these productions have gathered since the 2009 copyright incidents with the SGAE reignited familiar patterns of resistance against rural repression. The messages of defiance against what the locals construe as institutional exploitation, messages which rapidly spread over the digital media, affected both the communities' self-perception and their visibility. These actions contributed to a unique dynamic in the social identity of the residents by signalling shifts, however subtle, in the perception of place, community, and textual and cultural heritage. As performance scholar Diana Taylor observes:

> Spectacles ... function as the locus and mechanism of communal identity, the "imaginings" that constitute social systems. They reflect and (re)produce the spatial configurations of the imagined community, establishing both the parameters and organizational structures. (73)

In effect, the theatrical spectacles, which have incorporated banners, additional texts, and demonstrations in protest to the new taxes, are at the centre of a virulent media controversy that cannot easily be unravelled. The SGAE continues to demand copyright fees for works by early modern authors, authors whose works are considered under European law to be in the public domain. However, the SGAE states that these works are "adaptations" by contemporary authors, who must be paid. The municipal authorities of Fuente Obejuna argue that the productions faithfully preserve the original text and merely insert tableaus, props, and musical numbers that reframe the action. However, the mayor of Zalamea does admit to using adapted texts. Although the two festivals approach the original texts differently, both have similar objectives and structure: neither is intended as a money-making venture, but as a meaningful form of social interaction and shared cultural production. In fact, the actors insist that they receive no compensation and that, far from profiting from the performances, they suffer an economic burden since they donate their time, not only as actors but also as electricians, carpenters, painters, sound engineers, and administrators. Some have gone as far as to pay for tickets out of their own pockets to give to friends and acquaintances to encourage attendance.[12]

Despite the decidedly non-profit nature of these enterprises the result is identical for both towns, who are burdened by fees that threaten to make their productions unviable. According to the councils of Zalamea de la Serena and Fuente Obejuna, in 2009 the SGAE claimed 24,000 and 30,000 euros respectively to represent the classic Spanish dramas *El alcalde de Zalamea* and *Fuenteovejuna*. In both cases, the SGAE insisted that the exorbitant fees were a result of the town's failure to pay for related cultural activities since 1998. Headlines in the local, regional, and national press continued to tarnish the public image of the SGAE, which was regularly referred to as "inquisidores [inquisitors]," (Bensusan), "pirateria moderna (modern piracy]," (Blogger Atreides), "enemigos del pueblo [public enemies]," (Luis-Orueta), and as the new *Comendador*.[13] Despite the media frenzy and the number of blogs expressing popular indignation, payment (by instalment) of the bills was exacted by the SGAE (Agencia EFE, "La SGAE").

The consequences of the stormy events were, however, somewhat surprising. On the one hand the media, which regularly took sides in the controversy and consistently pointed to victims and villains in the conflict, continues to succeed in exposing irregularities and in damaging the public image of the SGAE. On the other hand, despite the catastrophic financial consequences of the scandal for the rural communities of Zalamea and Fuente Obejuna, who were penalized with fees that far surpassed their meagre profits, the residents and municipal representatives received the whirlwind of attention with a mixture of pride and exhilaration, which reframed the controversy as an opportunity rather than a loss. Arguably, the symbolic value added to their cultural capital, by gaining national attention and recognition, surpassed by far any economic adversity. The local reaction to the controversy reframes what is at stake for the residents: the economic penalty extracted by the SGAE had the unintended consequence of promoting the towns culturally.

To complicate things, the unpopularity of the SGAE reached its peak on 1 July 2011, not long after the towns had settled their accounts, and despite the fact that the mayors of Fuente Obejuna and Zalamea continued to organize their appeal. That day, the headquarters of SGAE in Madrid was raided and eight of its members, including the president, Teddy Bautista, were arrested on embezzlement charges.[14] The investigation committee reported irregularities from 1997 to 2011 and estimated that as much as 87 million euros were embezzled by members of the SGAE in this period.

When examining these events from a purely economic angle, it is not difficult to identify the root causes of the public outrage, and to draw comparisons to the scenes they were performing onstage. Both *Fuenteovejuna* and *El alalde de Zalamea* feature the historic residents sustaining losses and paying tributes to unfair and abusive masters (Ynduráin). The fact that material loss is presented in *Fuenteovejuna* as a reason for revolt is particularly poignant here. In the words of Juan Rojo, a peasant featured in the play:

> Si nuestras desventuras se compasan,
> para perder las vidas, ¿qué aguardamos?
> Las casas y las viñas nos abrasan,
> ¡tiranos son! ¡A la venganza vamos! (III, 1708–11)

> If our misfortunes be compounded, what do we await to give away our lives? They burn our houses and vineyards; they are tyrants! Let us go avenge ourselves!

El alcalde de Zalamea presents similar arguments against economic abuse perpetrated by military troops that pillage and raid fields and crops. Domingo Ynduráin best explains the economic burden on the medieval peasantry portrayed in these plays:

> En la Península, como en tantos otros lugares, la riqueza fundamental es la que proporciona la agricultura; y son los agricultores quienes pagan los impuestos con que la corona hace frente a sus necesidades; no hace falta recordar que los nobles no trabajan directamente en actividades productivas y que, en cualquier caso, nobles, hidalgos y religiosos no pagan pechos a la real hacienda. El aumento de las guerras interiores y exteriores, el desarrollo de los gastos suntuarios de la corte y otros factores provocan, por una parte, que muchos campesinos sean enrolados a la fuerza o con engaños ... y que, por otra, los pocos que quedan trabajando las tierras, realizando un trabajo productivo, vean cómo los impuestos aumentan de forma desmesurada. Ambos factores hacen que el campo quede despoblado.

In the Iberian Peninsula, like in so many other places, the main resource was agriculture; and the farmers themselves were supporting the crown by paying levies; needless to say, the nobility never produced anything from their work and, in any case, the aristocracy, nobility, and religious sectors did not pay taxes to the crown. The increase in domestic and international conflicts, the onerous court expenses, and other factors caused many peasants to be overcome by force or through fraud ... and burdened those few who worked the land with exorbitant and ever-increasing taxes. Both factors resulted in the abandonment of the fields.

Thus, both *Fuenteovejuna* and *El alcalde de Zalamea* give accurate portrayals of the abusive circumstances that rural areas regularly faced, mirroring, in part, the contemporary situations of Fuente Obejuna and Zalamea. Today's rural youth migrate to the cities in search of employment – rather than seeking patronage or enlisting in the military as in the time of the plays – and those remaining see their cultural labour, which they donate to the theatre festivals without pay, unduly taxed. The parallels have not escaped the locals; in Fuente Obejuna, for example, they refer to the SGAE as the new "Comendador" and residents pledge to fight, like the characters in their play, "Todos a una [all for one and one for all]" (R.V.A.). Zalameans, for their part, find new meaning in Calderón's lines, alluding to the president of the SGAE: "al Rey la hacienda y la vida se han de dar [To the crown we are obliged to give life and state]" (Haba), implying a resistance towards the dominance exerted by the SGAE and its leaders. The distancing effect of these lines, now pronounced onstage to conflate past and present figures of tributary authority, is not unlike that of the defamiliarizing moments of the epic theatre. The rupture of the fourth wall when the king becomes the SGAE succeeds in stirring contemporary audiences, audiences who continually encounter the analogy in the media, in local signage, and in social networks. In effect, the early modern texts have become part of the legitimizing discourse that aids locals in articulating contemporary resistance, both to centralized taxation and to cultural invisibility.

The iteration of these famous lines, which are now part of the popular discourse, reveals the power of citationality as a gesture of resistance. As Butler theorizes, the true impact of citationality as a gesture derives from the distance to the original context:

> Benjamin concludes that epic theater, which narrates deeds and engages in explicit commentary, is quotable, even marked and defined by its quotability. A character is constantly breaking out of the context of the play to speak didactically. But also, characters lift utterances from their functional purpose, and display them in quotable form. The citational dimension of

speech arrests its effectivity. The where and when of a quotation is always, to some extent, lost when it emerges for the purpose of display; when the citation stands apart from its function, the everyday context is suspended, backgrounded, even lost, and so the quotation becomes a gesture, that is, a truncated form of action that has lost the context for its intelligibility. (182)

Gesture, understood here as movement, kinetic intervention, and moments of embodied knowledge that reproduce and potentially interrupt structures of power, becomes particularly pertinent to the actors of Fuente Obejuna. The gesture of the nearly three hundred local actors who lit torches and displayed a protest banner after each performance may be read as a form of intervention that draws effectivity from the citational dimension of the traditional canon to draw attention to the new context: "Somos más de 5.000 habitantes = somos más de 5.000 autores. Fuente Obejuna, todos a una [We are more than 5,000 residents = we are more than 5,000 authors. Fuente Obejuna, all for one and one for all]" (R.V.A.).

The renewed call for unity as a form of resistance becomes at the same time a call for shared authorship of a canonical text, one that represents the past and which renders the people of Fuente Obejuna absolute protagonists and makers of their own history. Since the adapter of the script, Fernando Rojas, had formally renounced any fees attached to the copyright, the residents refused to accept the charges. The SGAE claimed that the amount was partly due to related cultural undertakings and former editions of the performance. The banner stated Fuente Obejuna's position clearly (R.V.A.). Through this gesture, cultural heritage had become a site for contesting the socio-economic present of these rural localities.

Given the economic underpinnings of this controversy, it would not be a stretch to frame it in terms of social justice as explained in a 2006 UN document entitled *Social Justice in an Open World: The Role of the United Nations*:

> The concept first surfaced in Western thought and political language in the wake of the industrial revolution and the parallel development of the socialist doctrine. It emerged as an expression of protest against what was perceived as the capitalist exploitation of labour and as a focal point for the development of measures to improve the human condition. It was born as a revolutionary slogan embodying the ideals of progress and fraternity.

While this definition contextualizes social justice as a form of resistance against exploitation, one relevant to the local actors and participants who offer their labour pro bono, it opens the debate as to the compensation of other types of labour: that of the artists who produce the cultural capital produced and consumed in the festivals. Thus, the controversy can be reframed to consider the types of labour under consideration here and their respective contribution to "the ideals of progress and fraternity."

The SGAE, barely able to cope with constant scandals, attacks, and mismanagement, has been unable to communicate successfully to the public the full import of the copyright laws. In fact, the SGAE managed to worsen its image by repeatedly exacting unpopular fees from disadvantaged collectives. The SGAE did not have far to fall in the public eye, embroiled as it was in a number of controversies, one of which was charging several amateur groups for the use of texts: high school students, disabled actors, and Saharawi immigrants, among others (Luis-Orueta). None of these fees were seen to promote ideals of progress or community.

Still, this controversy partially hinges on what Manuel Castells, a sociologist of information technologies, terms "horizontal communication," a dimension of autonomous expression of social meaning in the digital age that depends on communication among people through information systems, such as blogs, that are independent of the traditional media and nearly impossible to control vertically. This horizontal communication can expose corruption and unveil useful information; it can also distract public attention and divulge erroneous or malicious data. In the particular case under examination, the residents, aided by a sympathetic press, were able to question the copyright laws on popular theatre and create a web of protest, which continued for years after the fees had been settled and paid for. This resulted in obvious benefits to the festivals in the form of publicity.[15] The effects of this type of horizontal communication on governments and institutions such as the SGAE are undeniable, considering that the control of information is a fundamental source of power (Castells, "Grassrooting" 366). Once SGAE was construed as a "public enemy" in the popular imaginary, there was no official or press communication that could erase the damage done to its reputation. In fact, the controversy quickly received national and even global coverage, reaching the cultural section of the digital version of the BBC in 2009 and 2010, in accounts of Fuente Obejuna's rebellion and, later, the eventual liquidation of the town's debt with the SGAE (Redacción BBC Mundo, "Fuente Obejuna paga," "Fuente Obejuna se rebela").

The legal profession, in its eagerness to contain the damage and correct possible misinformation, published documents and academic articles exonerating the SGAE and blaming the scandal on the weakness of the press and the alarming reach of social networks. Carlos Rogel Vide and colleagues, in a manuscript entitled "En torno a la reforma de la Ley de Propiedad Intelectual," laments the scandal and attributes its magnitude to the tendency of the public to sensationalize and to the maliciousness of those who took advantage of the incident to promote political agendas:

> Centrándonos en el plano nacional – sólo en parte, porque las redes sociales todo lo internacionalizan – además de las críticas razonables, desaforadas o desmedidas entre la sociedad española y las redes sociales, los medios de comunicación han dedicado mucho espacio en la última década a escrutar, defender algunas veces, y a criticar ferozmente, otras, la labor de las entidades de gestión, su pobre imagen social y su falta de éxito en la concienciación social de los derechos de autor o, en el peor de los casos, sus desavenencias internas (nota 2: Junto a numerosas portadas ... contra los pueblos donde se representan por los propios vecinos de Fuenteobejuna, Zalamea u Olmedo los clásicos del siglo de oro situados en estas localidades, noticias que excitan una indignación descriptible, un sector de la prensa ha tomado en los últimos años una actitud militante en su contra, por la presunta alienación de la mayor entidad o de algunas de ellas con la izquierda o, en concreto con el partido socialista). (35)

If we focus on the national level – and we can only partially do so, since everything is internationalized once exposed in social networks – besides the reasonable and unreasonable criticism generated by Spanish society and social networks, we have the media to blame for the tarnished image [of the SGAE]: indeed, in the last decade they have dedicated much attention to scrutinizing the institution, sometimes to criticize it ferociously, sometimes to defend it, but mostly to comment on its internal disagreements, on its poor public image and on its incapacity to educate the public about copyright (footnote 2: much can be explained by the numerous headlines against the SGAE ... regarding the towns where site-specific Golden Age classics are represented by the residents, news that has provoked general public indignation. Then, there is the added factor of a sector of the press who, for years, has been assuming a militant position against [the SGAE] because of its presumed alignment with the left, or more specifically, with the socialist party).

Legal journals also published articles detailing professional opinions on the issue of taxation of popular theatre and the classics. Even these legal opinions,[16] which similarly legitimized the SGAE's rulings, did little to stop the general outrage against the institution and its most visible head, Teddy Bautista. The few journalists who, in an attempt to remain objective, supported the fee, could not fail to note the lack of tact and leadership of the institution and, on occasion, even included sarcastic commendations: "A Teddy la hacienda y la vida se han de dar [To Teddy, we are obliged to give our life and our estate]" (Algorri).

In terms of the dynamics of rural economies in the digital age, both Fuente Obejuna and Zalamea were able to benefit from the structures of the networked society. Castells can be invoked once again to help clarify the process. The sociologist proposes a duality, the space of flows and the space of places, to help reconceptualize changes in space and time in the digital age. Whereas the space of places can be understood as physical space conditioned by local proximity, the space of flows uses networks to organize decision making and enclaves or to exclude disempowered areas, reframing space into a logic of power. In the words of Castells, space of flows consists of "the material arrangements that allow for simultaneity of social practices without territorial contiguity. It is not purely electronic space ... It is made up first of all of a technological infrastructure of information systems, telecommunications, and transportation lines" ("Grassrooting" 364). However, though contemporary society is organized through processes that dominate its financial and political aspects, these processes depend on cultural codes and forms of socio-political organization that can, on occasion, supersede and ultimately resist the logic of the space of flows.

> Empirical evidence continues to show that new information and communication technologies fit into the pattern of flexible production and network organization – permitting the simultaneous centralization and decentralization of activities and population settlements – because different locations can be reunited in their functioning and interaction by means of the new technological system. This system is created from telecommunications, computers, and fast reliable transportation systems, as well as dispatching centers, nodes, and hubs. (363)

Castells observed in 1999, rightly, that most of the population would soon live in cities and form part of global networks of information. But he also anticipated that, thanks to increasing access to information technologies by classes and areas previously silenced from public discourse, there would be a potential for a shift of power due to what he terms the "grassrooting" of the space of flows.

The consortium created by the municipal authorities of Fuente Obejuna and Zalamea to include all municipalities affected by the copyright tax constitutes precisely one such "grassrooting" initiative. In 2010 the mayors of Fuente Obejuna, Zalamea, and Olmedo met to discuss the creation of a network of up to twenty towns that share site-specific early modern plays as cultural patrimony. The association would be dedicated to the appreciation of the theatrical spectacles as cultural and economic resources (Heras, "Crean una red"). In fact, this initiative was modelled after a regional consortium, Teatro pueblo a pueblo, created in the province of Fuente Obejuna with the purpose of using and promoting the theatrical language as a cultural resource for rural areas and as a means of territorial cohesion (EscenaTe).

In Castells' opinion, the eruption of peripheral voices on the internet, "with the creative cacophony of their social diversity, with the plurality of their values and interests, and given the linkage between places and information flows, transforms the logic of the space of flows, making it a contested space and a plural and diversified space" ("Grassrooting" 370). More important, he proposes that though the dominant structures in the space of flows will continue to ensure control over decision-making activities by bypassing isolated localities from the space of places, there will be more and more "trenches of resistance" created by the interface between places and information networks:

> The constitution of the space of flows was in itself a form of domination, since the space of flows, even in its diversity, is interrelated and can escape the control of any locale, while the space of places is fragmented, localized, and thus increasingly powerless vis à vis the versatility of the space of flows. The only chance of resistance for localities is to refuse landing rights for overwhelming flows – only to see that they land in the locale nearby, therefore inducing the bypassing and marginalization of rebellious communities. (365)

The residents of Fuente Obejuna and Zalamea have penetrated the space of flows by affirming their identity in unity against the SGAE, by flooding the net with blogs, by contacting the press, by turning the local into global, and by joining forces with sites that share their political goals despite geographic distance. All these factors constitute sources of social change in the information age that bypass the dynamics of the space of flows.

In the 2004 introduction to *The Cybercities Reader*, Stephen Graham summarizes Castells' thinking on the relationship between place, technology, and society, a relationship which poses a new form of digital capitalism that is "being challenged by a multitude of smaller scale social movements trying to maintain a sense of cultural identity and a measure of local political control" (Castells, "Space of Flows" 82). This tension between local and global is condensed in Castells' claim that "our societies are increasingly structured around the bipolar opposition of the Net and the Self" (82). By adopting new organizational structures based on the pervasive use of networked communication media, Fuente Obejuna and Zalamea have overcome the limitations of a rural space of places and have initiated a form of social development that allows them "to reaffirm their identities under the conditions of global change and instability" (82).

In effect, despite the apparently catastrophic financial consequences of the controversy for the rural communities of Zalamea and Fuente Obejuna, the residents and municipal representatives found ways of using the media and digital platforms to promote new forms of social and political organization, and to accrue financial gain through the promotion of the local tourist industry. In other words, the reappropriation of the canonical plays set in Zalamea and Fuente Ovejuna became opportunities to redefine the local sense of place and to reinsert the towns into the national cultural patrimony in which they were formerly invisible. After the SGAE placed them in the spotlight, the new context for rural resistance has launched them into the midst of a digital culture that had hitherto excluded them. As a result, the historic rural resistance becomes cited in a gesture of local/global resistance to authority. The power of citationality, which the residents invoke in their everyday lives as they respond "Fuente Obejuna, todos a una!" or, in Zalamea, "al Rey, la hacienda y la vida," becomes doubly significant when the gesture is shared to encompass all rural communities affected by the copyright fees and joined through information technologies. It is interesting that the Golden Age *comedia* becomes once again a site for cultural and political contestation, the chosen means to dispute unresolved tensions, and the popular gesture to point out the victims and villains of the digital age. The attention generated by the media in relation to the SGAE controversy succeeded in presenting these hitherto invisible localities as protagonists of their own history and as autonomous interpreters of their cultural patrimony. In retrospect, and according to the local reading of the events, despite having to pay the unfair fees, a more important goal was achieved: cultural justice was served.

NOTES

1 Although Lope de Vega's play contains the title spelled in two words *Fuente Ovejuna*, modern editions join them into one word as *Fuenteovejuna*. I refer to the play in the modern spelling. Any reference to the town or its residents will respect the current local spelling, Fuente Obejuna, which alludes to the area's wealth in bees (*abejas*) rather than sheep (*ovejas*).

2 These towns are engaged in activities of conceptualization of space in many ways. There is no question as to the vast logistic effort that the theatrical enterprise requires of communities such as Zalamea, which averages a mere 4,000 inhabitants, and stands prepared to receive annually an average of 1,500 visitors on the weekend of the festival. Each resident is prepared to reinscribe the historical events within city parameters, explaining the importance of spatial markers reinvested with symbolic value.

3 I draw here upon the well-known distinction established by Bourdieu between forms of cultural capital that help shape social organization: "Cultural capital can exist in three forms: in the embodied state, i.e., in the form of long-lasting dispositions of the mind and body; in the objectified state, in the form of cultural goods (pictures, books, dictionaries, instruments, machines, etc.), which are the trace or realization of theories or critiques of these theories, problematics, etc.; and in the institutionalized state, a form of objectification which must be set apart because, as will be seen in the case of educational qualifications, it confers entirely original properties on the cultural capital which it is presumed to guarantee" (242).

4 In Zalamea, for instance, reports of the 2007 production in the local press speak of an increased cast of 450 actors and about 350 collaborators offstage, and 600 actors are listed for 2011 (Caballero). Despite these numbers, the director claims that in 2014 more than 700 residents responded to the casting call but only about 300 attended rehearsals regularly and were allowed on stage (Nieto). In Fuente Obejuna, the director, Fernando Rojas, states that more than 300 people participated in the 2000 and 2009 editions (Cantador 7).

5 For an in-depth study of the implication of rural Golden Age festivals in the identity construction processes of the towns see García Martín's *Rural Revisions of Golden Age Drama*.

6 The director in Fuente Obejuna underlines that, besides the magnitude and spectacularism of a production that includes horses in battle and panoramic scenes of group action, what makes this theatre particularly impactful is the nature of the protagonists in light of the events that *Fuenteovejuna* presents: "refrendada por la historia y vivida por los protagonistas actuales, herederos, sin duda, de aquellos hombres y mujeres que sufrieron en sus carnes la injusticia, la violencia y la falta de respeto [[The events portrayed] are corroborated by history and lived by their current protagonists, inheritors of the men and women who suffered the very same injustice, violence and disrespect in their own flesh]" (Cantador 7). The director insists on the importance of the residents themselves, who give a unique projection to the original text, specific to this cast and setting.

7 Fuente Obejuna and Zalamea, which count approximately 5,000 and 4,000 residents respectively, have both experienced a decrease in population

of about 20 per cent and 25 per cent in the last decade. In the span of seven years the unemployment rate has nearly doubled in both towns to represent about 20 per cent of the population in 2014 (Fuente Obejuna Habitantes).

8 Paredes explains that the annual budget must cover the cost of 90 metric tons of metallic structure, 150,000 kilos of sand, 20,000 square metres for crafts markets and parallel activities and a 2,400-metre stage (Agencia EFE, Zalamea).

9 At the time of writing, the *Fuenteovejuna* festival in Fuente Obejuna has taken place in the following years: 1992, 1994, 1997, 2000, 2004, 2006, 2013, and 2016.

10 "Creemos que cada tres años está bien, ya que es algo muy costoso de hacer [We believe that once every three years is enough since it is so costly to do]" (Cantador).

11 Space of flows is a cultural abstraction of space and time created by sociologist Manuel Castells in an attempt to determine how new social structures emerge out of their interactions with the material foundations of the digital age. Castells introduces the term in his 1989 *The Informational City*, but he revisits this foundational concept in a number of writings that span over two decades. In his 2010 preface to the second edition of *End of Millennium*, Castells states that "in general, I stand by the conceptualization and interpretation that I proposed in this text 10 years ago." After inviting the reader to contrast the data collected during this period, he affirms that his new revisions are not, in his mind, "in contradiction with the original approach," but merely develop the concept further (*End of Millennium* xxiii).

12 One of the veteran actors of the Zalamea performance, who admitted to having no particular trade, having had jobs from postman and hardware dealer to waiter, admitted in his interview with me that in 2014 he had spent 185 euros in tickets so that friends would come to see the play (Delgado).

13 See the following articles, which make the reference to SGAE as the new "Comendador": Miguel Ortiz, "Fuente Obejuna todos a una contra la SGAE"; David Ballota, "Fuenteovejuna pide ayuda ante el acoso del comendador de la SGAE"; and Arcadi Espada, "¿Quién mató al Comendador?"

14 For a more detailed account see Fernando Lázaro, "Bautista y otros 8 miembros de la SGAE, detenidos por desviar fondos," and J. Romera and A. Semprún, "El auditor eleva a 87 millones el dinero que la SGAE desvió a la red de Neri."

15 The directors of the productions in Zalamea and Fuente Obejuna are among the first to recognize the enormous impact that the SGAE has had

in the diffusion and visibility of the community festivals and the towns which enact them. In my 2014 interview with Miguel Nieto, director of *El Alcalde de Zalamea*, he recognized that, thanks to the SGAE controversy, their last edition of the festival benefited from the free publicity given by the nearly forty different media representatives (Nieto). Fernando Rojas, director of *Fuenteovejuna* declared a similarly unprecedented success with help of the media in a 2009 interview with the newspaper *El público* (Villegas).

16 See, for instance, the article by Paloma Arribas, attorney of Abril Abogados, which supports the SGAE's right to tax the production to support the author of the adaptation and to protect artists and the free use of the public domain. Mariano Yzquierdo Tolsada, Professor of Civil Law at the Universidad Complutense de Madrid, reaches the same conclusion in a professional legal journal, without failing to note that though SGAE is right, the public outrage is caused, not surprisingly, by a president who fashions himself as an authoritarian emperor rather than as a responsible leader of a cultural society and who acts "como emperador custodio de tributos más que como una entidad de gestión de derechos ajenos [as an emperor managing tributes rather than as an entity managing public funds]."

PART THREE

Interviews

This section of the book is dedicated to six interviews with national and international theatre practitioners, from the United States, Mexico, and Spain, who specialize in Spanish Golden Age theatre. They are active in a wide range of areas, such as direction, acting, dramaturgy, production, management, and higher education. In the first interview, Ben Gunter, artistic director for Theater with a Mission in Tallahassee, Florida, discusses how he discovered and became passionate about the Spanish Golden Age *comedia*. Gunter talks about how some of his productions: among them, *El muerto* (Better Wed than Dead), *Nuevo mundo, descubierto por Cristobal Colón* (Lope's (small) New World), and *La elección de los alcaldes de Daganzo* (The Election of the Mayors of Daganzo) deal with critical social justice issues, such as gender and race disparity, and power imbalance. The second interview features dramaturg Harley Erdman and director Gina Kaufmann, both professors at the University of Massachusetts, Amherst. They discuss important issues they consider when producing a multifaceted play such as *La serrana de la Vera* (Wild Thing). These issues relate, for the most part, to religion, race, and gender non-normative behaviour. The third one was conducted with Sandra Arpa and Paula Rodríguez, actors, directors, and co-founders of the Spanish theatre company Teatro Inverso. They discuss what drove them to create their own company, one that focuses on an innovative way of producing Spanish Golden Age texts, and how they are committed to defying limits, exposing important social issues through their work, and making the audience reflect upon these issues. In the fourth interview Fernando Villa and Allan Flores, actor and director, respectively, of the Mexican theatre company EFE TRES Teatro, comment on the development and focus of their company. They focus on producing Spanish Golden Age texts performed by a minimalist cast – often by one or two actors – and with a clear social commitment in regard to connecting with the audience and conveying a message of justice and social change. In the fifth interview, Ian Borden, Associate Professor of Theatre Studies and Performance at the University of Nebraska, talks about his experience as a director and educator. He is also a sword fight director, which led him to Golden Age theatre and to collaborate with other scholars in the field. Likewise, Ian discusses his interest in women's equality issues and how he has treated these matters in his Golden Age productions. Our final interview features Natalia Menendez, actor, director, dramatist, manager, and adapter, who also directed the Festival Internacional de Teatro Clásico de Almagro (International Festival of Classical Theatre, Almagro), from 2010 to 2017. She emphasizes the social and psychological impact of theatre, pointing out the ways that theatre is both transformative and therapeutic. Natalia also discusses her contribution as director of the Festival de Almagro.

All interviews have been edited for length and ease of reading.

12 Ben Gunter (dramaturg and director), Theater with a Mission, Tallahassee, Florida

Interview conducted by Tania de Miguel Magro and Erin Cowling at the 2018 Symposium of the Association of Hispanic Classical Theater (AHCT) in El Paso, Texas.

Ben Gunter is the artistic director for Theater with a Mission, a volunteer organization based in Tallahassee, Florida. Theater with a Mission performs Spanish Golden Age plays translated into English, peppered with extracts from the original Spanish. Theater with a Mission's goal is to foster rediscovery of Florida's Spanish roots.

TANIA AND ERIN: Could you start by presenting yourself and talking about your relationship with Golden Age Spanish theatre?

BEN: I got involved in Golden Age theatre because my high school Spanish teacher used to have cultural Fridays, where we read plays out loud. We read some extracts from José Zorrilla's *Don Juan Tenorio*, and she told us that there was an original *Don Juan* that came from even further back. Later on, when I went to college, I took a course in Spanish Golden Age literature and read the original Don Juan: *El burlador de Sevilla* (The Trickster of Seville). After I graduated, for a while I practised theatre professionally. At the backstage of the Orlando Shakespeare Festival, I heard a couple of actors trashing a presentation by an egghead who only wanted to talk about rotting vegetation images in *Hamlet*. I thought that sounded really interesting because of all the production possibilities of rotting vegetation images in *Hamlet*. I found out from them what the name of that kind of egghead was: a dramaturg. Then I went back to Tallahassee and found out that I could study dramaturgy.

At grad school, I discovered *El burlador de Sevilla*, *Don Gil de las calzas verdes* (Don Gil of the Green Stockings), *Fuenteovejuna*,

La vida es sueño (Life Is a Dream), and other Spanish classics in translation. I was fascinated with the differences between the translations, and how translation made certain aspects of the play more visible while suppressing others. My dissertation topic was translating plays from the Spanish Golden Age for production in the United States. I reviewed ten translations of the *Burlador de Sevilla*. I got very interested in how translation could either present road blocks to production or help production along the way. I finished my degree during an economic crisis. There were no paying jobs of any kind. A bunch of friends and I got together and said: "Well, nobody is paying us to do anything ... Let's just go do what we really like to do." So, we went to Mission San Luis, which is the reconstruction of the most important Spanish mission in Florida. It's based in Tallahassee and it was active between 1656 and 1704. We started talking with them about using scenes from Spanish Golden Age plays to illustrate social issues that were very important in the life of the Mission.

In the Mission, there is a circular central plaza. On one side of the plaza is the Apalachee Native chief's house and the Apalachee Council House. On the other side is a Franciscan friary and a Franciscan church, and far off in another angle is the Spanish fort. In one location you had very disparate, multicultural points of view and backgrounds. That was a phenomenal place to start to look into things like what it means when cultures live side by side, how cross-cultural contact changes dynamics between people, and what kind of power struggles go on in a place where people live, all of which have social justice ramifications.

We started Theater with a Mission there and then. We were doing our own translations and developing plays like *Better Wed than Dead* by Francisco Bernardo de Quirós. It was the first English-language production of that play. On the surface it is a wonderful farce, it sparkles, it engages people in a formally funny gender warfare. At the same time, it lets people think about what it means when society says there is more value to a male imperative, which is a fundamental social justice problem, and it is still very current. We had responses from audience members who said that watching that play made them think about their relationships with their siblings, relationships between men and women, economic opportunities for women, and how cultures open or close doors to them. This is a play one might think has nothing to do with social justice because of its aesthetic distance, because it is four hundred years old, but it gave audiences the chance to face social justice issues that they had otherwise overlooked.

ERIN: Have your performances ever revealed something too controversial for the audience?

BEN: Oh yes. I'll talk about two examples. First, our condensation of Lope's *Nuevo mundo, descubierto por Cristobal Colón*, which we called *Lope's (small) New World*, which in itself is a controversial title. While working on a Christopher Columbus play, what we wanted to do was to get input from Native American tribes and experts in our region. We wanted our representation of Native culture to be accurate, respectful, and relevant. In some Native American communities, the minute we mentioned Christopher Columbus, the door to communication slammed shut. Columbus remains a figure of such controversy that he can't even be talked about. In some ways, this is similar to what happens with Andrew Jackson, the first territorial governor of Florida, an English-speaking ruler of Spanish-speaking people. Andrew Jackson is a similarly controversial figure in that area right now. In the Tallahassee area there are very active Native American communities, with very strong and conflicted opinions about colonization. Doing a play like Lope's *Nuevo mundo* brought a lot of those issues up.

Our approach was to use the illustrations of Timucua life in Florida that were published by Theodore De Bry in 1591, with a brief narration of Jacques Le Moyne's French expedition to Florida, which took place between 1564 and 1565. The Natives that we worked with in Tallahassee said Timucua culture has completely disappeared. We were able to interpret it with a freedom that is impossible when approaching, for example, Cree culture. They helped us open that door, and explore how to use those paintings to take body postures, to understand relationships between people and issues of social justice. In one of the stories Le Moyne tells about a Native kingdom that was established on an island, a city state that was at war with other Native tribes. The island people stole the bride of their worst enemy on her wedding day. According to Le Moyne's memoirs, those kinds of brides were particularly valued by Native culture. They were considered especially desirable and lovely. We used that at the opening of act 2, where Dulcanquellín steals Tacuana. We found a social justice issue that resonated with everybody and was imbedded inside a Native culture. It made the Native culture both more approachable and still foreign inside the performance. That was our goal in *Lope's (small) New World*, to invite people on a journey and to say: "the journey is going to take you someplace foreign." Then make the journey inviting enough so that people would decide to take it with us, and still keep the foreignness and the challenge. Our *Lope's (small) New World* actually ends with a freeze frame of the beginning of the war of vengeance that Dulcanquellín declares on the Spanish colonizers. We wanted to stop at that moment and make people think about what the future is for the people that they've come to respect and have affection for in the course of the play, the Native characters, the Spanish characters, the children, because we were able to have eight- and nine-year-old kids in our production, and kids are a great way to start making people think about things in a new light.

The second example took place in 2004, when I was working with two groups of middle school children in Gadsden County, a small rural county in the northern part of Florida, in a summer theatre workshop called "Cervantes on Stage." We started with *La elección de los alcaldes de Daganzo* (The Election of the Mayors of Daganzo), which has loads of social justice issues. The kids took clippings of things having to do with politics and social life and brought them in to help us with the translation. For us, *La elección de los alcaldes de Daganzo* turned into electing a sheriff in Podunk County, Florida. Our actors were living through the first contested election for sheriff in twenty years because the sheriff, who had been sheriff since everybody remembered, had decided to retire. It was a really interesting year to engage with a play that talks about how people get qualified for office, how they get voted into office, who has power, who are the insiders, and who are the outsiders. We did an acting exercise specifically based on that. We had them establish who are the insiders in your community and who are the outsiders, and it was really interesting how a sense of social justice and a sense of ethnicity played into that.

TANIA AND ERIN: Is there any time that a performance had a different effect on the audience than what you had envisioned? How did that maybe change the way you thought about that particular play?

BEN: I'll talk about that from the angle of my internal audience (like production committees and our organizers), and then from the perspective of the external audience.

When Theater with a Mission started working on *El Retablo [de las maravillas]* (The Marvellous Tableau), I thought that everybody in our selection committee was going to love the double levels, the many different ways that "limpieza de sangre" (blood purity) defines ethnicity and legitimacy. I thought people would like that double edge because it makes people uncomfortable, which is what satire is supposed to do. The reaction was completely different from what I expected. Our production committee said that we could not do anything that insults Jewish people. They said that they understood that people do productions of *The Merchant of Venice*, but that in the place where we live and the time where we live we could not do a production of *The Merchant of Venice* because people would consider it either reinscribing their prejudice against Jews, or representing a prejudice against them, which is much too entrenched, and much too unquestioned to be satirized lightly. Our production committee was otherwise wide open to the issue of legitimacy, so that became what our production is about. The one litmus test is whether your parents were married by a priest, which makes sense inside colonial Florida.

Regarding the external audience. In Act II of our *Nuevo Mundo*, there is a Native character who describes seeing a Spanish soldier on a Spanish warhorse for the first time. The description is presented like a mystery: Can you decode this puzzle? This creature has two heads, six legs, and a beard on his behind. The audience has to solve it for themselves. Part of the appeal to that for us was that in order to experience that performance you had to assume a Native's point of view, because after that experience, it's much more difficult for you to say "Natives are animals," "Natives are stupid," "Natives don't think." Because you've just been a Native, you just had that experience. We were really surprised when some audiences decided the creature was a kangaroo. We were really surprised at what seemed really obvious to us but was not necessarily obvious to an audience.

I think those two surprises, as a matter of fact, could be connected. The surprise of our production committee was that this play is too close to the world we live in because these prejudices are really active and embedded in the social injustices that we live with every day. In the case of the kangaroo, the audience was assuming that the play had nothing to do with the world they live in, like it was happening in a faraway land.

TANIA AND ERIN: If you could do anything you wanted, what would be the big project?

BEN: Can I give you more than one? I'll give you two or three. One play that we know that we want to do is *Castelvines y Monteses* (*Capulets and Montagues*) by Lope de Vega, because where we live, contrasts between English- and Spanish-speaking points of view are active parts of daily life. We are about to come up on two hundred years since Florida transitioned from being a Spanish "provincia" to being a U.S. territory. We want to make people aware of the implications of that: having a government change, having land ownership changed by fiat. All of the social ranking and justice implications they think they know, we want to give them a Spanish point of view on that.

We would also love to do *Amar después de la muerte* (Love after Death) by Calderón de la Barca, because it takes on that project of humanizing the demonized enemy. Even people of great goodwill find it permissible to demonize the Islamic Other, but it seems to me that Calderon's play does not settle for that. He makes Alcuzcuz funny, so irresistibly funny; also he makes the love between the rebellious Islamic couple absolutely irresistible. We are also really interested, third, in staging *La capeadora* by Luis Quiñones de Benavente, which now has an English translation. We think it brings up issues of social justice that are pertinent to our university community. There are two state universities and a state college in the area. Women academics do not make as much as their male counterparts while performing the same work. *La capeadora* puts front and centre that economic problem.

13 Harley Erdman (university professor, director, adapter, and translator of early modern theatre) and Gina Kaufmann (university professor, director), University of Massachusetts, Amherst

Interview conducted by Mina García Jordán, Erin Cowling, and Glenda Y. Nieto-Cuebas at the 2018 Symposium of the Association of Hispanic Classical Theater (AHCT) in El Paso, Texas.

Harley Erdman is a dramaturg, playwright, and professor at the University of Massachusetts, Amherst, whose translations of Spanish Golden Age plays have been published and produced for modern day audiences. These include works by Tirso de Molina, Ana Caro, Sor Marcela de San Félix, Feliciana Enríquez de Guzmán, and Luis Vélez de Guevara.

Gina Kaufmann is a professional theatre director and associate professor at the University of Massachusetts, Amherst. Her productions include adaptations based on works by Molière, Shakespeare, and Tirso de Molina. Kaufmann has directed some of Erdman's work, including his translation and adaptation of Tirso's Marta the Divine *(Marta la piadosa).*

Recently, both scholars worked on a production of Erdman's latest translation, Wild Thing *(La serrana de la vera), by Luis Vélez de Guevara.*

MINA, ERIN, AND GLENDA: What are the issues that come up over and over in your work having to do with social justice, and why do you think it is important to bring those up?

HARLEY: There is the aspect of the audience, and I think that is important. The most complicated and fascinating part, which might be invisible, is the collaborative process of working with a group of people in order to make a production work. For example, in *La serrana de la vera*, by Luis Vélez de Guevara, and in *Wild Thing*, our adaptation of this play, there is a lot of discontinuity, abrupt shifts of tone to struggle with. Gila (la serrana) is a heroine, a rebel, a hero, an icon, a murderess, a martyr; she goes over the top, and she is also a victim ... There is also a whole other level of that play that has to do with religion and race. It is something I am grappling with as a Jewish man, because Don Lucas de Caravajal, the captain, is perceived as a *nuevo cristiano* (New Christian). The reader can probably pick it up in our translation, but it is more explicit in the original Spanish text.

Another thing we are grappling with right now is if we see Gila as transgender according to our twenty-first century understanding of that. We know there was gender non-normative behaviour and certainly plenty of examples onstage and offstage in 1613. However, they didn't have the category "trans"; they had other categories. Then, what does it mean if we see Gila as trans and if the character is trans? Does that mean we should cast a trans actor in that role? Is that an ethical requirement? Is she really female? Is it more of a woman's story and not a trans story? But those are not mutually exclusive. Is she queer? Is she really in love with Isabel or is she platonically in love? What does that mean? We have to figure that out. We are going into a rehearsal process where there will hopefully be a dramaturg talking with people who are trans, and who have their own perspectives on the play. There are going to be actors of different sexual orientations. When the actors have done their own research and thinking, we will together figure it out. These kinds of issues are true for any production, not just for a Spanish *comedia*. However, I think they are highlighted in the *comedia* because in this kind of theatre gender is not subtle. Any company ends up grappling with this and the audience becomes an extension of that conversation as well.

The most important choice for me as a translator is about words, but about choosing the play that we will then produce. I base my decision on a play I really want to do, not because it is fun, not because it is great, but because it is something I want to work on for the next two or three years of my life. In order to achieve this, I have to get obsessed with something, with a question that will keep me going forward despite adversity and doubts.

GINA: One of the things that is really important to me is that, in theatre, we create an experience within a live community. Together, we have this opportunity within a live experience to expand our understanding, our empathy in relation to various stories, journeys, histories, points of view, and sexuality. There are opportunities to look to; as Brecht says, "Make the familiar strange." Theatre can do that within an experience where we are also being entertained. I am not interested in solely being entertained, but I do think it is important that we are entertained.

In a theatre, we laugh together, cry together, and have different reactions from one another. Comedy allows us to laugh and then the laughter opens us up to say "Oh!"

I think a lot about the ways that race, gender, and racial and gender hierarchies are being experienced in theatrical productions. What we are doing – no matter what time period it was written in or set in – is a piece about our present, because it is directed to all of us in the room. If it is a play that is set in 1613, and we decide to set it in the time it was written, that doesn't take away from what the production is about: it is about us now. In the particular case of *La serrana*, we face the question, What would it be like to feel that you were born in the wrong gender, but have no language to say, "I am transgender"? We have a different cultural experience around that now, but still have some of those same feelings about ourselves and our bodies. Who are we on the inside? I am really interested in expanding empathy in a lot of different ways. I think theatre does that in part because we are experiencing it live together.

MINA: Since you are both also professors, how is social justice present when you teach?

HARLEY: When I was younger, before Gina started teaching at UMass, I developed a lot of courses on theatre of the oppressed. I did very explicitly teach social justice, but in the last ten years I have gone back to working on the Spanish *comedia*. I am actually not very political in my work, but it is still complicated because, even in Massachusetts, the students come from different political backgrounds. I want to promote dialogue, and not just be up there saying "my side is right and your side is wrong." I don't think that is constructive. It is interesting how people of different political backgrounds might actually agree on some things. People of all different perspectives might also identify with something, no matter who they voted for. I think this is why I am attracted to the Spanish *comedia*, because it is multivalent. *Comedias* have multifaceted characters, something not always true in contemporary political plays.

ERIN: Is there any time that you started working on something and either the actors or the audience reacted to it in a totally different way than what you had envisioned? Did that change anything or have any implications for your future work?

GINA: I do think it is interesting the way the audience, here at El Chamizal,[1] responded when we did *Marta the Divine*, our production, and Harley's translation, of Tirso's *Marta la Piadosa*. The audience reacted so differently than when we did it in Amherst, Massachusetts.

ERIN: In what way was it different?

GINA: The cross-gender casting was a very big deal when we did it here.

HARLEY: There were two male actors; one was a male character and the other a female one who kissed on stage. It doesn't seem like a big deal. You know, what is the big deal?

GINA: Some members of the audience at Chamizal had a very loud vocal response, and not just at that moment. Someone shouted: "What is she doing? Oh my God!" Somebody near me said something like: "I can't believe they are doing this!" The extremity of their reaction was surprising to me. It just told me that it really does matter where you do things.

GLENDA: When I saw *Marta the Divine*, here at the Chamizal, at one point I forgot that Marta's sister was being performed by a male actor ... I started seeing her as what she was, a woman in love and a sister. However, that was not the case with many people at Chamizal. Have you had any blowback for exposing this on stage?

HARLEY: Yes. We had to send *Marta*'s script or a video in advance to National Park Services. They got very upset about it and wanted us to edit it. There was some really strong language in my translations, and they wanted to censor it. I was also trying to understand that it is a different community and a different world. It is not my world, or my community, and I did not want to offend anyone.

GINA: We did change it, though. We didn't have the section where he goes under her skirt.

HARLEY: We cut a few things out to make it more acceptable for a family-friendly audience. Even so, they put a warning sign on the door, because they were really worried. During the tech run before the show, they saw the two men kissing on stage and the word got out to the manager. They were really concerned and they resolved it by putting up signs that said: "Not appropriate for people under

---

1 Every spring, there is a Siglo de Oro Drama Festival at El Chamizal National Memorial Park in El Paso, Texas. Plays are in English or Spanish, free, and open to members of the community. The audience consists mostly of Latino families, often with small children, and school groups. This interview was conducted during the festival.

the age of 18." We kept the kiss! We were not going to cut it. They didn't ask us to cut that, but they made it clear they weren't happy. They got really nervous. We took off some of the more risqué stuff and a little of the strong language. I was okay with that. I don't feel like it violated the premise of the work.

GLENDA: Has anyone else asked you to eliminate a scene or edit the text because it can be controversial?

HARLEY: No, it is not normal. No, it is not part of the arts world. That is what is unusual about Chamizal. It is not an arts organization. It is a national park and they are understandably worried about losing their jobs, losing their budget, and the reputation of the park.

GINA: Going back to your original question. When I directed a production of *Tartuffe* at Shakespeare and Company (it was an adaptation into a 1950s musical), they got flak about it and I got letters from people who said I was being anti-Christian. I was a little confused by the vitriol of some of the letters. There was one handwritten letter saying, "Think about if there was a play that was anti-Jewish like this, no one would stand for it, but because you are mocking Christians, we all seem to think it's okay to laugh at Christians." I was surprised because *Tartuffe* is a play satirizing hypocrisy ... That is the only time I have ever gotten hate mail. People, based on their experience, their opinions, and who they are, are going to have responses that can be very surprising to the artists – in this case, this response had never occurred to me when I was working on the production.

MINA: You already talked a little bit about your next project. Do you anticipate any sort of resistance towards it?

GINA: I think it depends how we do it. I think that there will be if we bring *Wild Thing*[2] to Chamizal and we have a clearly transgender person in the central role. I am not sure how that will be taken. I think that it would be received very differently than if we choose to have someone who presents as female, and there are other choices. Every choice changes the story and changes audience reception to the story.

HARLEY: If people do see the character as trans and we don't have a trans performer, that is another complicated matter ... Also, there is the staging at the ending. Do we represent violence as an endpoint? What is the play saying? I'm generally okay with

---

2 The play was performed a year later at the 2019 Chamizal Festival.

my own personal world. I'm okay with an ironic or harsh ending. That is something else I can wrap my own imagination around, but most people don't and I am learning from that. I need to come up with a more affirmative idea. Do we escape having to see a terrible ending for Gila or is there something beyond that? I think that it is going to be a complicated conversation. I have talked to students about the ethics of staging tragedy. We are no longer in a tragic world, but we are still in tragic circumstances. We can't do tragedies as a way of reinscribing those endings where something horrible happens to the protagonist because she or he is a rebel.

Our students put together a version of Henrik Ibsen's *Hedda Gabler* that was very powerful. It was an all-female cast. They created three different endings to the play. One is the written ending where she commits suicide, and then they rewound it and had another ending where she ends up marrying. Which is not as bad as suicide, but also not a happy ending. They then dropped their roles and walked off the stage and into the audience as women of the twenty-first century and not as characters in the play. It is like they had broken free of the same constraints that forced Hedda to kill herself in 1890. It was very powerful, and I think *La serrana* brings exactly the same series of questions because she is a tragic, complicated, problematic, but fascinating tragic figure. But, does the end of her story have to be her death? Is that enough? We know we hit curtain end; we know we care about her. Is that enough to justify two hours of asking people to come experience this person, whether they are trans or female or whoever is a rebel against things that are still relevant today? What is the end point of that story?

MINA, ERIN, AND GLENDA: Could you tell us about what will be your next project after *Wild Thing (Serrana)*?

HARLEY: We have a new play, a new musical, a rock musical that we've written based on Tirso's *El Burlador de Sevilla*. It is set on a college campus. It is called *Legacy Boy*, and you can see where it goes from there … We have been working with a composer, Aaron Jones, for three years. We already have a product, a book, lyrics, and recordings. We are hoping to launch it professionally.

Essentially, it deals with race, class, and male privilege. It is very tough material. It is also very funny at times, but it is really about the situation in the United States right now and how it is represented by this one kind of legacy kid, in a small league liberal arts college who, like Don Juan, takes advantage of women and men, mostly women. Our ending is much more ambiguous.

14 Sandra Arpa and Paula Rodríguez (founders, actors, and directors), Teatro Inverso, Spain

Interview conducted by Mina García Jordán, Erin Alice Cowling, and Glenda Y. Nieto-Cuebas at the 2018 Symposium of the Association of Hispanic Classical Theater (AHCT) in El Paso, Texas.
  Translation by Ana Karen Rodas Garza and Erin Alice Cowling.
  Teatro Inverso is a two-woman production team that aims to build a new way to present classical theatre to modern audiences through the use of storytelling and adaptation. Paula Rodríguez and Sandra Arpa have been collaborating on a variety of projects since 2011. Their first show, Rosaura, *premiered in 2016.* Rosaura *explores the female characters of Calderón de la Barca's* La vida es sueño. *In 2019 they debuted their second production,* Wonders, *based on Cervantes' work, at Teatro Inverso.*

MINA, ERIN, AND GLENDA: Why did you decide to create Teatro Inverso? How did it all start?

PAULA: *Rosaura* came as a result of two elements, our desire to create our own work and to find our own artistic voices (as actors, directors, writers, and producers), and the effects of the economic crisis.

SANDRA: The economic crisis affected everyone in Spain. We lost any work prospects. We were young, trying to make a living, and it was a really tough moment.

PAULA: We felt uncertainty, like everyone in our generation. A lot of people left Spain, as I did at that time. In that context, and with our previous experiences as actors, we decided we wanted to take the reins in our own hands, to have control. We felt the need of having some sort of power, empowerment. We knew that as actors, as young women, we would be able to do things to achieve even more than we or society thought possible. We allowed ourselves to think for ourselves. We did not allow society to tell us what we had to do.

SANDRA: We, as actors, sometimes put ourselves into a passive position waiting for directors or producers (mostly male) to call us. Instead of that, we decided to take the initiative and trust in ourselves.

ERIN: What draws you to Golden Age theatre?

PAULA: The pieces have so many layers: poetical, philosophical, religious, historical, metaphorical, mythological ... There is always something new. I also think that, like other actors, we feel a deep connection with the verse and its musicality. Reading a poem is like reading a musical score. Poetry has a shape and limits, which becomes a starting point to create. We like to stretch limits. Maybe we are trying to shake up our own tradition, our own old ways of doing things, in our old country. Maybe we can shake up old things and change things.

MINA, ERIN, AND GLENDA: How is your work shaking up and changing things? Do you see your work as one that fights for social justice?

SANDRA: We want our voices to be the voices of women in a universal way. We are far from reaching social equality between men and women. It is difficult for us to find our own identity, our own place in the world, because we feel that we do not have equal rights. We also want to tackle other social and political issues, so when we travel, we adapt our production to the political situation.

PAULA: It is a question of creating a space where we can actually connect with the audience. We are not politicians, we are not professors, we are not trying to educate, we are not trying to indoctrinate, but we are trying to create a space in which we and our audiences can reflect together about what is happening now. We don't pretend to have the answers. We just question ourselves and our world about what is right or wrong. In our times, the most important thing we can do as citizens is to think, because everything is so confusing. The best way to search for social justice as theatre makers is to invite the audience to think about their reality and to offer new ways of looking into it. We talk quite openly about politics in *Rosaura*. *Life Is a Dream* is already a very political play. It is a reflection on freedom and what it means to be a good leader. Political comments are explicit in *Rosaura*, because as citizens and artists we need to be aware of what's happening now. We cannot just disconnect.

MINA: Do you choose a certain play to talk about certain issues, or do you find a play you like and then see what issues you can connect to the present?

PAULA: We start with the issues. With *Rosaura* we asked ourselves: what's happening to us right now? The answer was: we are lost. We didn't know how to be ourselves, how to be actors and women in our society without feeling rejected or that we were missing something. We felt part of, we are part of, a generation that is collapsing. All of these made us think about the character of Rosaura in *Life Is a Dream*. For our next project we want to reflect on issues of social media manipulation, fake news, technology, and the limits between reality and fiction. We are going to adapt different texts from Cervantes, including *El retablo de las maravillas*.

GLENDA: What reception is your work having in Spain?

SANDRA: We feel very appreciated; people like what we are doing, but it is difficult in Spain to work independently. There's some resistance towards this way of working.

GLENDA: Is there a specific situation that has made you feel rejected or inferior?

PAULA: I haven't felt like that. I think we are trying to do something quite new, to really go for it and explore, but sometimes I feel people are not ready for it. Audiences like *Rosaura*, and we connect with them, but maybe not with the professional theatre world. We have still not been able to open in Madrid.

GLENDA: Do you think it is because you are two women?

SANDRA: I think there are many factors. In Spain, in our profession, there are families, and if you are not part of one of the families, it's not so easy to find your space. I don't belong to any of these families, nor would I want to, because I want to be independent, but this also means I miss many opportunities. The other factor is that we are two women and we are not famous, we are not on TV. We just have a really good play and we want to do it.

PAULA: Every single time we arrive at a theatre in Spain, someone asks us: "where is the director?" Every time. Things are changing, there are female directors, but this is a world still dominated by men. People don't expect two women to be directing together. They expect us to be the actors, and that's it. They are not used to actors that are also directing, producing, and writing. In the theatre world the figure of the actor is boxed into this person that just waits for someone to give him or her an opportunity, and cannot be creative and independent.

MINA AND GLENDA: In twenty years, if we were to repeat this interview, what would you have hoped to have accomplished in terms of social justice?

SANDRA: I would like women to have space to create, to grow, in which we recognize and are recognized by each other at all levels (personal, social, economic, political). I hope we reach that level of not experiencing that sensation of inferiority. I want to see real empowerment. I want to have the sensation of being at ease wherever we might be, not having to search and fight for a space, but to be in a place where we are welcomed.

15 Fernando Villa Proal and Allan Flores (founders and directors), EFE TRES Teatro, Mexico City

Interview conducted by Erin Cowling and Tania de Miguel Magro at the 2018 Symposium of the Association of Hispanic Classical Theater (AHCT) in El Paso, Texas.
   Translation by Ana Karen Rodas Garza and Erin Cowling.
   EFE TRES Teatro *is a company from Mexico City, founded in 2012 by Fernando Villa Proal, Allan Flores, and Fernando Memije, that focuses on creating and performing minimalist adaptations of Golden Age theatre. Most of their productions consist of only one or two actors, and minimal props and decoration. Since their inception they have produced three shows:* El príncipe ynocente (The Innocent Prince), ¿Qué con Quique Quinto? (What's Up with Harry V?) (with Caberet Misterio), *and* El merolico (The Travelling Salesman), *all of which have been performed internationally, in Mexico, the United States, and Spain, and elsewhere. Villa Proal is an actor, adapter, and director, while Flores, who studied acting at the University of London, is primarily a director and producer for the company.*

ERIN AND TANIA: Can you tell us a little bit about the company?
FERNANDO: EFE TRES Teatro is a company we founded back in 2012. We got together with the hope of achieving a staging of Golden Age plays with specific goals: first of all, to adapt them for two actors; and second, to be able to connect these plays with twenty-first-century audiences, letting them know they are not old, out-of-date plays, but instead are very contemporary.
   At that time I was in my second year, fourth semester, in drama school, and I saw this play with two great actors about a troupe, a *ñaque* troupe, that goes from town to town having adventures. It was a very, very beautiful play, and we thought that we should do something like that, but with a classical play. I remember telling Fernando that we needed to have some kind of position to make

the plays connect to the present day. For instance, in most Golden Age comedies, everything turns out to be okay in the end, either because the king solves the situation (because he says it's okay) or because we discover that some particular character is a nobleman so he is entitled to do everything he did, as it is the case with Torcato.[1] Although we may think that this approach doesn't apply today, we all have a friend or have heard of someone trying to get out of a punishment because he is important or powerful, like the "Wolf of Wall Street" for example. That's what led us to these two prisoners, the only characters in *El príncipe ynocente*, and our profound concern with the idea of injustice.[2] We even used the soundtrack of the movie Robin Hood to emphasize that aspect, and also because we love that movie and it matched perfectly.

ALLAN: I think that beyond the political stance, the real struggle has been finding a constant in the plays that allowed us to manage two layers of fiction at the same time: the argument of the play, while opening a door to connect to the present audience, to invite them to participate, beyond their political or social stance, in a common pursuit that is shared with the actors on stage.

ERIN AND TANIA: Have you found any resistance when dealing with social justice topics onstage? Has anything come up that has been controversial for your audience or for yourselves?

FERNANDO: Not so much with *El Principe ynocente*. Just going one step back, with *El Principe ynocente* we realized that we didn't have to change anything in the play in order to make our position explicit. If we had not had this other plane of existence, the other fiction, the frame of the two prisoners, then it would have been much more difficult to show our position regarding this nobleman who gets away with everything. But the case with *Quique Quinto* is very interesting because in the play we actually ask the audience, "Do you have a voice?" Please raise your voice. It doesn't matter if you are five years old. It doesn't matter if you are an oppressed minority. It doesn't matter who you are. You have the right to raise your voice and say whatever you want to say, and whatever

---

[1] Torcato is the title character of Lope de Vega's *El príncipe ynocente*. Torcato is a peasant who seduces a noblewoman pretending to be man. He is about to be sentenced to death, but at the end everything is resolved because he turns out to be a prince.

[2] Their performance of *El príncipe ynocente* uses a frame in which two prisoners re-enact the play over and over to entertain themselves. This play is analysed in the essay by Erin Cowling.

you need, in terms of justice, in terms of what you are and what you want and what you need.

ALLAN: And besides, the character who utters those words, in this particular moment in the story, is young, doesn't know how to rule, doesn't listen to anyone, and is also named "Quique," or "Enrique." All of that reminds us of a president of a certain country we live in, which immediately connects with the audience, but we do it through fiction, which makes the play that much more powerful. **Fernando**: Mexico is a very conservative place where parents tell their children what to do, when to be quiet, how to behave, etc., and it's interesting to see the parents getting nervous when we invite their children to say "no" and they have to live with that, because we address children in our speech, to allow them to grow with that idea from a very young age.

ERIN: Is there anything you would have done differently, choices you would have made differently or are you happy with your trajectory?

FERNANDO: About what happens on stage, I wouldn't change a thing. I am very happy with these two plays. I believe that Jorge Dubatti said that "One of the ways to see that a play is a powerful play, and a good play, is the unspeakable." He talks about when you see a play and everything is just in the way it should be. It has everything it needs, and it has it in the specific intensity, so you don't get out of the play saying: "Oh I would have done this. Or this would have been better. Or maybe if they had." If you get out of the play and you're just whole, satisfied, then that's how you know the play has been good. I believe that *El Principe ynocente* and *Quique Quinto* are just like that. Everything they need is there, and they work, and I wouldn't change anything. I would like to show them to more people, to more audiences, and to exchange ideas not only in Mexico, in Spain, and here in El Paso, but I would have loved to travel a lot more. That's the only thing I would change for the future.

TANIA: Do you ever self-censor? For example, when you're preparing and you have an idea, do you ever say: "No this is too much. It's not going to work. It is going to make someone feel uncomfortable"?

FERNANDO: I actually believe that anything is achievable. You just have to find the correct approach and the correct way to show it, as long as it's not betraying your ideals. I have a sense of what works, and what doesn't work onstage, but that is different. I am actually very bold, and that sometimes is a double-edged sword. Sometimes being so bold can be counterproductive, but I would rather try, and risk it.

ERIN AND TANIA: What would you like to do if you could do anything with no limits? What would be your ideal?

ALLAN: I would love to do a project by Sor Juana with just women in the cast. It would probably be in the same format as *El Príncipe*, but with women because I would love to see that distinct sensitivity and how a text is approached from the perspective of women.

FERNANDO: With the other Fernando, we have been talking about doing *Lindo Don Diego* (The Lovely Don Diego). We still haven't worked out the details, but there's this possibility of working with a mainstream actor, and the three of us would do all the characters. I would love to do at some point *El Burlador de Sevilla* because I am intrigued about Don Juan as an ideal of a how to behave. I want to be that guy. I want to be the one who fools, I want to be powerful, I want to be the one who oppresses. Actually, I would like to perform this character, this god, to make this ideal crumble.

ERIN AND TANIA: He goes to hell at the end. But that's not the myth that endured. Nobody talks about the fact that he ended up in hell.

FERNANDO: A lot of people still want to be him. It has nothing to do with this, but like the *narcos* in Mexico. People want to be them. They don't care if they are actually putting themselves at risk because they are living a better life. Some people would take the risk to live like a king for two years rather than their whole life as a beggar. People want to be Don Juan; it doesn't matter if that takes them to hell. If people don't believe in him, if people don't like him, at least he is a powerful figure.

TANIA: Do you see yourselves and your profession as having some kind of social responsibility? And what is this responsibility, and do you actually think you can make a difference?

FERNANDO: Yes, I do. I don't know if I can make a difference. Well, actually yesterday we were talking about this. Someone who interviewed us asked: "A lot of young guys and girls went to the play, and they got out saying, 'Oh, I want to be an actor,' or 'Oh, I want to do theatre,' because of what they have just seen." If we are able to impress someone so much that after a performance they want to become actors, maybe we are able to change perspectives on a specific topic. In the matinee performance in El Paso, we were talking about feminist ideas and how a particular *entremés* supported the idea of a strong female figure, a woman who is portrayed in one very particular way. We understand that overgeneralization of the female figure can be counterproductive because it can be seen as a criticism. If you are not open to these subtleties, you are just like this Massachusetts politician (I don't know if it was a senator) who said, maybe a month ago, that women are supposed to be in the kitchen or knitting, but don't need to meddle in men's chores. So, if this guy were to see that play, he would say: "Yes! that's what women should be doing," and he wouldn't even think that we are criticizing that very idea. So yes, we do have a responsibility. Whatever we put on stage has to show very clearly what we want to say, and what we want you to think about with us, because this is a dialogue. Whatever we say here will resonate in our audience in what they are saying. That is how we have grown in these five years. When we were approached by the audience with ideas that they had while watching *El Príncipe ynocente* that had never crossed our minds, that is when we realize how much responsibility we have when we are onstage.

16 Ian Borden (associate professor of theatre studies), Johnny Carson School of Theatre and Film, University of Nebraska

Interview conducted by Tania de Miguel Magro and Erin Cowling at the 2018 Symposium of the Association of Hispanic Classical Theater (AHCT) in El Paso, Texas.

Ian Borden is an associate professor of theatre studies and performance in the Johnny Carson School of Theatre and Film at the University of Nebraska. He works primarily with English-language students, performing early modern Spanish plays in translation.

TANIA AND ERIN: Could you just start by telling us a little bit about your trajectory, what you do and why Golden Age?

IAN: A lot of the work that I've done as a performer has been in Shakespeare or related to Shakespeare. I'm also a fight director. I blame Ben Gunter for a lot of the fact that I'm in Golden Age. We were PhD students together. He was doing a workshop with middle school kids and he went, "Hey! Come do some fights and get paid." In 2009, I was invited to ASTR (the American Society for Theatre Research) to work with a group working on *Fuenteovejuna* doing some fights. There I met Amy Williamsen, and she said, "Hey, I got this play of a woman who fights." I was like "that's cool," and then I started reading more and down the rabbit hole I went.

TANIA AND ERIN: We are particularly interested in looking at Golden Age theatre pieces and how they expose issues related to social justice both in their own time and in contemporary adaptations.

IAN: Would you, just to help me out, tell me how you define social justice in theatre?

ERIN: That's a good question, because everyone perceives it from a different angle. Those that are working on adaptations are really looking at how they are connecting the pieces to issues going on today with gender, race, social inequality, etc.

TANIA: I am also thinking about the role of teaching. When we are teaching, sometimes issues come up and the students are able to understand things from their world's perspective through these plays and to talk in a more comfortable way.

IAN: The thing that I really notice working on Golden Age, of course, is women's equality issues. In my production of *Valor, agravio y mujer* (Courage, Betrayal, and a Woman Scorned) by Ana Caro, I had Ribete being played by Flora as disguised, which made for two women in disguise going into a men's world. That set up a whole other level of issues with the women on stage. Watching Flora take away Tomillo's clothes and then end up dressed as Ribete, it's very consciously placing gender construction literally onstage. To me the use of the sword is crucial. The sword defines a character in terms of masculinity and masculine power. Even when it is a woman who carries the sword, it creates a level of masculine idealized power or its lack. When men are not good with the sword, it takes them down.

ERIN: Have there been times when something didn't have the effect you expected and what did that tell you about your work or how did that change how you approached something?

IAN: The first script I did of *Valor, agravio y mujer* was with Amy Williamsen, and it was still very close to the original play. There was a huge amount of resistance from the other theatre faculty about putting this play on, as happens with a lot of Golden Age plays. One of the things that particularly struck me was that one of my colleagues, who I never would have thought of as not being a feminist, really disliked the character of Leonor. That's when I went to Amy and told her I was going to move away from close translation and turn more to adaptation. I played with the characters and that made a difference. In that play, though, there was some stuff that just happened. It was really interesting having the two women onstage. What started as just a clown routine, became something else. It became a visible construction: the balcony scene and the juxtaposition of the women and the men. But some of that just did not get the resonance that I expected. Now, there were also things that I didn't have an idea would have resonance that really hit people strong. You just can't tell the audience what to feel.

TANIA: I would like to go back to one thing you said about always finding resistance when you want to put on a Golden Age play.

ERIN: What sort of reasons do people give you?

IAN: Money, money, money. Bruce Burningham was putting a play up for inclusion in the repertoire, and they were basically saying, "Well, this is very much like Molière, so why don't we just do a Molière." Because Molière is recognized. When I talked to several different artistic directors of Shakespeare companies about this issue – particularly Bob Hall from Flat Water Shakespeare Festival – they all said that to get audiences into the unfamiliar is not going to work. A lot of the Shakespeare companies and a lot of the industry are predicated on people coming to see the familiar and they don't want to go to that next level, even the companies that are in the longer residence, like Chicago Shakespeare Theater or American Shakespeare Center. American Shakespeare has been really going since 2002; they are a recreation of Shakespeare's Blackfriars Theatre. They are just now starting to reach out to different kinds of plays and experiences. It takes a long time for a company to open up to that, even though Shakespeare companies are the best ones to do it. There is so much intrinsic resistance to the Siglo de Oro plays. They have been translated badly, people have seen and read them, and they kind of stank because they are textbook-close adaptations, and they just don't work that way. A lot of the translating work I've been doing is also about "let's make things more exciting, let's bring them into iambic pentameter," which makes the Shakespeare crowd recognize it.

ERIN: And in terms of pedagogy, how is it when you introduce these plays to students; what do you hear back from the students?

IAN: In my theatre program, as in many theatre programs, we are production based. Not just in what we do onstage and how we focus, but in what we are teaching. We are a school of theatre and film, and we teach mostly modern texts; we don't do any Golden Age at all. Our students have an introduction to theatre class, where the crazy professor, that's me, makes them read one Golden Age play. They do two history classes, one of which goes from Roman times through Shakespeare, and then Shakespeare on to today. I am not in charge of that. Maybe, if they are lucky, in their entire degree, they read one Spanish play. That's it.

TANIA: Can you talk a little bit about the reaction of your students? I imagine some of them know Shakespeare and for the first time they are doing Golden Age.

IAN: I brought some students with me to the Chamizal Festival. On the bus back from the show last night, they were going, "Hey, can you do a class on Golden Age theatre?" Once the students get exposed to it, particularly if they can put it up in some form or see it in the theatre, then they go, "These are really interesting." I find the resistance of the theatre scholars to Spanish Golden Age mystifying. As a PhD student in theatre studies, I had one single week on Spanish Golden Age. We read two plays. There were entire courses dedicated to Shakespeare.

ERIN: If you could do anything, either in the classroom or onstage, what would be your ideal?

IAN: Well, I am trying to set up right now what I'm pitching as *Bare Stage Classics*. Golden Age stages and Elizabethan stages were pretty darn empty, which means we don't need to worry about scene design. We would do a show per semester from the period. It would have to start with Shakespeare or it wouldn't get support. But once it started rolling, we can have Lope de Vega. Then, I'll also venture into Restoration England because part of my work is both Spain and England and how they cross over in that era.

TANIA: I was wondering if you think about teaching theatre as having a social responsibility.

IAN: Good theatre artists by nature have to have incredible empathy for anyone they come across. Most really great theatre artists are also really great people. There is always the exception to the rule. Part of doing this work is thinking about things in a very different way. There is a reason why there are not a lot of conservative, hard-core right-wing people who do this kind of work. It takes empathy to do it. Many of the people who are originally drawn to it tend to have alternative outlooks ... the number of gay men in theatre is legendary, the number of gay women in theatre is becoming more known. You can't be someone who works with all these types of people day in and day out and then go: "They are strange." It just doesn't happen. I teach a script and production class in which I try to choose a play or a film that makes everybody in the class face something from their experience. It may be gender related, or have to do with sexual orientation, ethnicities ... I still haven't found a Native American play that I like as a teaching tool, but other than that, I can find a way to make students find their own experiences within the theatre. Maybe that's where I find my transformative moment.

TANIA: Does your program offer any sort of general education classes for people who are not doing theatre? Can you talk about those classes?

IAN: Achievements-Centred Education, that's how we categorize General Studies. My Script Class is an ACE 2, which is the communications area. In that class I have theatre students, film students, and then general students. I had a baseball player last year who just went nuts for the class. He wrote this beautiful long letter about how much he enjoyed it and how he appreciated what I brought to it. The General Studies students tend to find it really interesting. Some of them become theatre minors.

17 Natalia Menéndez (director, actor, dramaturg), former director of Almagro Festival, Spain

The theatrical career of Natalia Menéndez has encompassed many roles. She has been an actor, director, dramatist, manager, and adapter. Natalia Menéndez was the director of the Festival Internacional de Teatro Clásico de Almagro from 2010 to 2017. Throughout her tenure as director, Natalia made significant changes to the festival, many of which had to do with adjusting the financial situation of the festival and expanding its reach, but she was also concerned with the social impact of the enterprise.

Interview conducted by Tania de Miguel Magro and Erin Cowling in a café in Madrid during the summer of 2018.

Translation by Tania de Miguel Magro.

TANIA: Let's start with a bold question. Does theatre have a social responsibility?

NATALIA: Of course. Maybe not all professions, but most, and particularly creative ones, have a social component. There is enough in this question for a dissertation, because it can be seen from many points of view: creating, the community of the scenario, the community of the audience, knowing that you can influence, manage, manipulate, transform groups of people. You can simply change their lives in two hours and make them smile. Just for that reason, I believe, we should be included in the Ministerio de Sanidad (Ministry of Health). I have said this publicly on many occasions. I mean it. I believe theatre and music should be part of the Ministry of Health, because we really improve the quality of life. One of the things I most enjoyed in Almagro, which I do when I direct, is, without being noticed, watch people enter the theatre (their faces; we all arrive as if we had been run over by the subway) and how they come out. It is like a facial peeling or a massage. The body language is completely different. We should analyse this. I have studied this because it interests me, and because it is a way of checking my work. I believe we help children understand themselves, old people find their way, disadvantaged people or abused women understand that they are not alone, and that there are other ways, and that they can talk about their situation. We show people issues that are occurring and talk about them so they can see other ways to understand or deal with such problems. I truly believe in the social aspect of theatre. It is therapeutic, not only for the audience or the actor who plays a certain role, but also for me. Reading and confronting plays has helped my brain, and my soul, and my body. Also, one can give back to the audience through meetings and workshops, and not just for professionals.

TANIA AND ERIN: During your tenure as director of the Festival de Almagro, what changes were implemented to ensure better access for non-traditional audiences?

NATALIA: Part of the social compromise of the Festival de Almagro was to become more accessible. We had up to seven spectacles for people with visual and hearing disabilities per year. All theatrical spaces were made accessible to people with limited mobility. Programs were printed in Braille, whenever possible, for the accessible shows. Starting in 2014 we organized accessible exhibits for people who are blind. We also created children's workshops for social inclusion, in which children without obvious disabilities got together with children with different capabilities, so they could get to know each other's worlds. In 2015 we started the Touch Tours, allowing people who cannot see to touch things like scenery. The first time the Compañía Nacional de Teatro Clásico performed an accessible play was at the Festival de Almagro, in 2012, at our request. We also increased discounts for unemployed people and large families. We started to work with national and international volunteers. We paid special attention to including low-income families from Almagro. I also met yearly with the women's reading club from the Almagro Public Library. There was an open competition to select three children from three local schools to become part of the Barroco Infantil jury. We have been the first festival to have a mixed jury: three children and three adults. Fortunately, this idea has since been copied by many other festivals.

TANIA: There is a general impression that young people go to the theatre less often than they did a generation ago. Why? What can be done?

NATALIA: Education has deteriorated. This has to be addressed from the bottom-up. This can be fixed by a state, a government, who understands that theatre is part of culture and that culture is part of the quality of life. From the president to the housewife (or house-husband, which is fortunately more and more frequent now), people have to be aware that theatre is culture and culture improves your life. It is not just the government. We are all responsible for making sure people have access to culture. From my position, I feel I did all I could, and the results were very good. I told myself, maybe it is not necessary to have young people go to the theatre for two and a half hours; let's create baroque micro-theatre, like a carrot, to get them in. There is no need to be such a purist. I am not a purist. Getting to know Cervantes through rap? Sure, why not? We had 9 million or I don't know how many millions of followers of that adventure in Mexico. I cried hearing rappers reciting lines from Cervantes. It was done so well. Want to make video productions about Dulcinea? Sure. Are you thinking about the idea of Dulcinea in contrast to Marcela? Great. To get people in the streets talking about Laurencia moves me. To facilitate little kids coming out of the theatre talking about Sancho, Don Quixote, or the two sisters in *La dama boba* (The Foolish Lady) moves me. This is an individual endeavour that then grows. It is not something you can say, "It has to be done by them." That is too easy. We all have a responsibility towards children and young people and the elderly. I have been working for a long time with the non-violent ascetic, and since 2010 we included in Almagro encounters with the non-violent aesthetic: philosophical meetings, learning how to treat the audience, how to behave during the festival.

TANIA: Can you explain some more about what you mean by a non-violent aesthetic?

NATALIA: Life is packed with violent aesthetics. It is easier to find violent aesthetics than to define a non-violent aesthetic. Why? Because it has not been allowed to exist officially because it does not make any money, or it makes less money. What I believe is that in creativity, in thought, in philosophy, in the way of existing, there are people that have provoked a non-violent aesthetic. This is to confront, to find, a way of living from a non-violent vocabulary. For example, onstage, I never use the word "conflict." There are words that are not in my vocabulary because I believe that they are not necessary. We can talk about disagreement, or something else, but without warmongering. In the same way, I told my team the Chinese proverb: If you do not know how to smile, do not open a shop. We do not have to show the sweat, but the smile. It's the same at work. There are words, actions, gestures through which you have to find harmony. Finding harmony in graphics, in colours, in sentences, in messages. It is not about fighting but contributing and communicating from a non-violent aesthetic of inclusion, of diversity, of appreciation for human beings. The social part of the Festival de Almagro was the most important one. To the extent of your capabilities, wherever you are, at work, you can use harmony and function from a certain place and call things by their name, not to cover up, not to hide, but to find whatever it is that favours light, and health, and improvement, not something that will leave you trapped in a state of shock that you don't know how to get out from. I try to provoke from my different positions that harmony.

TANIA AND ERIN: What do you think are the weak points of the festival?

NATALIA: The main one is economic: lack of funding for culture. This is not just something that happens with Almagro, but something that needs to be addressed in Spain. There are countries that have realized their culture could allow them to achieve many things, like putting them on the map, and I believe Spain could do this perfectly. Sometimes all it needs is a little push; it is a ridiculously small amount that you need to generate a profit. I realized that for every euro we spent, we got back between four and five, which is a very high return. Some politicians understood this, some not so much. That was the Achilles' heel. We could have achieved some more important things, like meetings with other countries, with a little more money.

TANIA AND ERIN: Have you ever experienced censorship? Have you ever self-censored to achieve something or to avoid problems?

NATALIA: No. There is no censorship, there is just lack of money. No one has ever censored my plays. But I, in my position, not as a censor, have decided that there are things that cannot be said. We cannot talk about jealousy in the twenty-first century. There are plays, like *Othello*, in which we should not talk about jealousy, but femicide. We must change and modify. It cannot be that in a Calderón play the wife gets killed and the husband goes to church for forgiveness and gets away with it. No, I think that is shameful. At the time it made sense, there was a certain mentality, and authors were showing cases and questions that reflected that mentality, that way of thinking and existing in the sixteenth and seventeenth centuries. But in the twenty-first century there are things we cannot keep. I mean, we can, but we shouldn't. I believe we must make changes and modifications to adapt to the twenty-first century. Not a version, an adaptation. To adapt to this century.

ERIN: In relation to this, can you explain what your process is for adapting a piece?

NATALIA: For me, all the elements that are related to questions of jealousy, or violence against women, or sexual abuse, or abuse of power, they all have to be treated with today's words. Fixing the verse is easy. There are authors, dramaturgs, and adapters who can do that work. What I cannot conceive of is that there are young companies that offered me plays like *El médico de su honra* (The Doctor of His Honour) and when I asked them about the ending, they were like, "Oh well, with the gestures and the gaze." No, no, no. When something is related to our times, and Golden Age is related to our times, there are things that need to be modified and treated. We don't walk and eat and breathe in the same way, then why should we keep words that meant something then, but now mean something else? In fact, adaptations to the twenty-first century that have been clear and transparent are the ones that achieved real success. Because I believe teens or people like us are not interested in going to a play where at the end a husband gets away with murder, or a military man destroys a town. For me, museum pieces have no interest. I only offer them when the plot and ending are not harmful. With Golden Age one has to be very cautious. And not only with Golden Age. Look at *Othello*. One of the most successful productions that has been done lately was one by the company Viajeinmóvil (2013), acted out with life-size puppets manipulated by two actors, talking about femicide and pain. For me there has been nothing like that. The same happens with Calderón. Cervantes is not so problematic, but Lope is. We need to give the "today"; otherwise Golden Age is too far away. Only mediocre creators don't do it. They do it as a business model, because in Spain, there was a time when putting on a classic was to make money (with the schools and such). But then you are not a creator, you are an accountant, an economist, or someone who does merchandising.

Bibliography

Abi-Ayad, Ahmed. "Argel: Una etapa decisiva en la obra y pensamiento de Cervantes." *Annali*, edited by Giuseppe Grilli, vol. 37, no. 2, 1995, pp. 133–42.
Abreu Gómez, Ermilo. *Sor Juana Inés De La Cruz: Bibliografía y biblioteca*. Imprenta de la Secretaría de Relaciones Exteriores, 1934.
Agencia EFE. "Ernesto Caballero traslada a Cervantes a los CIE en 'El trato de Argel'." *La Vanguardia*, 12 Sept. 2016, www.lavanguardia.com/vida/20160912/41260911822/ernesto-caballero-traslada-a-cervantes-a-los-cie-en-el-trato-de-argel.html.
– "La SGAE se pone al día con Fuente Obejuna." *El país*, 19 Aug. 2009, elpais.com/cultura/2009/08/19/actualidad/1250632804_850215.html.
– "Zalamea, Fuente Ovejuna y Olmedo, tres pueblos unidos por el teatro clásico." *Diario Sur*, 22 Oct. 2014, www.diariosur.es/agencias/20100720/mas-actualidad/cultura/ zalamea-fuente-ovejuna-olmedo-tres_201007202228.html.
Aguilar, Gaspar. *Expulsión de los moros de España por la S.C.R Majestad del Rey Don Felipe III, nuestro Señor*, edited by Manuel Ruiz Lagos. Editorial Guadalmena, 1999.
– "El gran Patriarca don Juan de Ribera." *Poetas dramáticos valencianos*, vol. 2, Real Academia Española, 1929, pp. 245–87.
Albuisech, Lourdes. *El alcalde de Zalamea*. Ayuntamiento de Zalamea, 10th ed., Aug. 2003. Playbill.
– "'Mezclar verdades con fabulosos intentos': Metateatro y aporía en *El gallardo español* de Cervantes." *Anales Cervantinos*, vol. 36, 2004, pp. 329–44.
Algorri, Luis. "Este es el hombre más odiado del verano: Teddy Bautista." *Tiempo de hoy*, no. 1817, 16 Oct. 2009, www.tiempodehoy.com/espana/este-es-el-hombre-mas-odiado-del-verano.
Altolaguirre, Manuel. *Obras completas*, edited by James Valender, vol. 1, Ediciones Istmo, 1986.

Aranda, J.F. "Manuel Altolaguirre y el cine (1959)." *Litoral*, no. 181/2, 1989, pp. 295–7.

Aristotle. *Poetics*. Translated and with a commentary by George Whalley, edited by John Baxter and Patrick Atherton, MQUP, 1997. *ProQuest Ebook Central*, ebookcentral.proquest.com/lib/utk/detail.action?docID=3330809.

Armas, Frederick A. de. *The Invisible Mistress: Aspects of Feminism and Fantasy in the Golden Age*. Biblioteca Siglo de Oro, 1976.

Armstrong-Roche, Michael. "Imperial Theater of War: Republican Virtues under Siege in Cervantes's *Numancia*." *Journal of Spanish Cultural Studies*, vol. 6, no. 2, 2005, pp. 185–203.

– "(The) *Patria* Besieged: Border-Crossing Paradoxes of National Identity in Cervantes's *Numancia*." *Border Interrogations: Questioning Spanish Frontiers*, edited by Benita Sampedro Vizcaya and Simon Doubleday, Berghahn Books, 2008, pp. 204–27.

Arribas de Hoyos, Paloma. "El Alcalde de Zalamea y SGAE." *Legal Today*, 7 March 2009, www.legaltoday.com/practica-juridica/civil/prop._intelectual/el-alcalde-de-zalamea-y-sgae.

Ashenfelter, Orley, and George E. Johnson. "Bargaining Theory, Trade Unions, and Industrial Strike Activity." *American Economic Review*, no. 59, 1969, pp. 35–49.

Avalle-Arce, Juan Bautista. "'*La Numancia*': Cervantes y la tradición histórica." *Nuevos deslindes cervantinos*, Ariel, 1975, pp. 247–75.

Aznar Soler, Manuel. "'El retablo de Eldorado'de José Sanchis Sinisterra." *Teatro español contemporáneo: autores y tendencias*, edited by Alfonso de Toro and Wilfried Floeck, Reichenberger, 1995, pp. 391–414.

Azorín Martínez Ruíz, José. *Diario de un enfermo*. Establecimiento Tipográfico de Ricardo Fe, 1901.

Bakhtin, Mikhail Mikhailovich. *The Dialogic Imagination*. Edited by Michael Holquist, translated by Caryl Emerson and Michael Holquist. U of Texas P, 1981.

Ballota, David. "Fuenteovejuna pide ayuda ante el acoso del comendador de la SGAE." *Genbeta*, 9 Feb. 2012, m.genbeta.com/activismo-online/fuenteovejuna-pide-ayuda-ante-el-acoso-del-comendador-de-la-sgae.

Barba, Eugenio. *Theatre: Solitude, Craft, Revolt*. Black Mountain P, 1999.

"The Battle for Burgos." *Workers Solidarity Movement*, 1 Jan. 2014, www.wsm.ie/c/battle-burgos.

Beasley-Murray, Jon, and Alberto Moreiras. "Subalternity and Affect." *Angelaki*, vol. 6, no. 1, 2001, pp. 1–4.

Behrend-Martinez, Edward. "An Early Modern Spanish Divorce Court and the Rhetoric of Matrimony (1654–1715)." *Disciplines on the Line: Feminist Research on Spanish, Latin American, and U.S. Latina Women*, edited by Anne J. Cruz, Rosilie Hernández-Pecoraro, and Joyce Tolliver, Juan de la Cuesta, 2003, pp. 145–66.

Benjamin, Walter. *The Origin of German Tragic Drama*. New Left Books, 1977.
Bensusan, Pilar. "La SGAE, inquisición intelectual." *Granada Hoy*, 17 Aug. 2009, www.granadahoy.com/opinion/articulos/SGAE-inquisicion -intelectual_0_ 287671556.html.
Blogger, Atreides. "Al abordaje! – La SGAE como piratería moderna amparada por el estado." *Occidente a la Deriva*, 11 Feb. 2010, www.occidentealaderiva .com/2009/08/sgae-o-la-pirateria-moderna-amparada.html.
Boal, Augusto. *Theater of the Oppressed*. Theatre Communications Group, 1985.
Bod, Rens. "How a New Field Could Help Save the Humanities." *Chronicle of Higher Education*, vol. 63, no. 25, Feb. 2017, www.chronicle.com/article /How-a-New-Field-Could-Help/239209.
Boronat y Barrachina, Pascual. *El Beato Juan de Ribera y el Real Colegio de Corpus Christi: Estudio histórico*. Vives y Mora, 1904.
Borowski, Mateusz, and Malgorzata Sugiera. "Storytelling as a Strategy of Strengthening Collective Bonds: Introduction." *Worlds in Words: Storytelling in Contemporary Theatre and Playwriting*, edited by Mateusz Borowski and Malgorzata Sugiera, Cambridge Scholars, 2019, pp. 76–89.
Bossy, John. "The Social History of Confession in the Age of the Reformation." *Transactions of the Royal Historical Society*, vol. 25 (1975), 21–38. JSTOR, www .jstor.org/stable /3679084.
Bourdieu, Pierre. "Forms of Capital." *Handbook for Theory and Research for the Sociology of Education*, edited by J.G. Richardson, Greenwood, pp. 241–58.
Boyle, Margaret. "Women's Exemplary Violence in Luis Vélez de Guevara's *La serrana de la Vera*." *Bulletin of the Comediantes*, vol. 66, no. 1, 2014, pp. 159–75.
Burkhart, Louise M., et al. *Aztecs on Stage: Religious Theater in Colonial Mexico*. U of Oklahoma P, 2011.
Bushnell, Rebecca. "A Companion to Tragedy: Introduction." *A Companion to Tragedy*, edited by Rebecca Bushnell, Blackwell, 2005, pp. 1–4.
Busquets, Jacinto. *Idea exemplar de prelados, delineada en la vida y virtudes del venerable varón, el Illmo. y Exmo. Don Juan de Ribera*. Patriarca de Antioquía, Arzobispo de Valencia, Real Convento de Nuestra Señora del Carmen, 1683.
Butler, Judith. "When gesture becomes event." *Interviews in Performance Philosophy: Crossings and Conversations*, edited by Anna Street, Julien Alliot, and Magnolia Pauker, Palgrave Macmillan UK, 2017, pp. 171–91.
Caballero, Ernesto. *Tratos*. Centro Dramático Nacional, 2016. Script.
Caballero, Pepe. "Todo el pueblo se vuelca en la XIV representación de '*El alcalde de Zalamea*.'" *Hoy, provincia Badajoz*, 15 Aug. 2007, p. 8.
Calame, Claude. "The Tragic Choral Group: Dramatic Roles and Social Functions." *A Companion to Tragedy*, translated by Dan Edelstein, edited by Rebecca Bushnell, Blackwell, 2005, pp. 215–33.
Calderón de la Barca, Pedro. *El alcalde de Zalamea*. Introduction by José María Díez Borque, Editorial Castalia, 1981.

- *El Gran Teatro del Mundo*. Edited by John J. Allen and Domingo Ynduráin, vol. 72, Crítica, 1997.
- "The Great Theater of the World." *Theater*, translated by Rick Davis, vol. 34, no. 1, 2004, Duke UP, pp. 128–51.

Campbell, Ysla. "El mercader amante de Gaspar de Aguilar: la imagen dramática del cambio." *El escritor y la escena: Estudios sobre el teatro español de los Siglos de Oro. Homenaje a Alfredo Hermenegildo*, edited by Ysla Campbell, Universidad Autónoma de Ciudad Juárez, 1996, pp. 27–35.

Campos, Prado. "*Tratos*: La inmigración, los CIE y Cervantes." *El Confidencial*, 12 Sept. 2016, www.elconfidencial.com/cultura/2016-09-12/tratos-cervantes-cie-inmigrantes-ernesto-caballero-teatro_1256486/.

Canavaggio, Jean. *Cervantès dramaturge: Un théâtre à naître*. PU de France, 1977.

The Canons and Decrees of the Sacred and Oecumenical Council of Trent. Edited and translated by J. Waterworth, London, Dolman, 1848. *Hanover Historical Texts Project*, history.hanover.edu/texts/trent/trentall.html.

Cantador, Francisco. "Cuando Fuente Obejuna se transforma en 'Fuenteovejuna.'" *Sierra Albarrana: Medio ambiente y sociedad*, no. 121, 2009, pp. 4–12.

Capeheart, Loretta, and Dragan Milovanovic. *Social Justice: Theories, Issues & Movements*. Rutgers UP, 2007.

Caro, Ana. *El Conde Partinuplés*. Edited by Lola Luna, Kassel, 1993.

Caro Baroja, Julio. "Honour and Shame: A Historical Account of Several Conflicts," *Honour and Shame: The Values of Mediterranean Society*, edited by J.G. Péristiany, Chicago: U of Chicago P, 1966.

Carrasco Urgoiti, Mª Soledad. "*El gallardo español* como héroe fronterizo." *Actas del III Congreso Internacional de la Asociación de Cervantistas (Menorca 1997)*, coordinated by Antonio Pablo Bernat Vistarini, U de les Illes Balears, 1998, pp. 571–81.

Carrión, Gabriela. *Staging Marriage in Early Modern Spain: Conjugal Doctrine in Lope, Cervantes, and Calderón*. Lewisburg, Bucknell UP, 2011.

Carrión, María M. *Subject Stages: Marriage, Theatre, and the Law in Early Modern Spain*. U of Toronto P, 2010.

Casa, Frank P. "Amor, riqueza y lealtad en El mercader amante." *El escritor y la escena: Estudios sobre el teatro español de los Siglos de Oro. Homenaje a Alfredo Hermenegildo*, edited by Ysla Campbell. U Autónoma de Ciudad Juárez, 1996, pp. 37–45.

Casalduero, Joaquín. *Sentido y forma del teatro de Cervantes*. Gredos, 1966.

Casey, James G. *The Kingdom of Valencia in the Seventeenth Century*. Cambridge UP, 1979.

Castells, Manuel. *End of Millenium*. 2nd ed., Wiley-Blackwell, 2010.

- "Grassrooting the Space of Flows." *The Global Resistance Reader*, edited by L. Amoore, Routledge, 2005, pp. 363–70.
- *The Informational City: Information Technology, Economic Restructuring, and the Urban-Regional Process*. Basil Blackwell, 1989.
- "Space of Flows, Space of Places: Materials for a Theory of Urbanism in the Informational Age." *The Cybercities Reader*, edited by Stephen Graham, Routledge, 2004, pp. 82–93.

Castillo, David R., and William Egginton. *Medialogies: Reading Reality in the Age of Inflationary Media*. Bloomsbury, 2016.

Castillo, Moisés R. "Apocalyptic Stages: Lope de Vega's *El Nuevo Mundo* and Cervantes's *La Numancia*." *Writing the End of Times: Apocalyptic Imagination in the Hispanic World*, edited by David R. Castillo and Bradley J. Nelson, *Hispanic Issues Online*, vol. 23, 2019, pp. 72–96.
- "Espacios de ambigüedad en el teatro cervantino: *La conquista de Jerusalén* y los dramas de cautiverio." *Cervantes*, vol. 32, no. 2, 2012, pp. 123–42.
- "¿Ortodoxia cervantina?: Un análisis de *La gran sultana*, *El trato de Argel* y *Los baños de Argel*." *Bulletin of the Comediantes*, vol. 56, no. 2, 2004, pp. 219–40.

Cerella, Antonio. "The Dehumanization of the Enemy." *The Philosophical Salon: Speculations, Reflections, Interventions*, edited by Michael Marder and Patrícia Vieira, Open Humanities P, 2017, pp. 34–6.

Cervantes, Miguel de. "El coloquio de los perros." *Novelas ejemplares*, edited by Harry Sieber, vol. 2, Cátedra, 2002, pp. 297–359.
- *Comedia llamada Trato de Argel*. Edited by Florencio Sevilla Arroyo and Antonio Rey Hazas. Planeta, 1987.
- *La conquista de Jerusalén por Godofre de Bullón, atribuida a Miguel de Cervantes*. Edited by Héctor Brioso Santos, Cátedra, 2009.
- *La destrucción de Numancia*. Edited by Ricardo Doménech, Taurus, 1967.
- "The Dog's Colloquy." *Exemplary Stories*, translated by Byc A. Jones, Penguin Books, 1972.
- "Entremés del retablo de las maravillas." *Entremeses*, edited by Miguel Herrero García, Espasa-Calpe, 1962, pp. 155–83.
- *El gallardo español. Obras Completas III, Edición Guanajuato*, edited by Florencio Sevilla Arroyo, Museo Iconográfico del Quijote / Centro de Estudios Cervantinos, 2013, pp. 149–93.
- "El juez de los divorcios." *Entremeses*, edited by Nicholas Spadaccini, Cátedra, 2004, pp. 97–110.
- *La Numancia*. Edited by Francisco Ynduráin, Aguilar, 1964.
- *Numantia: A Tragedy by Miguel de Cervantes Saavedra*. Translated from the Spanish with Introduction and Notes by James Y. Gibson, Kegan Paul, Trench & Co., 1885, *Internet Archive*, 30 July 2007, www.archive.org/stream/ numantiatragedy00cervuoft/ numantiatragedy00cervuoft_djvu.txt.

- *Poesías completas I: Viaje al Parnaso y Adjunta al Parnaso*. Edited by Vicente Gaos, Castalia, 1973.
- *Tragedia de Numancia. Obras Completas III, Edición Guanajuato*, edited by Florencio Sevilla Arroyo, Museo Iconográfico del Quijote / Centro de Estudios Cervantinos, 2013, pp. 73–109.

Childers, William. *Transnational Cervantes*. U of Toronto P, 2006.

Císcar Pallarés, Eugenio. *Moriscos, nobles y repobladores: Estudios sobre el siglo XVII en Valencia*. Alfons el Magnànim, 1993.

Cohen, Walter. *Drama of a Nation: Public Theater in Renaissance England and Spain*. Cornell UP, 1998.

Correa, Gustavo. "El concepto de la fama en el teatro de Cervantes." *Hispanic Review*, vol. 27, no. 3, 1959, pp. 280–302.

Cortadella i Morral, Jordi. "La *Numancia* de Cervantes: Paradojas de la heroica resistencia ante Roma en la España imperial." *Actas del XI Coloquio Internacional de la Asociación de Cervantistas (Seúl 2004)*, edited by Chul Park, U of Hankuk, 2005, pp. 557–70.

Covarrubias Horozco, Sebastián de. *Tesoro de la lengua castellana o española*. Madrid, Luis Sánchez, 1611. *Fondos digitalizados, Biblioteca de la Universidad de Sevilla*, http://fondosdigitales.us.es/fondos/libros/765/16/tesoro-de-la-lengua-castellana-o-espanola/.

- *Tesoro de la lengua castellana o española*. Edited by Felipe C.R. Maldonado and Manuel Camarero, Editorial Castalia, 1994.

Cowling, Erin. Review of 2016 International Siglo de Oro Drama Festival: *El príncipe ynocente*. Performance by EFE TRES Teatro, *Bulletin of the Comediantes*, vol. 69 no. 1, 2017, pp. 189–91.

Crispin, John. *Quest for Wholeness: The Personality and Works of Manuel Altolaguirre*. Albatros Hispanófila, 1983.

Cropanzano, Russell, Jordan H. Stein, and Thierry Nadisic. *Social Justice and the Experience of Emotion*. Routledge, 2011.

Cruz, Anne J. *Discourses of Poverty: Social Reform and the Picaresque Novel in Early Modern Spain*. U of Toronto P, 1999.

Cruz, Juana Inés de la. *Carta atenagórica y Respuesta a sor Filotea*. Linkgua digital, 2010.

- *The Divine Narcissus: El Divino Narciso*. Translated by Patricia A. Peters and Renée Domeier, U of New Mexico P, 1998.
- "Loa para el Auto Intitulado 'El Cetro de José.'" *Obras completas de Sor Juana Inés de la Cruz*, edited by Alfonso Méndez Plancarte and Alberto G. Salceda, vol. 4, Fondo de Cultura Económica, 1957.
- "Loa para el Auto Intitulado 'El Mártir del Sacramento, San Hermenegildo.'" *Obras completas de Sor Juana Inés de la Cruz*, edited by Alfonso Méndez Plancarte and Alberto G. Salceda, vol. 4, Fondo de Cultura Económica, 1957.

- *A Sor Juana Anthology*. Translated by Alan S. Trueblood, Harvard UP, 1988.
Cudd, Anna E. *Analyzing Oppression*. Oxford UP, 2006.
Daniel, Lee A. "Sor Juana's Baroque Martyr-*Auto*: *El Mártir del Sacramento, San Hermenegildo*." *Latin American Theatre Review*, vol. 28, no. 1, 1994, pp. 101–14.
"Defining Economic Justice and Social Justice." *Center for Economic and Social Justice*, 2017, www.cesj.org/learn/definitions/defining-economic-justice-and-social-justice/.
de Kock, Leon. "Interview with Gayatri Chakravorty Spivak: New Nation Writers Conference in South Africa." *ARIEL: A Review of International English Literature*, vol. 23, no. 3, 1992, pp. 29–47.
Delgado Llano, Bernardo, actor. *El alcalde de Zalamea*. Personal Interview, 23 Aug. 2003.
Delumeau, Jean. *Sin and Fear: The Emergence of a Western Guilt Culture, 13th–18th Centuries*. New York: St Martin's P, 1990.
Dopico Black, Georgina. *Perfect Wives, Other Women: Adultery and Inquisition in Early Modern Spain*. Durham: Duke UP, 2001.
Eden, Kathy. "Aristotle's *Poetics*: A Defense of Tragic Fiction." *A Companion to Tragedy*, edited by Rebecca Bushnell, Blackwell, 2005, pp. 41–50.
Egginton, William. "The Baroque as a Problem of Thought." *PMLA*, vol. 124, no. 1, 2009, pp. 143–9.
- *How the World Became a Stage*. SUNY P, 2002.
- "'Quixote,' Colbert, and the Reality of Fiction." *The Stone*, 25 Sept. 2011, www.opinionator.blogs.nytimes.com/2011/09/25/quixote-colbert-and-the-reality-of-fiction/.
- *The Theater of Truth: The Ideology of (Neo)Baroque Aesthetics*. Stanford UP, 2010.
Ehlers, Benjamin. *Between Christians and Moriscos: Juan de Ribera and Religious Reform in Valencia, 1568–1614*. Johns Hopkins UP, 2006.
Eisenberg, Daniel. "El convenio de separación de Cervantes y su esposa Catalina." *Anales Cervantinos*, vol. 35, 1999, pp. 143–9, analescervantinos.revistas.csic.es/index.php/analescervantinos/article/view/120/119.
Elliot, John Huxtable. *Imperial Spain*. Penguin Books, 2002.
Erdman, Harley, translator. *The Mountain Girl from La Vera*. By Luis Vélez de Guevara. Liverpool UP, 2019.
Escrivá, Francisco. *Vida de Illustrísimo y Excellentísimo Señor Don Juan de Ribera*. Patriarca de Antiochia y Arzobispo de Valencia, Pedro Patricio Mey, 1612.
"La escuela de los vicios." *Morfeo Teatro*, http://www.morfeoteatro.com/laescueladelosvicios/index.html. Accessed 22 Feb. 2018.
Espada, Arcadi. "¿Quién mató al Comendador?" *El mundo*, 22 Aug. 2009, www.elmundo.es/opinion/columnas/arcadi-espada/2009/08/18947085.html.
Fastrup, Anne. "Cross-cultural Movement in the Name of Honour: Renegades, Honour and State in Miguel de Cervantes' Barbary Plays." *Bulletin of Spanish Studies*, vol. 89, no. 3, 2012, pp. 347–67.

Fernández, Enrique. "*Los tratos de Argel*: Obra testimonial, denuncia política y literatura terapéutica." *Cervantes*, vol. 20, no.1, 2000, pp. 7–26.

Ferns, Chris. *Narrating Utopia: Ideology, Gender, Form in Utopian Literature*. Liverpool UP, 1999.

Figueroa, Melissa. "La expulsión de los moriscos en *El gran Patriarca don Juan de Ribera* de Gaspar Aguilar: Un festejo a medias." *Bulletin of the Comediantes*, vol. 66, no. 2, 2014, pp. 27–44.

Fiume, Giovanna. "'Illud quod est caput omnium: L'espulsiones dei moriscos e la canonizazione di Juan de Ribera." *Estudis, Revista de Historia Moderna*, no. 39, 2013, pp. 215–50.

Flores, Allan, Fernando Memije, and Fernando Villa Proal. *Proyecto El príncipe ynocente*. n.d. T.S. Collection of EFE TRES Teatro.

Frankena, William K. "The Concept of Social Justice." *Social Justice*, edited by Richard B. Brandt, Prentice-Hall, 1962, pp. 1–29.

Frías, Brisa. "Ciudad Juárez se quita el sombrero." *El Diario*, 9 March 2013, p. A16.

Friedman, Edward. *Spanish Captives in North Africa in the Early Modern Age*. U of Wisconsin P, 1983.

"Fuente Obejuna – Habitantes desde 1900 hasta 2016." 23 July 2013, www.foro-ciudad.com/cordoba/fuente-obejuna/mensaje-11459159.html.

Galeano, Eduardo. *Las palabras andantes*. Siglo Veintiuno Editores, 1993.

Gamboa, Pepa, director. *"Fuenteovejuna" por las mujeres del barrio del Vacie (Sevilla)*. 5 Oct. 2016, www.youtube.com/watch?v=ztDurCMPHes.

— Personal Interview. 19 June 2018.

Garcés, María Antonia. *Cervantes in Algiers: A Captive's Tale*. Vanderbilt UP, 2002.

García-Martín, Elena. *Rural Revisions of Golden Age Drama: Performance of History, Production of Space*. Bucknell UP, 2017.

García Puertas, Manuel. *Cervantes y la crisis del Renacimiento español*. U de la República, 1962.

Garcilaso de la Vega, El Inca. *Comentarios reales de los incas*. V. 1. Edited by Aurelio Miró Quesada. Biblioteca Ayacucho, 1976.

Gaylord Randel, Mary. "The Order in the Court: Cervantes' *Entremes del juez de los divorcios*." *Bulletin of the Comediantes*, vol. 34, no.1, 1982, pp. 83–95. *Project Muse*, doi:10.1353/boc.1982.0011.

Gerli, E. Michael. "Aristotle in Africa: History, Fiction, and Truth in *El gallardo español*." *Cervantes*, vol. 15, no. 2, 1995, pp. 43–57.

Gil Ambrona, Antonio. "La violencia contra las mujeres: Discursos normativos y realidad." *Historia Social*, vol. 61, 2008, pp. 3–21. *JSTOR*, www.jstor.org/stable/40658113.

Gili Gaya, Samuel. *Tesoro lexicográfico 1492–1726*. Consejo Superior de Investigaciones Científicas, 1947.

Gómez-Robledo, Marina. "Burgos Activists Hunker Down against Construction Project." *El País*, 13 Jan. 2014, elpais.com/elpais/2014/01/13/inenglish/1389607345_906072.html.

González de Salas, José Antonio. *Nueva idea de la tragedia antigua*. 1633.

Graham, Stephen. Introduction. *The Cybercities Reader*, edited by Stephen Graham, Routledge, 2004, pp. 81–2.

Greer, Margaret R. "Imperialism and Anthropophagy in Early Modern Spanish Tragedy: The Unthought Known." *Reason and Its Others: Italy, Spain, and the New World*, edited by David R. Castillo and Massimo Lollini, Vanderbilt UP, 2006, pp. 279–95.

– "Spanish Golden Age Tragedy: From Cervantes to Calderón." *A Companion to Tragedy*, edited by Rebecca Bushnell, Blackwell, 2005, pp. 351–69.

Grossi, Verónica. "Subversión del Proyecto Imperial de Conquista y Conversión de las Américas en la 'Loa Para El Divino Narciso' de Sor Juana Inés de la Cruz." *Revista Canadiense de Estudios Hispánicos*, vol. 28, no. 3, 2004, pp. 541–64.

Gutiérrez Galindo, Blanca. "Creatividad y democracia: Joseph Beuys y La crítica de la economía política." *Anales del instituto de investigaciones estéticas*, vol. 35, no. 103, 2013, pp. 99–140.

Haba, Raúl. "A la SGAE, la hacienda y la vida, pero no el honor." *Hoy.es*, 22 Oct. 2014, www.hoy.es/20090822/sociedad/sgae-hacienda-vida-pero 20090822.html#frm_art_ rectifica.

Halliwell, Martin. "Picaresque." *Encyclopedia of the Novel*, edited by Paul Schellinger, Routledge, 1998.

Halperin Donghi, Tulio. *Un conflicto nacional: Moriscos y cristianos viejos en Valencia*. Institució Alfons el Magnànim, 1980.

Hamilton, Earl J. "Las consecuencias económicas de la expulsión de los moriscos." *Actas del I Congreso de Historia de Andalucía: Andalucía Moderna*, Caja de Ahorros, 1978, pp. 69–84.

Hanisch, Carol. "The Personal Is Political: The Women's Liberation Movement Classic with a New Explanatory Introduction." *Women of the World, Unite! Writings by Carol Hanisch*, Jan. 2006, http://www.carolhanisch.org/CHwritings/PIP.html.

Harvey, L.P. *Muslims in Spain, 1500 to 1614*. U of Chicago P, 2005.

Henry, Melanie. *The Signifying Self: Cervantine Drama as Counter-Perspective Aesthetic*. Modern Humanities Research Association, 2013.

Heras, Eva M. "Crean una red de pueblos con montajes de teatro populares." *Diario de Córdoba*, 21 July 2010, www.diariocordoba.com/noticias/cordobaprovincia/crean-red-pueblos-montajes-teatro-populares_573964.html.

– "La SGAE demanda a Fuente Obejuna unos 32.000 euros." *Diario de Córdoba*, 14 August, 2009, www.diariocordoba.com/noticias/cultura/sgae-demanda-fuente-obejuna-32-000-euros_502402.html.

Hermenegildo, Alfredo. *La "Numancia" de Cervantes*. Sociedad General Española de Librería, 1976.
Hernández-Simón, Javier. "Joven Compañía Nacional de Teatro Clásico: Fuente Ovejuna de Lope de Vega." *Compañía Nacional de Teatro Clásico*, 2016, teatroclasico.mcu.es/2016/06/22/fuente-ovejuna-2016/.
Hicks, John R. *The Theory of Wages*. Macmillan, 1963.
"Historia del Festival de Almagro." *Festival de Teatro Clásico de Almagro*, festivaldealmagro.com/es/seccion/historia-festival-almagro/.
"Honra." *Diccionario de autoridades*, Gredos, 1963.
Hughes, Gethin. "*El gallardo español*: A Case of Misplaced Honour." *Cervantes*, vol. 13, no. 1, 1993, pp. 65–75.
Hulme, Peter. "Introduction: The Cannibal Scene." *Cannibalism and the Colonial World*, edited by Francis Barker et al., Cambridge UP, 1998, pp. 1–38.
Hutcheon, Linda. *A Theory of Adaptation*. Routledge, 2006.
Hyman, Colette. *Staging Strikes. Workers' Theatre and the American Labor Movement*. Temple UP, 1997.
I.L.H. "Morfeo convierte en teatro los discursos políticos de Quevedo." *Diario de Burgos*, 31 Jan. 2014, www.diariodeburgos.es/noticia/ZF3D0F5E3-A182-1A9914779C0F D3A7FBEE/20140131/morfeo/convierte/teatro/discursos/politicos/quevedo.
Jiménez, Juan. *Vida del Beato Juan de Ribera*. Imprenta de Joseph de Orga, 1798.
Johnson, Carroll B. "*La Numancia* y la estructura de la ambigüedad cervantina." *Cervantes: Su obra y su mundo*, edited by Manuel Criado de Val, EDI-6, 1981, pp. 309–16.
Kagan, Richard L. "A Golden Age of Litigation: Castile, 1500–1700." *Disputes and Settlements: Law and Human Relations in the West*, edited by John Bossy, Cambridge UP, 2003, pp. 145–66.
– *Lawsuits and Litigants in Castile 1500–1700*. U of North Carolina P, 1981.
Kahn, Aaron M. *The Ambivalence of Imperial Discourse: Cervantes´s La Numancia within the "Lost Generation" of Spanish Drama (1570–90)*. Peter Lang, 2008.
Kartchner, Eric J. "Dramatic Diegesis: Truth and Fiction in Cervantes's *El gallardo español*." *Yearbook of Comparative and General Literature*, vol. 47, 1999, pp. 25–35.
King, Willard F. "Cervantes' *Numancia* and Imperial Spain." *Modern Language Notes*, vol. 94, no. 2, 1979, pp. 200–21.
Kock, Leon de. "Interview with Gayatri Chakravorty Spivak: New Nation Writers Conference in South Africa." *ARIEL: A Review of International English Literature*, vol. 23, no. 3, 1992, pp. 29–47.
Lapeyre, H. *Géographie de l'Espagne morisque*. S.E.V.P.E.N., 1959.
Lauer, A. Robert. "*La Numancia* de Cervantes y la creación de una conciencia fundacional nacional." *Comentarios a Cervantes: Actas del VIII Congreso*

Internacional de la Asociación de Cervantistas (Oviedo 2012), edited by Emilio Martínez Mata and María Fernández Ferreiro, Fundación María Cristina Masaveu Peterson, 2014, pp. 986–96.

Lázaro, Fernando. "Bautista y otros 8 miembros de la SGAE, detenidos por desviar fondos." 1 July 2011, www.elmundo.es/elmundo/2011/07/01/espana/1309537638.html.

León, Fray Luis de. *La perfecta casada*. Edited by Mercedes Etreros, Taurus Ediciones, 1987.

Lewis-Smith, Paul. "Cervantes' *Numancia* as Tragedy and as Tragicomedy." *Bulletin of Hispanic Studies*, vol. 64, 1987, pp. 15–26.

Long, Anthony A. "Stoic Communitarianism and Normative Citizenship." *Social Philosophy and Policy*, vol. 24, no. 2, July 2007, pp. 241–61.

López Pinciano, Alonso. *Philosophia Antigua Poética*. Venta y libreria nacional y extranjera de hijos de Rodriguez, 1894.

López Rejas, Javier. "Caballero firma un trato con Cervantes." *El Cultural*. 9 Sept. 2016, m.elcultural.com/revista/escenarios/Caballero-firma-un-trato-con-Cervantes/38496.

Lorenzo Pinar, Francisco Javier. "La mujer y el Tribunal diocesano en Zamora durante el siglo XVI: Divorcios y nulidades matrimoniales." *Studia Zamorensia*, vol. 3, 1996, pp. 77–88. *Dialnet*, dialnet.unirioja.es/servlet/articulo?codigo=297290.

Luis-Orueta, Fernando de. "Las 54 reclamaciones que convirtieron a la SGAE en el 'enemigo del Pueblo.'" *La información*, 12 July 2011, www.lainformacion.com/arte-cultura-y-espectaculos/las-54-reclam.

Luna, Lola. Introducción. *Valor, agravio y mujer*, edited by Lola Luna, Castalia, 1993.

Lundelius, Ruth. "Paradox and Role Reversal in *La serrana de la Vera*." *The Perception of Women in Spanish Theater of the Golden Age*, edited by Anita Stoll and Dawn Smith, Bucknell UP, 1991, pp. 220–44.

Magnier Heney, Grace. "Ambiguity in *La Expulsión de los moros de España* by Gaspar Aguilar." *Actes du Ve Symposium International d'Études Morisques sur: Le Ve Centenaire de la Chute de Grenade, 1492–1992*, edited by Abdeljelil Temimi, CEROMDI, 1993, pp. 766–8.

Magraner Rodrigo, Antonio. *La expulsión de los moriscos, sus razones jurídicas y consecuencias económicas para la región valenciana*. Instituto Valenciano de Estudios Históricos, 1975.

Maiorino, Giancarlo, editor. *The Picaresque Tradition and Displacement*. U of Minnesota P, 1996.

Maravall, José Antonio. *La cultura del barroco. Análisis de una estructura histórica*. Ariel, 2012.

Marchante-Aragón, Lucas A. "The King, the Nation, and the Moor: Imperial Spectacle and the Rejection of Hybridity in *The Masque of the Expulsion of the*

Moriscos." *The Journal for Early Modern Cultural Studies*, vol. 8, no. 1, 2008, pp. 98–133.

Marini Palmieri, Enrique. "Notas a la 'Loa' del Divino Narciso, auto sacramental de Sor Juana Inés de la Cruz." *Revista De Literatura*, vol. 71, no. 141, 2009, pp. 207–32.

Mariscal, George. *Contradictory Subjects: Quevedo, Cervantes, and Seventeenth-Century Culture*. Cornell UP, 1991.

Márquez Villanueva, Francisco. *Moros, moriscos y turcos de Cervantes: Ensayos críticos*. Ediciones Bellaterra, 2010.

– *El problema morisco (desde otras laderas)*. Libertarias, 1991.

Martín Fernández, Ángel Luis. Personal Interview 22 Aug. 2014.

McKendrick, Melveena. *Theatre in Spain: 1490–1700*. Cambridge UP, 1989.

Méndez Plancarte, Alfonso, and Alberto G. Salceda, editors. *Obras completas de Sor Juana Inés de la cruz*, vol. 4, Fondo de Cultura Económica, 1951.

Menéndez y Pelayo, Marcelino. *Historia de los heterodoxos españoles II*. Librería Católica de San José, 1880.

Miguel Magro, Tania de. "Fragmentarismo ideológico en *El trato de Argel*." *Cervantes*, vol. 35, no. 1, 2015, pp. 181–202.

Miller, David. *Social Justice*, Oxford UP, 1976.

Mintz, Jacqueline Ann. "A Comparative Study of Shame in Spanish and English Renaissance Drama." U of California, Berkeley, 1982, Dissertation.

Morales, Ambrosio de. *Corónica general de España*. Alcalá de Henares, Juan Iñíguez de Lequerica, 1574.

Mujica, Bárbara. *A New Anthology of Early Modern Spanish Theater*, Yale UP, 2014.

Negro, Francisco. "Cervantes' *El coloquio de los perros*: A Theater Production by Morfeo Teatro." Adapted and directed by Francisco Negro, Reimagining the Spanish *Comedia* in the Transmedia Age Conference, Ohio Wesleyan University, Delaware, OH.

– "El coloquio de los perros." 2011. Theatrical script.

– "Re: Entrevista." Received by Glenda Y. Nieto-Cuebas, 24 Nov. 2017.

Nieto, Miguel. Personal Interview. 23 Aug. 2014.

Núñez, Cristina. "Labotika 'retoca' *La serrana de la Vera*." *Hoy*, 26 Aug. 2017. www.hoy. es/caceres/labotika-retoca-serrana-20170826001818-ntvo.html.

OECD *Economic Survey of Mexico 2017*. 2017, www.oecd.org/eco/surveys/economic-survey-mexico.htm. Accessed 13 July 2017.

Ohanna, Natalio. *Cautiverio y convivencia en la edad de Cervantes*. Centro Estudios Cervantinos, 2011.

Ortiz, Miguel. "Fuente Obejuna todos a una contra la SGAE." *Papel en Blanco*. 20 Aug. 2009, www.papelenblanco.com/divulgacion/fuente-obejuna-todos-a-una-contra-la-sgae.

Ovid. *Metamorphoses*. Translated by Frank J. Miller. Harvard UP, 1958.

Ovidio. *Metamorfosis*. Translated by Eli Leonetti Jungl, Espasa-Calpe, 1994.
Patterson, Charles. "Jesuit Neo-Scholasticism and Criollo Consciousness in Sor Juana's *El Mártir del Sacramento, San Hermenegildo*." *Hispania*, vol. 96, no. 3, 2013, pp. 460–8.
Peale, George. "El Acto I de *La Serrana de la Vera* de Vélez de Guevara: Hacia una poética del bufón." *El escritor y la escena V: Estudios sobre teatro español y novohispano de los Siglos de Oro: Homenaje a Marc Vitse*, Universidad Autónoma de Ciudad Juárez, 1997, pp. 141–58.
Pedraza Jiménez, Felipe B. "La expulsión de los moriscos en el teatro áureo: Los ecos de un silencio." *Textos sin fronteras: Literatura y Sociedad*, 2, edited by H. Awaad and M. Insúa, *Ediciones Digitales del GRISO*, 2010, pp. 179–200, hdl.handle.net/10171/ 14259.
Pérez-Romero, Antonio. *The Subversive Tradition in Spanish Renaissance Writing*. Bucknell UP, 2005.
Peters, Patricia A., and Renée Domeier, translators. *The Divine Narcissus/El divino Narciso*, University of New Mexico Press, 1998.
Piñero, Pedro Manuel, and Virtudes Atero. "El romance de *La serrana de la Vera*: La pervivencia de un mito en la tradición del Sur." *DICENDA. Cuadernos de Filología Hispánica*, no. 6, 1987, pp. 399–418.
Pitt-Rivers, Julian. *Honour and Shame: The Values of Mediterranean Society*. Edited by J.G. Péristiany, U of Chicago P, 1966.
Puppinck, Grégor. "ECHR: No Right to Divorce." *European Center for Law and Justice*, Jan. 2017. eclj.org/marriage/echr/ cedh-la-cour-confirme-labsence-de-droit-individuel-au-divorce.
Rampell, Catherine. "A Really Horrible Boss Gets His Just Desserts." Review of *Fuenteovejuna*, directed by Julian Mesri, *New York Times*, 26 Feb. 2013, p. C3.
Rawls, John. *A Theory of Justice*. Harvard UP, 1971.
Redacción BBC Mundo. "Fuente Obejuna paga su deuda." *BBC Mundo*, 22 Jan. 2010, www.bbc.com/mundo /cultura_sociedad/2010/01/100122 _fuenteovejuna_deuda.
– "Fuente Obejuna se rebela." *BBC Mundo*, 19 Aug. 2009, www.bbc.com/ mundo/cultura_sociedad/2009/08/090819_derechos_fuenteovejuna_np.
Reed, Cory A. "Cervantes and the Novelization of Drama: Tradition and Innovation in the *Entremeses*." *Cervantes: Bulletin of the Cervantes Society of America*, vol. 11, no. 1, 1991, pp. 61–86. *Cervantes Society of America*, www. hnet.org/~cervant/csa/artics91 /reed.htm.
– "Dirty Dancing: Salome, Herodias, and *El retablo de las maravillas*." *Bulletin of the Comediantes*, vol. 44, no. 1, 1992, pp. 7–20.
Reglá, Juan. *Estudios sobre los moriscos*. Anales de la U de Valencia, 1964.
Reizábal Garrigosa, María Socorro. "La crisis financiera de la ciudad de Valencia en el siglo XVII: Las repercusiones inmediatas de la expulsión de

los moriscos." *Pedralbes. Revista d'Història Moderna*, vol. 13, no. 1, 1993, pp. 521–34.

Ríos, Sara. "Gamonal: ocho días que hicieron de Burgos el epicentro de la protesta ciudadana." *20 Minutos*, 18 Jan. 2014, www.20minutos.es/noticia/2033313/0 /gamonal-vecinos/burgos/protestas-ciudadanas/.

Robalino, Gladys. Review of "El coloquio de los perros de Miguel de Cervantes." Directed by Francisco Negro, *Bulletin of the Comediantes*, vol. 67, no. 1, 2015, pp. 174–5.

Rodríguez Cuadros, Evangelina. "La espantosa compostura: El canón de la tragedia del Siglo de Oro desde el actor." *Hacia la tragedia áurea: Lecturas para un nuevo milenio*, edited by Frederick A. de Armas, Luciano García Lorenzo, and Enrique García Santo-Tomás, Iberoamericana, 2008, pp. 181–218.

Rogel Vide, Carlos, et al. *En torno a la reforma de la Ley de Propiedad Intelectual*. Editorial Reus, 2013.

Rojas Villandrando, Agustín de. *El viaje entretenido*. Emprenta [sic] Real, 1603. Biblioteca Virtual Universal, www.biblioteca.org.ar/libros/ 154442.pdf. Accessed 1 Sept. 2016.

Romera, J., and A. Semprún. "El auditor eleva a 87 millones el dinero que la SGAE desvió a la red de Neri." *El economista*, 29 Nov. 2011, www.eleconomista.es/empresas-finanzas/noticias/3566939/11/11/El-auditor-eleva-a-87-millones-el-dinero-que-la-SGAE-desvio-a-la-red-de-Neri.html.

R.V.A. "La tradición se convierte en reivindicación: 'Somos 5.000 habitantes, somos 5.000 autores. Fuente Obejuna, todos a una.'" *El Mundo*, 20 Aug. 2009, www.elmundo.es/ elmundo/2009/08/20/andalucia/1250760687.html.

Sabàt de Rivers, Georgina. *En Busca de Sor Juana*. Facultad de Filosofía y Letras, U Nacional Autónoma de México, 1998.

Salas Barbadillo, Alonso Jerónimo de. *Fiestas de la boda de la incansable malcasada*. Madrid, Viuda de Cosme Delgado, 1622.

Sánchez Escobar, Juan José. "Las aportaciones de Gaspar de Aguilar al proceso de formación de la comedia barroca." *Teatro y Prácticas Escénicas II: La Comedia*, edited by José Luis Canet Vallés, Tamesis Books Limited, 1986, pp. 132–55.

— "Gaspar Aguilar: El proceso de construcción de una dramaturgia inorgánica." *Cuadernos de Filología. Literaturas: Análisis*, vol. 3, no. 1–2, 1981, pp. 125–52.

Sánchez Seoane, Loreto. "Paula Bonet: 'Estoy cansada de que lo universal sea lo masculino.'" *El Independiente*, 3 Apr. 2018, https://www.elindependiente.com/ tendencias/2018/03/04 / paula-bonet-estoy-cansada-de-que-lo-universal-sea-lo-masculino/.

Sanchis Sinisterra, José. "La condición marginal del teatro en el Siglo de Oro." *Primer acto*, vol. 186, 1980, pp. 73–83.

- "Por una dramaturgia de la recepción." *ADE Teatro: Revista de la Associación de Directores de Escena de España*, vol. 41–2, 1995, pp. 64–9.
- "Sobre la revisión crítica de los clásicos." *Primer acto*, vol. 43, 1963, pp. 63–4.
- *El retablo de Eldorado: Trilogía Americana*. Edited by Virtudes Serrano, Cátedra, 1996, pp. 252–362.

Scholz, Sally J. "The Challenge of Systemic Oppression; The Dangerous Divorce of Civil and Domestic Spheres: Institutional Violence." *Institutional Violence*, edited by Deane W. Curtin and Robert Litke, Rodopi, 1999.
- *Political Solidarity*. Pennsylvania State UP, 2008.

Serralta, Frédéric. "Juan Rana homosexual." *Criticón*, vol. 50, 1990, pp. 81–92.

Serrano, Virtudes. "Introducción." *Trilogía americana*, by José Sanchis Sinisterra, edited by Virtudes Serrano, Cátedra, 1996, pp. 9–77.

Silleras-Fernández, Núria. *Chariots of Ladies: Francesc Eiximenis and the Court Culture of Medieval and Early Modern Iberia*. Cornell UP, 2015.

Simerka, Barbara. *Discourses of Empire: Counter-Epic Literature in Early Modern Spain*. Pennsylvania State UP, 2003.

Sirera, Josep Lluís. "Las 'comedias de santos' en los autores valencianos: Notas para su estudio." *Teatro y Prácticas Escénicas*, vol. 2, *La Comedia*, edited by José Luis Canet Vallés, Tamesis Books, 1986, pp. 187–228.
- "Mercaderes, campesinos y jornaleros en el teatro de Gaspar Aguilar." *Modelos de vida en la España del Siglo de Oro*, vol. 1, edited by Ignacio Arellano and Marc Vitse, Iberoamericana, 2004, pp. 553–65.

"Social Justice in an Open World: The Role of the United Nations." *United Nations Department of Economic and Social Affairs*, 2006, https://www.un.org/esa/socdev/documents/ifsd/SocialJustice.pdf.

Solodkow, David. "Mediaciones del Yo y Monstruosidad: Sor Juana o el 'Fénix' Barroco." *Revista Chilena de Literatura*, vol. 74, 2009, pp. 139–67.

Soufas, Teresa Scott. "Ana Caro Mallén de Soto." *Women's Acts: Plays by Women Dramatists of Spain's Golden Age*, edited by Teresa Scott Soufas, UP of Kentucky, 1997.
- *Dramas of Distinction: A Study of Plays by Golden Age Women*. UP of Kentucky, 1997.
- "Introduction." *Women's Acts: Plays by Women Dramatists of Spain's Golden Age*, edited by Teresa Scott Soufas, UP of Kentucky, 1997.
- "Repetitive Patterns: Marrying Off the 'Parthenos' in Ana Caro's *El conde Partinuplés*." *Engendering the Early Modern Stage: Women Playwrights in the Spanish Empire*, edited by Valerie Hegstrom and Amy R. Williamsen. UP of the South, 1999, pp. 93–106.

Sourvinou-Inwood, Christiane. "Greek Tragedy and Ritual." *A Companion to Tragedy*, edited by Rebecca Bushnell, Blackwell, 2005, pp. 7–24.

"Spain Austerity: Spending Protest Grips City of Burgos." BBC News, 17 Jan. 2014. www.bbc.com/news/world-europe-25775122.

Sprinceana, Iulia Andrea. "Staging History, Fantasizing Reality: José Sanchis Sinisterra's *The Eldorado Puppet Show* through Miguel de Cervantes's *The Marvelous Puppet Show*." *Text & Presentation*, vol. 10, 2013, pp. 54–68.

Stackhouse, Kenneth. "Beyond Performance: Cervantes's Algerian Plays, *El Trato de Argel* and *Los Baños de Argel*." *Bulletin of the Comediantes* vol. 52, no. 2, 2000, pp. 7–30.

Stapp, William A. "*El gallardo español*: La fama como arbitrio de la realidad." *Anales Cervantinos*, vol. 17, 1978, pp. 123–36.

Stiegler, Brian N. "The Coming of a New Jerusalem: Apocalyptic Vision in Cervantes's *Numancia*." *Neophilologus*, vol. 80, 1996, pp. 569–81.

Stroud, Matthew. "Homo/Hetero/Social/Sexual: Gila in Vélez de Guevara's *La serrana de la Vera*." *Plot Twists and Critical Turns: Queer Approaches to Early Modern Spanish Theater*, Bucknell UP, 2007, pp. 121–40.

Syverson-Stork, Jill. *Theatrical Aspects of the Novel: A Study of Don Quixote*. Albatros, 1986.

Taylor, Diana. *Disappearing Acts: Spectacles of Gender and Nationalism in Argentina's "Dirty War."* Duke UP, 1997.

"El teatro pueblo a pueblo." *EscenaTe*, edited by María Fernanda Cosín, 2013, escenate.es/ ?project=el-teatro-pueblo-a-pueblo.

Thompson, Peter E. *The Triumphant Juan Rana: A Gay Actor of the Spanish Golden Age*. U of Toronto P, 2006.

Torres Morera, Juan Ramón. *Repoblación del reino de Valencia después de la expulsión de los moriscos*. Ayuntamiento de Valencia, 1969.

Torres Nebrija, Gregorio. "Manuel Altolaguirre, dramaturgo." *Segismundo*, vol. 13, 1977, pp. 349–79.

Tusell, Javier. *Spain: From Dictatorship to Democracy, 1939 to the Present*. Translated by Rosemary Clark, John Wiley and Sons, 2011. Wiley Online Library, DOI 10.1002 /9780470690031.

The Universal Declaration of Human Rights, United Nations, 1948. http://www.un.org/en/universal-declaration-human-rights/.

Usón, Víctor. "El rap que crea rimas con Cervantes." *El País*, 13 Nov. 2016, https://elpais.com/cultura/2016/10/09/actualidad/1475996908_363509.html.

Valdés Aragonés, Isabel. "Support for Burgos Rebels Spreads to Other Spanish Cities." *El País*, 16 Jan. 2014, https://elpais.com/elpais/2014/01/16/inenglish/1389869248_ 650001.html.

Valencia, Felipe. "*Furor, industria* y límites de la palabra poética en *La Numancia* de Cervantes." *Criticón*, vol. 126, 2016, pp. 97–110.

Valencia, Pedro de. *Consideraciones de Pedro de Valencia, su coronista, sobre las enfermedades y salud del reino*. Biblioteca Nacional de España, Madrid, MS 7845, ff. 103–117.

Valender, James. "Guiones de cine: Introducción." *Obras completas*, by Manuel Altolaguirre, edited by Valender, vol. 2, Ediciones Istmo, 1986, pp. 323–48.

Vega Carpio, Lope Félix de. *El arte nuevo de hacer comedias en este tiempo*. Edited by J. de José Prados, Consejo Superior de Investigaciones Científicas, 1971.
- *Arte nuevo de hacer comedias en este tiempo*. Edited by Erique García Santo-Tomás, 2nd ed., Cátedra, 2009.
- *Fuenteovejuna*. Edited by Juan Mª Marín, Cátedra, 1997.
- *El príncipe inocente*. Edited by by Tania de Miguel Magro and Erin Cowling, Agilice Digital, 2019.
- *El príncipe ynocente*. Adapted by Fernando Memije and Fernando Villa, directed by Allan Flores, performances by Fernando Villa and Juan Carrillo, 2 Apr. 2016, Chamizal National Park, El Paso.

Vélez de Guevara, Luis. *The Mountain Girl from La Vera*. Translated by Harley Erdman, Liverpool UP, 2019.
- *La serrana de la Vera*. Edited by William Manson and C. George Peale, Juan de la Cuesta, 2002.
- "La serrana de la Vera." *A New Anthology of Early Modern Spanish Theater*, edited by Bárbara Mujica, Yale UP, 2014, pp. 235–87.
- *Wild Thing of La Vera*, translated by Harley Erdman, Liverpool UP, 2018.

"Videocreación Dulcinea." *Festival de Teatro Clásico de Almagro*, http://festivaldealmagro.com/es/proyectof/7/acercate-a-cervantes-video-art-contest-dulcinea/.

Vill, A.S.R. "Descarnado y desencantado Cervantes." *El correo de Burgos*, 19 Jan. 2011, http://www.elcorreodeburgos.com/noticias/cultura/descarnado-desencantado-cervantes_13900.html.

Villa Proal, Fernando. "Ñaque del siglo 21, una conversación con EFE TRES y su acercamiento a los clásicos." Association for Hispanic Classical Theater, 21 April 2017, Hilton Garden Inn, El Paso, TX. Interview/Round Table.

Villegas, Rafael. "El conflicto con la SGAE nos ha traído publicidad." *El público: Córdoba* 20 Aug. 2009, www.publico.es/245319/el-conflicto-con-la-sgae-nos-ha-traido-publicidad.

Vitoria, Francisco de. *Relecciones del estado, de los indios y del derecho de la guerra*. Porrúa, 1996.

Vivar, Francisco. "El ideal *pro patria mori* en *La Numancia* de Cervantes." *Cervantes*, vol. 20, no. 2, 2000, pp. 7–30.

Vives, Juan Luis. *The Education of a Christian Woman: A Sixteenth-Century Manual*. Edited by Charles Fantazzi, U of Chicago P, 2000.

Weiner, Jack. "*La Numancia* de Cervantes y la alianza entre Dios e Israel." *Neophilologus*, vol. 81, 1997, pp. 63–70.

Weissgerber, Barbara F. "Introduction: Gender and Sovereignty in the Age of Isabel." *Isabel Rules: Constructing Queenship, Wielding Power*, U of Minnesota P, 2004, pp. xi–xxvi.

Wheeler, Duncan. *Golden Age Drama in Contemporary Spain: The Comedia on Page, Stage and Screen*, U of Wales P, 2012.

Wild Thing. By Luis Vélez de Guevara, directed by Gina Kaufmann, translated by Harley Erdman, U of Massachusetts Amherst Theater Department, 10 Apr. 2019, Siglo Theater Festival, Chamizal National Memorial, El Paso, TX.

Williams, Bernard. *Shame and Necessity*. U of California P, 1993.

Ynduráin, Domingo. "'El alcalde de Zalamea': Historia, ideología, literatura." Biblioteca Virtual Miguel de Cervantes, 2012, www.cervantesvirtual.com/obra/el-alcalde-de-zalamea-historia-ideologia-literatura/.

Yzquierdo Tolsada, Mariano. "El alcalde de Zalamea, la alcaldesa de Fuente Obejuna, la SGAE y lo que no es la SGAE." *La tribuna del derecho*, 16 Oct. 2009, libros-revistas-derecho.vlex.es/vid/alcalde-alcaldesa-fuente-juna-sgae-285685773.

Zanelli Velásquez, Carmela. "La Loa de 'El Divino Narciso' de Sor Juana Inés de la Cruz y la Doble Recuperación de la Cultura Indígena Mexicana." *La literatura novohispana: Revisión crítica y propuestas metodológicas*, edited by José Pascual Buxó and Arnulfo Herrera, U Autónoma Nacional de México, 1994, pp. 183–200.

Zimic, Stanislav. *El teatro de Cervantes*. Castalia, 1992.

Žižek, Slavoj. *The Sublime Object of Ideology*. Verso, 1989.

Contributors

Moisés R. Castillo is Associate Professor of Early Modern and Colonial Studies in the Department of Hispanic Studies at the University of Kentucky. He has a BA in philosophy from the Universidad de Granada, Spain, and a PhD in Hispanic literature from the University of Minnesota. He is the author of *Indios en escena: La representación del amerindio en el teatro del Siglo de Oro* (Purdue University Press, 2009), and a guest editor of the special number of *Romance Quarterly* (vol. 61, no. 2, 2014) devoted to Cervantes's *Exemplary Novels*. He has written numerous chapters in edited volumes and articles in refereed journals. His research focuses on Golden Age theater and Cervantes studies. Currently, he is writing a book on the Cervantine *comedias*, and preparing an edited volume, *Essays in Memory of John Jay Allen*. He is the recipient of the College of Arts and Sciences Outstanding Teaching Award in the Humanities 2015–16 at the University of Kentucky.

Jaclyn Cohen-Steinberg is Associate Professor (Teaching) of Spanish at the University of Southern California in Los Angeles. She has been at USC for eight years. Previously, she was Visiting Assistant Professor at Towson University in Towson, Maryland. Jaclyn received her PhD from Johns Hopkins University in 2011. Dr Cohen-Steinberg's main areas of interest and research are Spanish Golden Age theatre and short stories, with an emphasis on Spanish women writers.

Erin Alice Cowling is Assistant Professor of Spanish at MacEwan University in Edmonton, Alberta. Her current research interests lie in how marginalized characters are portrayed, as well as how modern performances can inform and expand our understanding of early modern plays. She is the author of a forthcoming book on chocolate in early modern literature. She has published in a number of journals, including *Bulletin of the Comediantes*, *Hispania*, and *Hipogrifo*.

Tania de Miguel Magro has a PhD from Stony Brook University and is Associate Professor at West Virginia University. Her publications deal mainly with the work of Agustín Moreto, the figure of Juan Rana, and short theatre. She has prepared critical editions of Lope de Vega's *El príncipe inocente* and Moreto's *Los engaños de un engaño* and *La misma conciencia acusa*. She is currently working on a monograph that analyses representations of domestic violence, violence against homosexuals and "effeminate" men, and of abuse of sex workers by their pimps in *jácaras* and *entremeses*. The recurring themes of her work are power struggles, subversion, and the reaffirmation of authority. She writes on how theatre portrays, questions, and/or supports social, political, religious, and gender conventions.

Melissa Figueroa is Assistant Professor of Spanish in the Department of Modern Languages at Ohio University. She is interested in exploring dramatic representations of Moriscos and how theatre became a medium for the construction of minorities affected by the emergence of Spanish imperialism during the early modern period. She has published in the *Bulletin of the Comediantes*, the *Journal of Spanish Cultural Studies*, and *ehumanista/Conversos*.

Mina García Jordán, born in Málaga, Spain, is Associate Professor in the Department of World Languages and Cultures at Elon University, where she teaches Spanish language and literature. Dr. García Jordán's research interests include the role of literature in the expansion of the Spanish empire, early modern Spanish literature, transatlantic studies, and Latin American colonial culture and literature, with special attention to the role of the Other (e.g., *conversos*, Moriscos, and witches). She has authored many articles and book chapters as well as numerous conference papers. Her first book, entitled *Magia, Hechicería y Brujería: Entre La Celestina y Cervantes* was published by Editorial Renacimiento (Seville, Spain) in 2010. Her second book, *Idolatry and the Construction of the Spanish Empire*, was published by the University of Colorado Press in 2018.

Elena García-Martín is Associate Professor at North Central College, where she specializes in Spanish studies and Spanish drama, with interests in minority cultures and comparative cultural studies. Her latest work has appeared in the *Bulletin of the Comediantes*, *Hispanic Research*

Journal, Comedia Performance, and *Romance Quarterly.* Overall, her research focuses on issues of social justice in contemporary theatre. Other ongoing projects include the investigation of pedagogies in mixed-language classrooms, a study about theatres of inclusion, and the publication of her book titled *Rural Revisions of Golden Age Drama.*

Francisco Javier López-Martín is Associate Professor of Spanish at Denison University and teaches Spanish literature and language, critical theory, and writing. His specialty area is sixteenth- and seventeenth-century Hispanic transatlantic literature and history with emphasis on the representation of time, space, and the dynamics of power between America and Spain. He is also interested in European humanism during the sixteenth century, Spanish Golden Age theatre and digital humanities. Some of his publications include "Violencia, neoplatonismo y aristotelismo en La Aurora en Copacabana," "Definiendo las reglas del juego: Calderón y el espacio virtual," "Crisis y catarsis en el teatro calderoniano: del rito de paso a la tragedia española," and his book *Representaciones del tiempo y construcción de la identidad entre España y America (1580–1700).*

Harrison Meadows is Assistant Professor of Spanish in the Department of Modern Foreign Languages and Literatures at the University of Tennessee, Knoxville. His research focuses on early modern Iberian theatre and its role in the intellectual and cultural history of the West, on which he has published recent articles in *MLN* and *Romance Quarterly.* Dr Meadows also collaborated with John Slater (University of California–Davis) to publish an annotated edition of Pedro Calderón de la Barca's *En la vida todo es verdad y todo mentira* and *Sueños hay que verdad son* through Cervantes and Co.'s European Masterpiece Series, and spent 2017–18 on fellowship at the University of Tennessee Humanities Center. He received his PhD at the University of Colorado Boulder.

Glenda Y. Nieto-Cuebas is Associate Professor at Ohio Wesleyan University. Her current research focuses on contemporary productions of seventeenth-century texts, with special emphasis on censorship and social issues. She is also working on several pedagogical projects and publications focused on how experiential learning can help students better analyse the Spanish *comedia* through non-traditional means.

Charles Patterson is Associate Professor of Spanish at Western Washington University. He taught previously at Stephen F. Austin State University, and received his PhD from the University of Texas at Austin.

His research focuses on Golden Age Spanish theatre, as well as modern performances, translations, and adaptations of these early modern works. His articles have appeared in journals such as *Hispania*, *Bulletin of the Comediantes*, and *Comedia Performance*. He has also published an edition of Lope de Vega's *La dama boba* and a volume of translations of Miguel de Cervantes' plays titled *Cervantes's Eight Interludes*. One of the highlights of his career was directing a production of Cervantes' *El retablo de las maravillas* (The Stage of Wonders).

Index

abuse of power, 241
abused women, 238
adaptation, 4–11, 16, 26, 30, 64, 120–1, 128, 133–5, 136n9, 137, 139, 141, 143–4, 148, 150, 153–4, 158, 175, 178–9, 181, 196, 208, 217, 221, 223, 227, 232–4, 241, 252
Adjunta al Parnaso. See under Cervantes, Miguel de
Africa, 79, 157–8, 166, 170
Aguilar, Gaspar: *El gran Patriarca don Juan de Ribera*, 10, 68, 70, 71, 78, 80; *El mercader amante*, 70, 81nn6, 11; *Expulsión de los moros de España*, 78; *La fuerza del interés*, 70, 77; *La suerte sin esperanza*, 81n6
allegory, 7, 57, 61, 63, 65, 66
Almagro, 8, 210, 237, 239; festival, 238, 240; public library, 238
Altolaguirre, Manuel, 11, 175, 178–83, 185, 189–90; *Las maravillas*, 11, 175, 178–83, 185, 189
Amar después de la muerte. See under Calderón de la Barca, Pedro
Amerindians, 92, 187
annulment, 36–7, 43, 45, 51nn4, 5
Apalachee, 212
Apollo, 42–4

Aquinas, Thomas, 54–5, 67n7
Aristotelian, 6, 50
Aristotle, 21, 23–5, 28, 33n6, 54, 95; *Poetics*, 21, 25
arrepentimiento, 111, 115n15
Arte nuevo de hacer comedias. See under Vega, Félix Lope de
Association of Hispanic Classical Theater (AHCT), 4, 122, 211, 217, 212, 223, 227, 232
audience, xiii, 4–5, 8–12, 15–29, 31–2, 47–9, 53, 65–6, 68, 74, 76–80, 82, 84, 91, 119–30, 132–5, 140–2, 145–6, 152–3, 158, 160, 162, 164–5, 169–70, 179, 185, 188–9, 191, 196, 199, 209–10, 212–15, 217–25, 227–9, 231, 234, 237, 238–9
auto (*sacramental*), 10, 53–67, 98–9

Bernardo de Quirós, Francisco: *El muerto* (Better Wed than Dead), 209, 212
Bakhtin, Mikhail, 120, 126, 128, 136n8
ballad tradition, 16, 26–7, 32n1, 33n8
baroque, 20–2, 24, 28–9, 31, 56, 83, 124, 126, 239
Barroco Infantil, 238
Benedict XIV, 69

Index

bizarra, 20
blood purity, 46, 175–7, 179, 181, 189, 215
Boccacio, 38
body language, 237
Bourdieu, Pierre, 192, 194, 206n3
Brecht, Bertoldt, 218
Brechtian, 4
burlesque, 34, 36–8, 40–1, 44, 50
Butler, Judith, 199

Caballero, Ernesto, 11, 158–9; *Tratos*, 11, 157–8, 164, 173n2
Calderón de la Barca, Pedro, 10, 55, 70, 103, 114n3, 216, 223, 240–1; *Amar después de la muerte* (*Love After Death*), 70, 216; *El alcalde de Zalamea*, 192–3, 195, 198–9, 208; *El gran teatro del mundo*, 55; *El médico de su honra*, 35, 241; *La vida es sueño* (*Life Is a Dream*), 103, 212, 223
Cantar de los Cantares. See under León, Fray Luis de
capitalism, 70, 183
Caro Baroja, Julio, 108–9
Caro Mallén de Soto, Ana, 10, 98–100, 105–6, 108, 110, 112–13, 113n2, 217, 233; *El Conde Partinuplés*, 10, 98–100, 109, 111, 113, 114n3; *Valor, agravio y mujer*, 99, 113n2, 114n3, 233
Carta atenagórica. See under Cruz, Sor Juana Inés de la
Castells, Manuel, 196, 201, 203, 207n11
Castelvines y Monteses (Capulets and Montagues). See under Vega, Félix Lope de
Castro, Guillén de, 51n2; *Los malcasados de Valencia*, 51n2
Catholic, 9, 34–5, 37, 42–5, 50, 57–8, 61, 65, 82, 96n6, 162–3; Catholic Church, 34, 43–4, 68, 76; Catholic doctrine/dogma, 35, 37, 42, 44
Catholic monarchs (*los reyes católicos*), 16, 20, 25, 32n5, 72. See also Isabel (la católica); Fernando (el católico)
cautionary tale, 18, 19, 22. See also exemplarity
censales (loans), 76
censorship, 28, 140, 142, 229, 240, 263
Cervantes, Miguel de, 10–11, 34, 41, 49–50, 51n7, 82–95, 95–6n3, 96nn4, 5, 6, 97nn12, 13, 137–40, 143–4, 147–8, 153–4, 156n20, 157–60, 162–73, 175–9, 181, 183, 185, 189–90, 214, 223, 225, 239, 241; *Adjunta al Parnaso*, 49; *Don Quixote*, 48, 142, 174n8, 239; *El coloquio de los perros*, 11, 137, 138, 139, 140–3, 145, 147–56; *El gallardo español*, 10, 83, 84, 86, 89, 93, 94, 95n1, 95–6n3, 96n4; *El juez de los divorcios*, 34, 36, 41, 49–50; *El retablo de las maravillas* (The Marvellous Tableau), 11, 175–9, 181, 183, 185, 189, 225; *El trato de Argel*, 11, 86, 89, 93, 96n9, 157–73; *La conquista de Jerusalén por Godofre de Bullón*, 83, 86, 89, 92, 93, 96n7; *La elección de los alcaldes de Daganzo* (The Election of the Mayors of Daganzo), 209, 214; *La gran sultana doña Catalina de Oviedo*, 86, 89, 93; *La Numancia*, 10, 83, 86, 87, 88, 89, 91, 93, 94, 95n1, 96n7, 178; *Los baños de Argel*, 86, 89, 93; *Ocho comedias y ocho entremeses nunca representados*, 49, 83
Chamizal National Memorial Park, 220, 220n1, 221, 221n2
Charles I, 92
Christian slaves, 159–60

Christianity (Christian faith), 20, 160–4, 171, 173nn3–4
chronotope, 120–1, 126, 128, 133, 135
class (social class), 9–10, 134, 137–8, 148–9, 153–4, 155n6, 183, 194, 203, 222
collective bargaining, 9, 74–5
Colón, Cristóbal (Columbus, Christopher), 213
comedia burlesca, 36
comedia de enredo, 10
comedia doméstica, 36
comedia of captives, 83, 86
comedia/romance fronterizo, 83, 85
Compañía Nacional de Extremadura de Teatro y Kabaret (Labotika), 30
Compañía Nacional de Teatro Clásico, 30, 238
conquest, 10, 54, 56–8, 60–1, 64–6, 80n1, 83, 86, 175, 91, 93, 183–6, 188, 189–90
conservatism, 140–1
conversos, 106, 262
Corónica general de España. See under Morales, Ambrosio de
corruption, 136n3, 139, 141–2, 149, 154, 180, 201
Countess of Paredes de Nava, 65
Covarrubias y Orozco, Sebastián de, 102–3, 111, 115nn14–15; *Tesoro de la lengua castellana o española*, 102
Creole, 55, 60–1, 64–5
cross-dresser, 37
Cruz, Sor Juana Inés de la, 10, 53–8, 60–1, 63–6, 66n3, 67nn6–7, 9, 230; *Carta atenagórica*, 53, 58, 60; *El cetro de José*, 54; *El divino Narciso*, 53–4, 58, 60–3, 65, 67n9; *El mártir del sacramento*, 54, 58; *La Respuesta a Sr. Filotea de la Cruz*, 53, 58
cultural capital, 192, 194, 196, 206n3
currency: blanca, 71–2; real, 72, 74

De Fuenteovejuna a Ciudad Juárez, 8
De institutione feminae Christianae. See under Vives, Juan Luis
dehumanization, 95, 149, 154, 156n10
depopulation, 73
desengaño, 17, 122, 126–8, 135
desvergüenza, 102–3, 113
Diálogo de la verdadera honra militar. See under Urrea, Jerónimo de
Diccionario de Autoridades, 102
disabilities: blindness, 238; Braille, 238; limited mobility, 238; vision and hearing, 238
disadvantaged people, 76, 145, 238
divorce, 10, 34–8, 41–5, 47, 50, 51nn1, 6, 52n7
Don Gil de las calzas verdes. See under Molina, Tirso de
Don Juan Tenorio. See under Zorrilla, José
Don Quixote. See under Cervantes, Miguel de
double characters, 163, 168–9
Duke of Gandía (Carlos de Borja), 77, 81n10
Duke of Lerma (Francisco de Sandoval y Rojas), 69

economic: crisis, 212, 223; inequality, 6, 31, 54, 57, 60, 66, 68, 70–1, 76, 79, 113, 136n3, 138–9, 154, 156n10, 233; opportunities for women, 212; profit, 70, 74, 77–9, 194–5, 197, 240; stagnation, 70, 76
EFE TRES Teatro (ETT), 11, 119–22, 124–6, 128, 130, 132–5, 136nn5, 9, 209; *El príncipe ynocente*, 119, 121, 122, 126–8, 135–6n1, 227–8, 228n1, 229, 231
El burlador de Sevilla. See under Molina, Tirso de

El castigo sin venganza. See under Vega, Félix Lope de
El cetro de José. See under Cruz, Sor Juana Inés de la
El coloquio de los perros. See under Cervantes, Miguel de
El Conde Partinuplés. See under Caro Mallén de Soto, Ana
El descasamentero. See under Salas Barbadillo, Jerónimo de
El desdén con el desdén. See under Moreto, Agustín
El gallardo español. See under Cervantes, Miguel de
El gran Patriarca don Juan de Ribera. See under Aguilar, Gaspar
El gran teatro del mundo. See under Calderón de la Barca, Pedro
El juez de los divorcios. See under Cervantes, Miguel de
El lindo don Diego. See under Moreto, Agustín
El mártir del sacramento. See under Cruz, Sor Juana Inés de la
El médico de su honra. See under Calderón de la Barca, Pedro
El mercader amante. See under Aguilar, Gaspar
El muerto. See under Bernardo de Quirós, Francisco
El príncipe inocente. See under Vega, Félix Lope de
El retablo de Eldorado. See under Sanchis Sinisterra, José
El retablo de las maravillas. See under Cervantes, Miguel de
El trato de Argel. See under Cervantes, Miguel de
Encomium Matrimonii. See under Erasmus Desiderius
Enríquez de Guzmán, Feliciana, 217
entremés, 35–8, 40, 46–9, 83, 190n4, 231

Erasmus Desiderius: *Encomium Matrimonii*, 45
ethics, 93, 95, 191, 222
European Union, 34
exclusion, 11, 138, 144, 147, 149, 179
exemplarity, 18–21, 25. *See also* cautionary tale
Expulsión de los moros de España. See under Aguilar, Gaspar

femicide, 240–1
feminist, 6, 9, 231, 233
Fernando (el católico) (Ferdinand, the Catholic), 16, 18–20, 22, 25, 32–3n5, 87, 92
Fiestas de la boda de la incasable malcasada. See under Salas Barbadillo, Jerónimo de
Flemish, 92
fragmented text, 160
Franco, Francisco, 7–8, 173n5, 194
free will, 53, 58–60, 65–6, 163, 168
freedom, xii–xiii, 7, 40, 53, 59, 102, 112, 121, 135 158–60, 162, 164, 175, 213, 224
Fuenteovejuna. See under Vega, Félix Lope de
Fuenteovejuna en el frente, 1936, 8

gender, 4–7, 9–10, 15–16, 30–1, 45, 99, 106, 109, 113, 138, 209, 212, 218–19, 233, 235; cross-gender, 220; disparity, 209; expression, 15–16, 31; identity, 15–16, 25, 104, 138; non-binary, 31; non-normative, 209, 218; warfare, 212. *See also* transgender
González de Salas, José Antonio, 21, 33n6; *Nueva idea de la tragedia antigua*, 33n6
guilt, 98, 100, 104–7, 111–13, 114nn5, 6, 115n12, 132, 158

Habsburg dynasty/Habsburgs, 87–8, 92
hagiography/hagiographic, 10, 68, 71, 81n2, 165
hamartia, 24
Hamlet. See under Shakespeare, William
Hedda Gabler. See under Ibsen, Henrik
hegemonic, 53–5, 58, 60–1, 63–4, 69, 80
heresy, 38
historical drama, 10
homosexuality/homosexual, 16, 30, 36–7, 187–8
honour, 17, 23, 24, 35, 40, 70, 80–1n2, 84, 86, 94, 96n4, 98, 101–4, 106–13, 127, 131, 134, 241
honra, 35, 84, 96n4, 102–3, 131, 241
horizontal communication, 201
humanities, 3–5; crisis of, 3
humanization of the enemy, 83, 94
hunger, 150–3, 157

Ibsen, Henrik: *Hedda Gabler*, 222
identity, 5, 15–17, 20, 25, 28–31, 39, 84, 87–9, 91, 96n6, 104, 138, 145, 156n11, 161–2, 168, 192, 196, 204–5, 206n5, 224. See also gender
ideology/ideological, 6, 9, 15, 18, 22–4, 26–31, 35, 69, 78, 80n1, 81n10, 89, 95, 111, 139, 183–5, 194
immigration, 157, 161, 167, 169, 173n5
inclusion, 25, 40, 234, 238, 240
Indigenous, 10, 54–7, 59, 61–2, 64–5, 186–7
Industrial Revolution, 71, 200
inequality, 6, 9, 11, 31, 54, 56–7, 60, 66, 68, 70–1, 76, 79, 113, 136n3, 138–9, 152–4, 156n10, 175, 189, 233
injustice, 7–11, 24, 38, 41, 45, 50, 54–5, 57, 71, 79, 83, 89, 98, 100–1, 104, 112–13, 119, 126–7, 134–5, 137, 139, 148, 156n10, 160, 165, 168–9, 175–8, 182–3, 186, 188–90, 206n6, 215, 228
Inquisition (Spanish), 106, 176, 189
Institutio foeminae christianae. See under Vives, Juan Luis
Isabel (la católica), 16, 20, 22, 24–5, 27, 32n5, 33n5, 218
Islam, 69, 95, 160, 163, 171, 216
Italian, 38, 159

jornaleros (workers), 71–2, 75
Joven Compañía Nacional de Teatro Clásico, 8
justice, xi, xiii, 6–7, 15, 22–3, 34–5, 43–6, 50, 53, 55, 57, 68, 93–4, 100, 104–5, 110, 122, 126, 130–2, 135, 136n8, 175–6, 187, 190, 210, 216, 229; blind, 6; commutative, 65; criminal, 10; cultural, 205; distributive, 53–5, 58, 65; divine, 6, 43; legal, 6, 22; poetic, 19; social, 4–7, 9–11, 34–5, 50, 53–4, 70, 80, 83, 100, 104, 112–13, 119, 134, 139, 148, 154, 157, 167–8, 170, 172, 175, 179, 182–3, 185, 191, 200, 209, 212–14, 216–17, 219, 224, 226, 228, 232. See also injustice

La capeadora. See under Quiñones de Benavente, Luis
La conquista de Jerusalén por Godofre de Bullón. See under Cervantes, Miguel de
La elección de los alcaldes de Daganzo. See under Cervantes, Miguel de
La fuerza del interés. See under Aguilar, Gaspar
La gran sultana doña Catalina de Oviedo. See under Cervantes, Miguel de

La Numancia. See under Cervantes, Miguel de
La perfecta casada. See under León, Fray Luis de
La Respuesta a Sr. Filotea de la Cruz. See under Cruz, Sor Juana Inés de la
La serrana de la Vera. See under Vélez de Guevara, Luis
La suerte sin esperanza. See under Aguilar, Gaspar
La vida es sueño. See under Calderón de la Barca, Pedro
labour, 71, 73, 76, 80, 201; conditions, 68, 71–2, 75–6, 79; cultural, 199; exploitation, 79, 200; movement, 80
labrador(es) (farmers), 55, 72–5, 77, 79
Las maravillas. See under Altolaguirre, Manuel
Lazarillo de Tormes, 148–9
León, Fray Luis de, 45, 106–7; *Cantar de los Cantares*, 178; *La perfecta casada*, 45, 107
limpieza de sangre (blood purity), 175–7, 179, 181, 189, 215
loa, 10, 53, 56–61, 63–5, 66n3, 67nn5, 6, 7
Lope de Aguirre, traidor. See under Sanchis Sinisterra, José
Lope's (small) New World, 209, 213–14
López Pinciano, Alonso, 21, 33n6; *Philosophia Antigua Poética*, 33n6
Los baños de Argel. See under Cervantes, Miguel de
Los malcasados de Valencia. See under Castro, Guillén de
Los moriscos de Hornachos, 70

Madrid, 41, 53–4, 57, 65, 114n3, 155n6, 157–8, 193, 198, 208n16, 225, 237
male imperative, 212
marginalization, 138, 149, 196, 204

Marquesa de la Laguna, 65
martyrology, 45, 164–5
McCarthyism, 181
Metamorphoses. See under Ovid
Mexico, 56, 61, 65, 66n3, 119, 136n3, 175, 178–9, 184, 190n2, 209, 227, 229–30, 239
micro-theatre, 239
mimesis, 25
Ministerio de Sanidad (Ministry of Health), 237
Molière, Jean-Baptiste Poquelin, 217, 234; *Tartuffe*, 221
Molina, Tirso de, 23, 99, 178, 217; *El burlador de Sevilla* (The Trickster of Seville), 23, 32n4, 211–12, 222, 230; *El condenado por desconfiado*, 178; *Don Gil de las calzas verdes* (Don Gil of the Green Stockings), 211; *Legacy Boy*, 222; *Marta la piadosa* (Marta the Divine), 217, 220
Moor, 83, 85–6, 93. *See also* morisco
Morales, Ambrosio de, 87; *Corónica general de España*, 87
More, Thomas, 41; *Utopia*, 41
Moreto, Agustín, 39; *El desdén con el desdén*, 39; *El lindo Don Diego*, 230; *No puede ser*, 39
Morfeo Teatro, 11, 137, 139–44, 146, 148, 154n2, 155n9, 156n10
morisco, 10, 68–70, 73–9, 80n1, 81nn4, 9, 83, 85, 88, 92, 160
mujer esquiva, 39
mujer varonil, 101, 114n7
Muslim, 79, 80n1, 84–6, 98, 170–2

ñaque, 122, 124, 128–9, 133, 135, 227
narcos, 230
Naufragios de Álvar Núñez. See under Sanchis Sinisterra, José
No puede ser. See under Moreto, Agustín

non-traditional audiences, 238
non-violent aesthetic, 239–40
Norte de la poesía española, 68, 70, 81nn6, 11
novella, 38, 40
Nueva idea de la tragedia antigua. See under González de Salas, José Antonio
Nueva recopilación, 37, 52n11
nuevo cristiano (new Christian), 70, 79, 176–7, 179, 218
Nuevo mundo descubierto por Cristóbal Colón. See under Vega, Félix Lope de
Numancia (city), 87–91

Ocho comedias y ocho entremeses nunca representados. See under Cervantes, Miguel de
old Christians, 73, 78
oppression, 80, 149, 153–4, 158; racial, 9; systemic, 137–9, 154, 156n10–11
Othello. See under Shakespeare, William
Other, 10, 37, 54, 83, 86, 89, 93–5, 157, 171, 184, 216
Ovid (Publius Ovidius Naso): *Metamorphoses*, 63, 67n9

Philip II, 36, 87–8, 91–2, 96n9, 159, 169, 172
Philip III, 69, 172
Philosophia Antigua Poética. See under López Pinciano, Alonso
Picaresque, 148, 150, 156n13
pícaro, 122, 136n9, 149–50, 156n14
Poetics. See under Aristotle
Portonopeus de Blois, 100, 114n6
Portugal, 8, 268
poverty, 129, 137, 142, 149, 153, 156n13, 172, 183
power imbalance, 209

privilege, 20, 22, 27, 48, 67n7, 81n9, 103, 108, 134, 138–9, 142, 144, 148–9, 153, 172, 176–7, 222
production, 3, 8–9, 11, 21–2, 30–1, 33n5, 53, 74, 78, 80, 82, 119, 122–4, 126, 128, 132–4, 136n1, 137, 139–42, 144, 147, 150, 173n1, 192–7, 203, 206nn4, 6, 207n15, 208n16, 209–12, 214–15, 217–21, 223–4, 227, 233–5, 239, 241

queer, 218
Quevedo, Francisco de, 56, 141–2, 155n9; *El buscón*, 139; *La escuela de los vicios*, 139
Quiñones de Benavente, Luis, 216; *La capeadora*, 216

race, 4–6, 9–10, 34, 179–80, 182, 189, 209, 217, 219, 222, 233
Renaissance, 6, 107
Repertorio Español, 8, 119–20
responsibility, 12, 143, 157, 162, 165, 169, 230–1, 235, 237, 239
Ribera, Juan de, 10, 68–71, 75–6, 78–9, 81n3
rite, 57, 60–1, 65–6
Robin Hood (Disney), 132–4, 228
Rojas, Fernando, 200, 206n4, 208n15
romance Morisco, 83, 85
Rome, 67n7, 87–9, 91–4

Salas Barbadillo, Jerónimo de, 10; *El descasamentero*, 10, 34–6, 38–50; *Fiestas de la boda de la incasable malcasada*, 38, 45–6, 48, 50, 52n8
San Félix, Sor Marcela de, 217
Sanchis Sinisterra, José, 11, 175, 183–5, 188, 190, 190n2–3; *El retablo de Eldorado*, 11, 175, 183–90, 190n2; *Lope de Aguirre, traidor*, 184; *Naufragios de Álvar Núñez*, 184;

Tragientremés en dos partes (see *El retablo de Eldorado* above); *Trilogía Americana*, 184
Scipio Aemilianus, Publius Cornelius, 87, 88, 89, 91–2, 94
sexual abuse, 168, 241
sexuality, 16, 30–1, 36–7, 218
SGAE (Sociedad General de Autores y Editores Españoles), 11, 191–2, 196–202, 204–5, 207nn13–14, 207–8n15, 208n16
Shakespeare, William, 217, 232, 234–5; *Hamlet*, 211; *The Merchant of Venice*, 215, *Othello*, 240–1
shame, 73, 98–113, 114n5, 166; shameful, 24
shared/common humanity, 83–6, 93
social order, 16, 20, 22, 29, 135
space of flows, 196, 203–5, 207n11
(Spanish) Civil War, 7–8, 178, 184
stage props, 76, 126, 129, 133, 144–5
strike, 69–72, 74–5, 78–80
subaltern, 38, 54–5, 64–5

Tartuffe. See under Molière, Jean-Baptiste Poquelin
Teatro Inverso (theatre company), 209, 223; *Rosaura*, 223–5
Tesoro de la lengua castellana o española. See under Covarrubias y Orozco, Sebastián de
Tesoro lexicográfico, 111, 115n14
testimony, 44, 158, 160, 164–5
The Merchant of Venice. See under Shakespeare, William
Theater with a Mission (volunteer organization, Tallahassee, FL), 209, 211–12, 215
theatre of the oppressed, 219
Theogenes, 89–93
Thomistic, 58–9

Touch Tours, 238
tragedy, 10, 15, 21, 24–6, 28, 31, 33n6, 86–7, 89, 160, 164, 190n4, 222
Tragientremés en dos partes. See under Sanchis Sinisterra, José
transgender, 218–19, 221
translation, 16, 31, 120, 212, 214, 217–18, 220, 233
Tratos. See under Caballero, Ernesto
trauma, 25, 158, 160, 164, 184
Trilogía Americana. See under Sanchis Sinisterra, José

UMass Amherst Theater: *Wild Thing* (adaptation of *La serrana de la Vera*), 31
Urrea, Jerónimo de: *Diálogo de la verdadera honra militar*, 96n4
utopia, xi, xiii, 10, 34–52

Valor, agravio y mujer. See under Caro Mallén de Soto, Ana
Vega, Félix Lope de, 5, 7, 9, 11, 21, 25, 50, 56, 83, 119–21, 124, 126–7, 130, 135, 136n2, 235; *Arte nuevo de hacer comedias*, 119, 124, 194; *Castelvines y Monteses*, 216; *El castigo sin venganza*, 35, 119; *Nuevo mundo descubierto por Cristóbal Colón*, 96n7, 209, 213; *El príncipe inocente*, 11, 119–24, 126–9, 134, 135–6n1, 228; *Fuenteovejuna*, 7–9, 119–20, 134, 192, 205n1, 211; *La dama boba*, 119, 239
Velázquez, Diego (de), 149
Vélez de Guevara, Luis, 15–33, 217; *La serrana de la Vera*, 10, 15–33, 209, 217, 219, 221–2
vergüenza, 101–3, 108–9, 113
Viajeinmóvil (theatre company), 241
violence, 241

Virgin Mary, 160, 171
virtue, 6, 20, 39, 42, 83, 85–6, 89, 92, 94, 95, 101–3, 107, 145
Vitoria, Francisco de, 6, 66n2
Vives, Juan Luis, 106–7; *Institutio foeminae christianae*, 45
voice, xi–xiii, 11, 20, 38, 40–1, 46, 53–5, 79, 85, 89, 93, 105, 110, 122–3, 133, 137, 143, 147, 153–4, 156n10, 164–5, 204, 223–4, 228
volunteers, 191, 211, 238

wealth gap, 71

Zorrilla, José: *Don Juan Tenorio*, 211
Zurbarán, Francisco de, 149

Toronto Iberic

CO-EDITORS: Robert Davidson (Toronto) and Frederick A. de Armas (Chicago)

EDITORIAL BOARD: Josiah Blackmore (Harvard); Marina Brownlee (Princeton); Anthony J. Cascardi (Berkeley); Justin Crumbaugh (Mt Holyoke); Emily Francomano (Georgetown); Jordana Mendelson (NYU); Joan Ramon Resina (Stanford); Enrique García Santo-Tomás (U Michigan); Kathleen Vernon (SUNY Stony Brook)

1 Anthony J. Cascardi, *Cervantes, Literature, and the Discourse of Politics*
2 Jessica A. Boon, *The Mystical Science of the Soul: Medieval Cognition in Bernardino de Laredo's Recollection Method*
3 Susan Byrne, *Law and History in Cervantes'* Don Quixote
4 Mary E. Barnard and Frederick A. de Armas (eds), *Objects of Culture in the Literature of Imperial Spain*
5 Nil Santiáñez, *Topographies of Fascism: Habitus, Space, and Writing in Twentieth-Century Spain*
6 Nelson Orringer, *Lorca in Tune with Falla: Literary and Musical Interludes*
7 Ana M. Gómez-Bravo, *Textual Agency: Writing Culture and Social Networks in Fifteenth-Century Spain*
8 Javier Irigoyen-García, *The Spanish Arcadia: Sheep Herding, Pastoral Discourse, and Ethnicity in Early Modern Spain*
9 Stephanie Sieburth, *Survival Songs: Conchita Piquer's* Coplas *and Franco's Regime of Terror*
10 Christine Arkinstall, *Spanish Female Writers and the Freethinking Press, 1879–1926*
11 Margaret Boyle, *Unruly Women: Performance, Penitence, and Punishment in Early Modern Spain*
12 Evelina Gužauskytė, *Christopher Columbus's Naming in the* diarios *of the Four Voyages (1492–1504): A Discourse of Negotiation*

13 Mary E. Barnard, *Garcilaso de la Vega and the Material Culture of Renaissance Europe*
14 William Viestenz, *By the Grace of God: Francoist Spain and the Sacred Roots of Political Imagination*
15 Michael Scham, *Lector Ludens: The Representation of Games and Play in Cervantes*
16 Stephen Rupp, *Heroic Forms: Cervantes and the Literature of War*
17 Enrique Fernandez, *Anxieties of Interiority and Dissection in Early Modern Spain*
18 Susan Byrne, *Ficino in Spain*
19 Patricia M. Keller, *Ghostly Landscapes: Film, Photography, and the Aesthetics of Haunting in Contemporary Spanish Culture*
20 Carolyn A. Nadeau, *Food Matters: Alonso Quijano's Diet and the Discourse of Food in Early Modern Spain*
21 Cristian Berco, *From Body to Community: Venereal Disease and Society in Baroque Spain*
22 Elizabeth R. Wright, *The Epic of Juan Latino: Dilemmas of Race and Religion in Renaissance Spain*
23 Ryan D. Giles, *Inscribed Power: Amulets and Magic in Early Spanish Literature*
24 Jorge Pérez, *Confessional Cinema: Religion, Film, and Modernity in Spain's Development Years, 1960–1975*
25 Joan Ramon Resina, *Josep Pla: Seeing the World in the Form of Articles*
26 Javier Irigoyen-García, *"Moors Dressed as Moors": Clothing, Social Distinction, and Ethnicity in Early Modern Iberia*
27 Jean Dangler, *Edging toward Iberia*
28 Ryan D. Giles and Steven Wagschal (eds), *Beyond Sight: Engaging the Senses in Iberian Literatures and Cultures, 1200–1750*
29 Silvia Bermúdez, *Rocking the Boat: Migration and Race in Contemporary Spanish Music*
30 Hilaire Kallendorf, *Ambiguous Antidotes: Virtue as Vaccine for Vice in Early Modern Spain*
31 Leslie Harkema, *Spanish Modernism and the Poetics of Youth: From Miguel de Unamuno to La Joven Literatura*
32 Benjamin Fraser, *Cognitive Disability Aesthetics: Visual Culture, Disability Representations, and the (In)Visibility of Cognitive Difference*
33 Robert Patrick Newcomb, *Iberianism and Crisis: Spain and Portugal at the Turn of the Twentieth Century*
34 Sara J. Brenneis, *Spaniards in Mauthausen: Representations of a Nazi Concentration Camp, 1940-2015*
35 Silvia Bermúdez and Roberta Johnson (eds), *A New History of Iberian Feminisms*

36 Steven Wagschal, *Minding Animals in the Old and New Worlds: A Cognitive Historical Analysis*
37 Heather Bamford, *Cultures of the Fragment: Uses of the Iberian Manuscript, 1100–1600*
38 Enrique García Santo-Tomás (ed), *Science on Stage in Early Modern Spain*
39 Marina Brownlee (ed), *Cervantes'* Persiles *and the Travails of Romance*
40 Sarah Thomas, *Inhabiting the In-Between: Childhood and Cinema in Spain's Long Transition*
41 David A. Wacks, *Medieval Iberian Crusade Fiction and the Mediterranean World*
42 Rosilie Hernández, *Immaculate Conceptions: The Power of the Religious Imagination in Early Modern Spain*
43 Mary Coffey and Margot Versteeg (eds), *Imagined Truths: Realism in Modern Spanish Literature and Culture*
44 Diana Aramburu, *Resisting Invisibility: Detecting the Female Body in Spanish Crime Fiction*
45 Samuel Amago and Matthew J. Marr (eds), *Consequential Art: Comics Culture in Contemporary Spain*
46 Richard P. Kinkade, *Dawn of a Dynasty: The Life and Times of Infante Manuel of Castile*
47 Jill Robbins, *Poetry and Crisis: Cultural Politics and Citizenship in the Wake of the Madrid Bombings*
48 Ana María Laguna and John Beusterien (eds), *Goodbye Eros: Recasting Forms and Norms of Love in the Age of Cervantes*
49 Sara J. Brenneis and Gina Herrmann (eds), *Spain, World War II, and the Holocaust: History and Representation*
50 Francisco Fernández de Alba, *Sex, Drugs, and Fashion in 1970s Madrid*
51 Daniel Aguirre-Oteiza, *This Ghostly Poetry: Reading Spanish Republican Exiles between Literary History and Poetic Memory*
52 Lara Anderson, *Control and Resistance: Food Discourse in Franco Spain*
53 Faith Harden, *Arms and Letters: Military Life Writing in Early Modern Spain*
54 Erin Alice Cowling, Tania de Miguel Magro, Mina García Jordán, and Glenda Y. Nieto-Cuebas (eds), *Social Justice in Spanish Golden Age Theatre*

www.ingramcontent.com/pod-product-compliance
Lightning Source LLC
Chambersburg PA
CBHW030307080526
44584CB00012B/481